The British Bus Heritag

STANDERWICK & SCOUT

by

Peter and Judith A. Deegan

Venture *publications*

© Venture Publications Ltd August 1994.

ISBN 1 898432 13 9

All rights reserved. Except for normal review purposes no part of this book may be reproduced or utilised in any form or by any means, electrical or mechanical, including photocopying, recording or by an information storage and retrieval system, without the prior written consent of Venture Publications Ltd, PO Box 17, Glossop, Derbyshire, SK13 9FA.

Companion Volumes

Ribble Volume One
Ribble Volume Two

Front Cover Illustration

Standerwick operated many distinctive vehicles during its history, none more so than the double-deck coaches which it used on long distance services. One of the Leyland Atlantean Gay Hostess vehicles is seen in service in the early 'sixties coming into Bolton bus station to pick up passengers before resuming its southbound journey to London.

Photograph Peter Eckersley courtesy Photobus

Typeset and produced electronically for the Publishers by
Mopok Graphics, 128, Pikes Lane, Glossop, Derbyshire
Printed and bound in Great Britain

CONTENTS

Foreword 4
Acknowledgements 5
Introduction 6
1. Coaching in Lancashire 10
2. W. C. Standerwick 1904-1925 14
3. W. C. Standerwick Ltd 1925-Nov 1932 18
4. W. C. Standerwick Ltd Group Nov 1932-Feb 1935 24
5. W. C. Standerwick Ltd Group Feb 1935-Sep 1939 29
6. W. C. Standerwick Ltd Sept 1939-Oct 1968 36
7. Standerwick & Scout joint express operations
Sept 1940-Oct 1968 48
8. W. C. Standerwick Ltd Oct 1968-Apr 1974 58
Fleet List of Standerwick 1910-1939 66
Fleet List of Standerwick 1940-1974 68
9. Scout Motors 1919-Apr 1933 70
10. Scout Motor Services Ltd Sept 1939-1968 79
Fleet List of Scout Motors 1919-1939 93
Fleet List of Scout Motor Services Ltd 1940-1961 94
Fleet List of Scout Motor Services Ltd 1962-1968 95

Appendices :

I. C. Smith Motors & Jos. Bracewell Ltd 96
Fleet List of Jos. Bracewell (Blackpool) 99
II. J. W. Dewhurst & Co Ltd Wood Bros. (Blackpool) Ltd 100
Fleet List of Wood Bros. (Blackpool) Ltd 103
III. Wm. Salisbury & Sons Ltd (and J. E. Jenking) 104
Fleet List of Wm. Salisbury & Sons Ltd 106
Fleet List of John E. Jenking 107
IV. Wright Bros. (Burnley) Ltd 107
Fleet List of Wright Bros. (Burnley) Ltd 110
V. Some other Ribble Group Acquisitions: 111
(a) Wm. Armitage & Sons Ltd 111
(b) Walker Taylor & Sons Ltd 111
(c) Armitage & Walker Taylor Yorkshire Expresses
and closure of businesses 113
Fleet List of Wm. Armitage & Sons Ltd 113
Fleet List of Walker Taylor & Sons Ltd 114
Index 115
Photographic Credits 116

FOREWORD

Several publications have in recent years been devoted to the history and operations of Ribble Motor Services Ltd, and these have mentioned in passing that the company purchased and continued as a subsidiary the Blackpool-based operator W. C. Standerwick Ltd. This company was a substantial coaching company in its own right, and was a pioneer of motor coaching and also in the introduction in 1927 of long-distance expresses. The important contribution made by this subsidiary of Ribble to the development of road transport has not to date been fully acknowledged, and to remedy this omission – and to record a further aspect of Ribble's activities – this volume has been produced.

There have been many volumes recording the histories of companies owned and operated by the large Combines that dominated the transport industry from its formative days; there have been histories written concerning the operations of businesses conducted by individual families. The story of Standerwicks does not fit conveniently into either category, however, as the business was conducted by a Blackpool family for close on half of its existence, and by the Associated Companies for the remainder, although for many of the latter years it still retained the guiding hand of one of its founders, and even after his retirement from service it managed to retain more than its share of individuality.

Nor was this all: although Standerwicks was the retained 'name' in Ribble coaching it absorbed the operations of several competitors, some of which were substantially larger than itself, and the 'foibles' of some of these were also incorporated into the overall Standerwick operation, not least those of the extremely active C. Smith Motors section of Jos. Bracewell Ltd, under the guidance of Bracewell's son-in-law – Frank Briggs – who remained in management with Standerwicks until three years prior to the 'killing off' of the business under the guise of National Bus Company's corporate image.

The final few years apart, Standerwicks was in many ways a typical Blackpool coach operator, one of over two hundred individuals and companies that have sought to run motor coaches in the resort, and the story that follows is in many ways typical of the Blackpool breed of coachmen. While all the businesses had their own stories to tell, we would wish this history to stand as a tribute to all the Blackpool coachmen, who at the peak in the 'twenties together provided seasonal employment for a great number of men (over 1,000 people are understood to have been employed in Blackpool's coaching industry around 1930).

Although remembered as a Blackpool operator, Standerwicks also became a substantial East Lancashire operator which for a time was much larger than the Burnley-based unit that survived until the final transfer to National Travel. Indeed it may well have become a northern coaching equivalent to the 'Royal Blue' fleet of the Western and Southern National companies, had the Traffic Commissioner not regarded with such suspicion the 1935 policy intentions of the Ribble company.

In the final years Standerwicks absorbed much of the operations of Scout Motor Services of Preston, which had been a competitor and then partner in the London expresses; for the final eight years it had been a Ribble subsidiary alongside Standerwicks, and in view of the long and important operational life of Scout the present volume sets out the history of this undertaking also; the period of joint London operation is covered in a separate chapter to avoid repetition.

In view of the important contribution to Standerwicks by certain of the absorbed businesses this history concludes with a series of Appendices detailing the pre-purchase activities of these highly competitive and astutely-run businesses. Most of the businesses so detailed were run for a time as subsidiaries (or investments) of Ribble and for this reason are worthy of attention as a part of the overall history of Ribble's activities that have received little attention to date. It should be mentioned here that Ribble also operated as a subsidiary Howard Coaches Ltd, an excursion operator based in Southport following the acquisition of the share capital in August 1954: this company was not associated in any way with Standerwicks and cannot therefore form a part of this history, but its separate continuation under Ribble ownership is hereby acknowledged.

ON HIRE TO
W. C. STANDERWICK LTD.

ACKNOWLEDGEMENTS

The immense help afforded to the authors in the collation of information over a period of over ten years for this volume is gratefully acknowledged. The project was conceived during the years in which National Travel controlled Blackpool's Coliseum Coach Station and we were fortunate in being able to talk to certain former Standerwick employees at that time. In particular we received much help from Bob Mackay (then Blackpool Manager) and the Chapel Street clerk (Peter Wright), and we were welcomed into the home of Frank Briggs, who gave much patient help and encouragement to the fledgling project although he was not in good health in his retirement. Sadly, he did not live to see the results of our work, but we hope that the story we have discovered would have been approved had he seen the work.

We have also been able to make contact with members of the families of certain of the absorbed businesses, and in particular gained much background knowledge from Dorothy Jenkinson (a niece of William Salisbury) who recalled for us much of the atmosphere of the coachman's life, remembering the visits of 'Johnny Jenks' to the Salisbury house for Sunday tea, notwithstanding the cut throat operation between their respective businesses

We would also wish to acknowledge the kind help and encouragement of Bruce Maund (himself a former member of the Standerwick team) in the later stages of the project; Bruce has been instrumental in discovering answers to certain outstanding matters from his researches into Ribble's activities. Other help with queries has been forthcoming from Chris Heaps, John Nye and the late John Hughes: all are colleagues from the Omnibus Society's North Western and Yorkshire Branch. The comprehensive timetable collection of that Society has been consulted, and the issue-date of many of the un-dated issues verified from archive research in the Reference Libraries of several branches of the Lancashire Library. These confirmations have come in the main from the advertisement pages of various newspaper micro-fiches in Blackpool, Preston, Blackburn, Burnley and Rossendale: fortunately most of the subject businesses of this history were prolific advertisers. A helpful and detailed report from David Grisenthwaite enabled much background detail to be added to the story of the commencement of the Keswick-London route in 1952.

The enormous contribution of the photographers is gratefully and individually acknowledged in the appropriate section, but here we would wish to add our thanks to the Garth Dawson Studio in Accrington for their sympathetic help in restoring certain of the older views used.

ABOUT THE AUTHORS

Peter Deegan first discovered his interest in transport towards the end of the Second War, when he realised that he had been more interested in a journey from Manchester to Lancaster on a North Western Bristol single-decker (in the black-out) than in the visit to the Castle that was the object of the school trip. Subsequently attempting to discover the history of North Western's Urmston depot, he was introduced to a former Mid-Cheshire employee, who recounted a story that subsequent more detailed research has demonstrated had little bearing on the truth. The lesson that 'second-hand' research does not always pay has never been forgotten, and a prelude to setting pen to paper is invariably an extended period of research, to seek accurate and often obscure sources of information that can be pieced together – jig-saw fashion to assemble a picture of the subject. Judith Deegan's interest in transport is of more recent origin, and initially stemmed from a choice of sitting in an archive or becoming a 'grass-widow'; the visits soon resulted in the number of researchers doubling as they 'leap-frogged' volumes or micro-fiches. Now much of the entire production is shared, and the end result is a product of end-to-end collaboration and co-operation. Both authors have been employed in the Banking industry, although an offer of early retirement has enabled Peter additional time to seek wider sources for the research projects being undertaken.

Previous Publications: by Judith and Peter Deegan
Welsh Highland Wonderland – The Welsh Highland Railway in Pictures – Pride Books
The Yellow Road (Yelloway Motor Services Ltd) – Pride Books
Rossendale and Hyndburn Transport – 75 years of Transport – Omnibus Society
The Picture Postcard – an Early View of Transport – Omnibus Society
Travelling Around The Fylde – Communications

: by Peter Deegan
Introducing 'Russell' – the story of a steam locomotive – Welsh Highland Railway

INTRODUCTION

Motor Coaching has been a prominent part of the travel industry for most of the current century resulting in significant changes to the travelling habits of the British public. Although motors were available in the final years of the nineteenth century they failed to make any impact in the United Kingdom, not least because the then current legal requirements restricted heavy motors to four miles per hour and involved use of a pedestrian flag-man. The Heavy Locomotives Act 1903 eased these conditions, permitting heavy motors to travel at a maximum speed of 12 mph, reflecting development of mechanical traction at that time. In spite of subsequent improvement to design and safety, this limit remained until 1929, when as a precursor to the Road Traffic Act of 1930, pneumatic-tyred coaches were permitted to operate at 20 mph, increasing to a maximum of 30 mph in 1931. This maximum was to remain until the new motorways brought further relaxations, finally resulting in the current limits: 60 mph on ordinary roads, 70 mph on motorways

Not unnaturally, many operators in the 1920's chose to ignore the out-of-date legal requirements, running generally (though illegally) at an average speed of 24-25 mph, allowing a journey from Manchester to Blackpool to be undertaken in a little over two hours (to remain within the 12 mph limit would have resulted in a journey time exceeding five hours). The resulting Magistrate's Court fines were treated as a business overhead, as a necessity to secure – and retain – a viable passenger loading.

Prior to the 1930 Act, licensing of passenger vehicles was in the hands of local authorities (under powers granted by the Town Police Clauses Act 1847). This authority, to issue licences to 'ply for hire', was originally intended to regulate the horse-carriage trade, which was essentially local in character, and subsequent extension to include motor buses and coaches (which was at least inter-urban and often long-distance in character) was to lead to much allegation of injustice. A modification in 1921 permitted an aggrieved operator to appeal to the Minister of Transport, but long winded Appeals procedures only partly met the complaints, and all too often the Minister's powers were insufficient to remedy matters

The 1930 Act swept away the anomalies of the earlier system, appointing Traffic Commissioners responsible for licensing in specific areas through Traffic Courts, eventually providing a fairer system of considering applications, albeit not without some political input in the decision-making process. Long-distance operation was (to some extent) hampered by the need to make application to several Area Commissioners, although as the system settled down improved methods of handling such matters followed often bitter experience.

The earliest motor coaches were almost inevitably motorised versions of the horse charabanc, open to the elements and with the driver positioned behind a front-mounted engine (normal-control). He was seated on the first of several rows of bench seats, tiered to enable passengers in the rear to have a forward view over the heads of those in front. Those at the back sometimes required a ladder to reach their seats! Llandudno Motor & Garage Co Ltd purchased six Dennis charabancs in 1906, and DB147 is seen leaving the Craig-y-Don boarding establishment in July 1910. The photograph shows the original tiered design, with a rudimentary folding hood, but little safety protection apart from the arm-rest at the end of each row. An early development was the fitting of doors to each row, to prevent passengers falling out as the chara (or sharry, as it became familiarly known), bounced over the many un-made roads of the day.

The 1903 Heavy Locomotives Act had opened the door to the motor coach becoming a viable proposition, and by 1906 many towns were handling applications for motor coach licences on a routine basis. The onset of World War I slowed progress, as many vehicles had latterly been made available to operators as 'subsidy' chassis, on which the government had a lien in the event of war; these were commandeered in 1914 for use by the military. Quite apart from a downturn in demand, with vast numbers of men in the armed forces, there was the question of replacement of the lost fleets; certain types (such as the Tilling Stevens petrol electric chassis) were not considered suitable for war use, and these enjoyed increased sales at this difficult time.

The period up to the end of the Great War may be regarded as the pioneer era for motor coaching, as operators struggled with untried and primitive machines, learning by trial and error the vagaries of their trade. General demobilisation after 1918, however, brought about a return to more normal conditions, but with an important difference: heavy use of motors in the war-fields had proved a valuable testing-ground, and development of vehicles had been rapid under the difficult conditions encountered by the military. Many ex-military chassis were brought back to the UK for sale to operators, and a Disposals Unit at Slough handled thousands of AEC and Daimler chassis; Leyland Motors re-purchased its own vehicles and re-furbished them before offering them to operators as effectively new machines. Many ex-soldiers, newly trained in the driving and maintenance of motor vehicles, were looking for work, assisted by their demobilisation pay: it was hardly surprising that a large number turned to a trade connected with motors on their return to civilian life, and the heavy motor industry entered into a major period of growth from 1919, with hundreds of new motor coach operators entering the business over a very short period of time.

It was, perhaps, a sign of a more hardy era that one of the chief selling points for the charabancs was that travel was in the open air. These machines brought a new mobility to many people who had not been able to take excursions over such distances before. Up to 1921, when inflation and the effects of the 1920 Coal Strike brought large increases in rail fares, charabanc travel had been more expensive than rail, but after a short period of parity in 1921 the vast upsurge in popularity of motor coaching brought further economies. Road fares continued to fall (partly as a result of increasing competition), until the

The torpedo charabanc was a pre- Great War design, which had a flat floor and enclosed sides. The doors were generally fitted to the nearside only. Collapsible side-screens were available, and a light frame-work could be erected from the rear, attaching to the top of the driver's windscreen to enable a canvas hood to be stretched over the passengers in inclement weather. A scene of frantic communal activity as rain threatened to spoil the day may well be imagined, although in changeable weather the side screens and framework might well be left in place, leaving only the hood to be secured in place as required. A long-bonneted Leyland belonging to S. & J. Wood Ltd of Blackpool (probably FR1716) is seen at the Botanic Gardens, Southport about 1921, not long after the fleet name 'Seagull' had been adopted. The Wood family – 'incomers' from Hyde – had originally been horse-operators, adding motor charas prior to the Great War, and were to maintain a strong presence in the South Shore area of Blackpool.

Alighting from charabancs was a relatively rapid procedure, with a separate door for each row of four or five seats. The descent from a torpedo charabanc was normally by way of two or more running boards, which usually continued over the rear wheel aperture by way of removable boards. Note the brass grab-handles, and the gentleman at the rear holding his wife's umbrella and handbag as she prepares to descend. The small number plate immediately in front of this gentleman is a local authority licence plate, in this case licence number 161.

The final stage of coach development was the fully-enclosed body, from about 1928, although the 'fresh-air' image still held partial sway by way of an opening roof. Several systems were used, but the sliding panel was to become the standard variety, surviving into the 1950s before a system of opening vents was substituted. The accent was now increasingly on luxury travel, the enclosed body enabling more comfortable upholstered seats to be fitted, and electric interior lighting became standard. Veneered panelling and mirrors improved the image further, with electric or hot water heating systems becoming standard, after a brief flirtation with system that warmed the air by feeding in the hot exhaust gases! Certain specialised operations were maintained by coaches fitted with toilet/washroom compartments by 1930, and vehicles began to be fitted with radio by 1933. This Leyland TS2 example of 1931, FV1499, was operated by Standerwicks on its London express, and the Burlingham coachwork had entrance doors at front and rear plus an emergency door at front off-side. A wooden framework supported a roll-back canvas roof to maintain the fresh-air image – when the weather permitted! Warm-air heating was also available. Twenty-six plush seats were fitted, and hanging luggage racks were available for passengers' belongings as seen below. Glass shades covered each of the electric lights fitted to the window frames, and a well-equipped toilet compartment was positioned at the nearside rear corner. The 1930 Act brought about certain changes to specifications. The speed limit was increased to a more realistic 30 mph and it was no longer permitted for a passenger on a normal-control coach to sit to the right of the driver. It seems incredible today that the driver had been permitted to sit in a central position on the bench seat, being totally unable to give hand signals in an era when direction indicators were not commonly in use.

railways were obliged to offer reduced bargain excursion rates to regain some part of the lost traffic. In 1920, the return fare from Manchester to Blackpool stood at 13/6d by both road and rail, but by 1928 the road fare dropped (in some cases) to 2/6d, while the rail excursion fare was perhaps double that figure.

The growth of coaching was checked by the Transport Act of 1930, which brought a regulated era to the industry: at least to those operators who wished to provide scheduled services or excursions and tours, with the new Traffic Courts assessing each application, and it became most difficult for new businesses to secure licences, apart from the expedient of purchasing the businesses of existing licence holders. The Act provided, however, a period of stability for existing operators although not all could adapt to the new climate, and many chose to sell to others who wished to trade in the altered environment.

The Second World War proved to be another bad time for coaching, and it was to be 1946 before the industry again began to re-equip itself as conditions commenced a long period of improvement. For some years there was a return to the pre-war buoyancy in the industry, but the surge of new motor car sales as the 1950s progressed began to have its effect upon the coaching industry, leading to reducing passenger figures on both express and excursion workings. The industry was forced to retrench, and the number of operators providing excursions steadily reduced, although many found other forms of coaching work.

Within Blackpool, none of the 'founding' families remain in control of their original businesses, although the Jackson family remain as an operator, and the present generation (Samuel) currently (1993) operates excursions from a stand (Hornby Road/Coronation Street) that was earlier in the licensed 'portfolio' of his father John.

As the 1920s progressed the torpedo charabanc was succeeded by the all-weather coach, equipped with continuous side panels and retractable windows, but still retaining a canvas hood. Entry and exit was often by means of front and rear doors, with seats now arranged in pairs on each side, and a central gangway along the length of the coach. In many cases the driver now sat alongside the engine, forward-control, and was often in a compartment away from his passengers. This photograph includes two all-weather coaches, the Albion behind the cloche hatted ladies is unidentified, but the Leyland Lioness at rear is understood to be Standerwick's sole example of this marque, FR8973, purchased in 1928 and sold in the following year. The third machine is a Dennis, probably some eight years old, and now up-dated with pneumatic tyres.

In 1951 a new type of chassis – with the engine fitted under the floor – came into service, returning many drivers to a position within the passenger compartment, while an increase in permitted length improved capacity from 31 or 33 passengers to 41. Standerwicks operated a fleet of 30 of these Leyland-bodied Leyland Royal Tiger coaches equipped with centre-entrance bodies, purchased in three batches during 1951 and 1952. Number 146 was the first of the final batch of 10, and is seen passing under the York City walls while engaged on excursion duties. Subsequent changes to the maximum permitted length have brought seating capacities up to 53 or more, with such variations as rear-mounted engines and double-decked coachwork, and have continued to move forward the improving image of the modern coach.

CHAPTER 1

COACHING IN LANCASHIRE

At a glance, the pre-1974 County of Lancashire was ideal for the developing coach industry, with many industrial towns and a considerable population, almost none having any personal transport other than the bicycle. The years following the Great War saw a tremendous upsurge in coaching and the number of coach operators recorded in the county exceeds that in any other area; however, a closer look reveals that the scope for profitable operation was limited in all the inland towns, most mills and factories working a 5½-day week, leaving only Sunday as potentially available for excursions and even this day was partly restricted by religious considerations.

There was profitable trade at holiday periods, particularly August Bank Holiday weekend, but the busiest period was undoubtedly during individual Wakes Weeks, when factories closed throughout each town; a similar holiday was in September-October, although often closure did not extend to a full week. At these times traffic was many times in excess of local operators' capacity, it being necessary to hire coaches from neighbouring towns. Even this traffic was at the mercy of bad weather, and a persistently wet Wakes might prove the final crisis, leading to bankruptcy of smaller operators. After a brief flirtation with larger machines, many operators settled for less risky smaller coaches; within a medium sized town, such as Accrington, the most popular coach throughout the 'twenties was the 14-seater.

Large-scale operators, such as Lancashire United Tramways Ltd, with a three dozen-strong coaching fleet which failed to make profits and was progressively converted to omnibuses, and Swift Fleet Motors Ltd, Salford which was forced into liquidation, were paralleled by many unsuccessful small businesses. Those that did succeed were managed by men of unusual enterprise, who cast their nets over a considerably wider area than their home town to find work. This could be achieved by making coaches available for hire elsewhere, but another method was to undertake 'raids' on particular towns to secure unlicensed traffic, in the hope that retribution in the form of prosecution might either be avoided, or at least a light penalty inflicted. Holt Bros (Rochdale) Ltd's 'Yellow Coaches' were well-known exponents of this method in the later 'twenties, with a catchment area that extended from Preston to Oldham, and Burnley to Manchester.

Within Lancashire one major region that proved an exception to the overall traffic malaise comprised the coastal towns to which the holidaymaker hurried for his Wakes Week enjoyment. While Southport and Morecambe

Despite the unwillingness of Blackpool Council to sanction stands for motor coaches in the first years of the century, the march of progress could not be halted. Edward Butterworth a horse-chara operator established in 1865 is credited with bringing the first true motor charabanc, a Commer machine registered FR527, into operation in Blackpool, by June 1911, and running it from private land within his York Street stables. Although no illustration of this machine in Butterworth's ownership has yet come to light, the photograph shows the chara under the subsequent ownership of Jack Cordingley, Haslingden, when it was named *Hazeldene*. It is seen about 1915 in Lower Deardengate, Haslingden. The second Blackpool motor charabanc was the chain-driven Karrier purchased by Walter Clinton Standerwick, which entered service by August 1911.

derived much benefit from these annual migrations, by far the largest number of visitors headed for Blackpool. Each mill-town held its Wakes by rota, with perhaps one large town and a couple of smaller ones on holiday each week from June until August, after which the Autumn Holidays repeated the process until the end of October. With thousands of visitors in seaside towns each week, coach excursions were extremely popular entertainment, and coastal coach operators secured enormous traffic from constantly-changing holiday populations, with prosperous owners operating modern and comfortable large machines to attract even more trade.

Surprisingly for a Borough whose motto is 'Progress', Blackpool Council was reluctant to license motor coaches in the town, although it could do little to bar incoming traffic arriving from more progressive towns – and indeed the resort found the motor traffic a valuable addition to the substantial numbers arriving by rail. The first recorded instance of a motor charabanc operator in the town was the August 1906 application by Motors (Blackpool) Ltd for licences to ply from 80 Central Beach. Recalled later by Mr W. Blackhurst, Blackpool Motor Coach Owner's solicitor, the machines were described as having 'six forward and six reverse gears'; they were reputed to have been able to travel as fast backwards as forwards. Whatever the truth, the application was summarily dismissed.

It was 1913 before Blackpool's Watch Committee issued its first motor coach licences, following which a steadily increasing number was approved, until World War I brought a down-turn as many vehicles were commandeered by the Military, and the needs of the War years resulted in reduced demand for pleasure traffic. Remaining fleets were hit by petrol shortages in the latter years of the war, many charas running on town gas with huge bags fitted on to the hood framework. Operators used Poulton Gas Works and those running excursions to the Lake District took their charas and passengers via the Lancaster Gas Works to refill en route.

After a brief post-war period in which Blackpool rewarded its ex-servicemen by awarding licences freely, the Council became alarmed at the number of street-side stands in use, many now having to be shared by rival operators and, in 1920, renewals were made with much acrimony. Notice was given that street stands would not be made available for the 1921 season. This threat brought the operators together, under the banner of Commercial Motor Users' Association, to plead for deferment, and the Council agreed to issue licences for a further year on a 'one stand – one vehicle' policy. Although the larger or more responsible took steps to provide themselves with off-street loading places, some street stands continued, albeit on a reducing basis, until 1933, when a further final attempt at abolition was made by the Corporation, this time seeking to use the Traffic Commissioners to achieve its purpose.

In pre-motorway days many hotels served as popular refreshment stops for excursion coaches. Lakes-bound trips usually stopped in Carnforth, where both the Carnforth and County Hotels welcomed coaches. The rear coach in the latter's parking ground is a Burlingham-bodied machine owned by Gore's Tours, Southport. An experienced man could do very well here: on the Keswick excursion there would be a free snack and cigarettes at Carnforth on the morning halt where, like most coach stops, there was a drivers' room. En route to the Lakes, the driver would extol the virtue of a boat trip on Lake Windermere: passengers would be dropped at Bowness Pier, and picked up again at Waterhead, Ambleside, the driver receiving a commission from the boatman. And so it went on: a man who performed extra little services and took the trouble to learn some history and geography need never touch his pay packet in the high season. The longer day excursions were taken by senior seasonal men and the pecking order decreased, with new men taking the local circulars. There was no training: they found their way by following other coaches although, in later years Standerwick drivers were issued with route books describing the range of excursions licensed to the company.

Blackpool Motor Coach Owners' Association was established in 1922, when 156 charabancs were operated by members: by 1929 some 270 enclosed coaches were operated by 52 owners, only one machine still running on solid tyres. Of the 52 members, the largest fleet was 24 coaches, and there were several owner-drivers. Ten per cent of coaches were licensed all year, chiefly in connection with express services, 55per cent for six summer months, and 10 per cent from July to September only. In this peak period, typically, 130 coaches per day ran on local circulars, 40 to Southport, 35 to Morecambe, 35 to Windermere and Keswick, 25 on expresses and five on extended tours. Express numbers were much greater at weekends, as were extended tours in the spring and autumn periods.

The growth of the resort's fleet led to over-provision, resulting in certain excursions to inland towns developing into expresses, with traffic commencing at either end and often at intermediate places also. Several Blackpool operators thus secured new traffic by conveying holiday-makers to and from the resort as well as catering for their excursion needs whilst the visitors were staying in the town. Much work was undertaken on hire to inland operators; some Blackpool operators established inland bases as adjuncts to their coastal operations.

The Blackpool coaching fraternity was divided into a number of categories: the prime group who comprised the Blackpool and District Motor Coach Owners' Association was inevitably one of (a) operators born and bred in Blackpool ('sand-grown'uns'); (b) those who moved to Blackpool and commenced their business ('in-comers'); (c) those who had purchased a business owned by an operator in categories (a) or (b). There was a fourth category: an operator who was established elsewhere, but who set up a base in Blackpool, utilising coaches that he worked into the town to provide excursions and other traffic in competition with the previous categories. This latter class was *persona non grata* in the local coaching industry, was excluded from the Owners' Association, and could expect united opposition to any applications, whether to Council or Commissioners.

With so many competing private and public excursion stands, it was inevitable that methods of 'persuading' passers-by to join particular coaches developed: these included agencies at boarding houses, the landlord or landlady receiving commission for bookings, clients being collected from their lodgings. However, the mainstay of the stand was the tout, a special breed of man akin to a modern-day bingo caller. Officially barred by the terms of both Hackney Carriage and later Road Service Licences, the most skilful were worth their weight in gold: some produced wonderful chalk boards, and others had the ability to spirit passengers aboard, almost against their wishes. Few stayed with one operator for more than a season or two, but turned up somewhere different each year. For a time, Coronation Street was enlivened by a character in the dress of John Bull, complete with Union Jack waistcoat, extolling the virtues of Wood Brothers trips; a Scots character wore a parson's collar and front while he walked up and down the white line in the middle of Chapel Street for Standerwicks, calling out "Bleasdale Fells, Southport, Morecambe" in guttural Glaswegian. This tout also had a habit of helping himself to an unallocated Leyland coach, hiding it in a side street for production when the available coaches had been loaded and demand was still strong, then persuading the controller to let him drive it. One day his efforts were in vain when they decided to teach him a lesson by getting another driver to take it and hide it somewhere else!

From 1930 until the motorway age, day excursions to Gretna Green, Scarborough and Llandudno were at the limit of the range of coaches without very early starts which could not be managed by holiday-makers bound by the strict breakfast routines of hotels and boarding houses. In the middle range were Keswick, Windermere, the Five Lakes Tour, York, Harrogate and Chester. Half-day trips to Southport and Morecambe were popular, and there were morning, afternoon and evening short runs round the Fylde. Throughout the year, there were trips to race meetings: each operator had his regular clientele, and there was great consternation when a regular found that the coach was fully booked. "It's not a day out, it's my living", said one anxious punter, so an illegal stool was surreptitiously placed in the gangway for him.

The sheer volume of Blackpool excursion traffic before the motor car age is difficult to comprehend at this distance. Fleetwood Market was a perennial attraction and, on at least one occasion, Standerwicks alone sent off at least 100 loads, morning and afternoon, in one day. Having done two Fleetwoods, a driver would then do an evening trip round the Fylde, or to Bleasdale Fells – three lots of tips in one day! During the Illuminations it was customary to run a trip to Morecambe Lights and on to Blackpool Lights, all on one ticket; apart from bringing in more revenue, the initial queue for Blackpool Lights was avoided as it had cleared before the coach returned from Morecambe. On a really busy night, there could be almost 100 Standerwick loads for this double trip, using Ribble coaches and various other companies' vehicles spending the night in Devonshire Road Garage. When one considers that the other operators were equally busy, it will be realised that thousands of passengers were carried daily.

The chapters following detail not only the history of the Standerwick and Scout businesses, but also give some account of their competitors and several businesses that were absorbed into the original firms.

During the 'fifties and 'sixties, Ribble and joint operators were organising Easy Way Holidays to many resorts: the package included travel to and from the chosen resort, accommodation with some meals and a programme of day excursions on the vehicles of the local operator. Blackpool was a popular venue for these holidays, and the excursionists were, of course, booked on Standerwicks, who picked them up from their hotels and conveyed them to the appropriate stand. Hundreds of passengers were booked for these day trips. Other Easy Way holidaymakers were conveyed by Standerwick expresses to London for onward travel to the south coast resorts. This post-war package traffic was not a new idea, for Standerwicks operated such an inclusive package as early as 1931, extending it to Wood Bros and Bracewell in 1933, utilising seats on their expresses from London, and their Blackpool excursions; this traffic is known to have continued in operation until at least 1936. The Easy-Way leaflets to Ramsgate for 1963 (above), and to Blackpool for 1964 (top right) are illustrated, and the Standerwick tours operated for Summer 1932 (right).

In Conjunction with

OUR BLACKPOOL SERVICE

We have organized the following:

4 and 8-DAY TOURS

—of—

BLACKPOOL

—and the—

ENGLISH LAKES

Itinerary.

4 DAYS TOUR — **Price 4 Guineas**

1st. DAY. Leave London at 8.30 a.m. by De-Luxe Motor Coach, via Coventry—Lunch, thence Knutsford for Tea, and on to Blackpool in time for Dinner.

2nd DAY. The Morning free, suggest stroll along glorious Sea front. Afternoon:- Drive to Sunny Southport, England's Seaside Garden City, and back in time for Dinner.

3rd DAY. After Breakfast, we start off for a Whole-Day Tour by Coach (packed Lunch provided) to the Famous English Lakes, embracing Keswick, Windermere, Grassmere, Rydal Water and Derwent Water, finest Scenery in Europe.

4th DAY. Board Coach from Hotel for Newcastle-U-Lyme for Lunch, thence St. Albans for Tea, arriving London at approximately 7 p.m.

8 DAYS TOUR — **Price 7 Guineas**

This Tour includes the above Itinerary, with the addition of a Grand Steamer Trip to Douglas, Isle of Man, allowing 2½ hours ashore.

Various alternative tours can be arranged to the Wye Valley, Devon, Cornwall and the English Lakes. Details on application

THE HOTELS.

The Hotels included in the Itineraries have been very carefully selected for comfort and catering, but are in every case establishments where the traveller who has possibly limited his or her travelling requirements to one suit-case would not feel any discomfort from the lack of an extensive wardrobe

CHAPTER 2

Walter Clinton STANDERWICK 1904-1925

Walter Clinton STANDERWICK was born in 1873, the son of Arthur and Elizabeth Standerwick: he had one sister, Miss M. E. Standerwick, who assisted her parents in the family glassware business, located for some years on Talbot Road, close to Dickson Road and later in Queen Square. The business exists, but is no longer in the hands of the family. Walter had a younger brother – Edward Victor (Vic) – who was to figure largely in the Standerwick coaching business.

Walter established himself in the carriage business and operated at least one horse landau from a Mews Stable on Coronation Street, now under the Winter Gardens frontage, from 1904. After a couple of years he purchased the licensed horse charabanc of R. Strickland, securing the transfer in October 1906 of the Hackney Carriage Licence issued by Blackpool Watch Committee. Strickland and his brother had earlier been horse omnibus proprietors, running two omnibuses between Talbot Square and Marton in 1899. Following closure of the horse-bus route on commencement of the Corporation's new electric tramway, the Stricklands had gained licences for horse charabancs and by 1906 were running from the Victoria Hotel Stables at Central Promenade/Brunswick Street junction. The latter, lying immediately north of Chapel Street, is no longer a highway but still has pedestrian access from the Promenade.

In May 1907, Standerwick received approval for his chara stand to be re-located outside Central Drive Livery Stables at Central Drive/Chapel Street corner, to which he had moved. The Watch Committee allocated him specific routes for excursions to eliminate alleged racing by rival proprietors: (a) via Poulton-le-Fylde and Gardeners Arms to Thornton Church, returning via Cleveleys and Bispham; (b) via St Annes and Lytham to Wrea Green, returning via Little Marton. As a new licensee, Standerwick was on trial, with his licence reviewed six-weekly, but he must have proved satisfactory for he received an annual licence after only two short-period grants.

In common with many horse proprietors, Standerwick's business included removals, certainly by March 1911. This enabled horses and men to be retained in service over winter months, as the busy holiday season precluded many residents from moving from the resort during the summer, making winter-period removals a useful second-string business.

Standerwick was a very interested observer of the continuing battle to secure licences for motor charabancs but, in common with others, was reluctant to commit himself to the high capital outlay if the machine might only operate from within the confines of his stables. However, when Edward Butterworth committed the not inconsiderable sum of £750 on his Commer chara by June 1911, Walter Standerwick was persuaded by brother Vic to follow suit, and Karrier FR530 was delivered to his Central Drive premises within a couple of weeks of the rival Commer. Nor was this all; the Standerwicks were also interested in the continuing debate regarding licensing of motor taxicabs in Blackpool and, once the Watch Committee gave way to the pressure, were in the vanguard of applications to run the new machines, securing on 25th August 1911 one of the first such licences to be issued.

In May 1912, Walter was advertising he had on hand 'a number of the latest motor charas, fitted with the latest torpedo bodies' and had placed in service a second vehicle: this was a Leicester-built Alldays and Onions, registered FR621. The year 1912 must have been a difficult year operationally, for in that year the Central Drive Livery

Walter Clinton Standerwick's first motor charabanc entered service in mid-1911: this was a Huddersfield-built Karrier FR530 with a chain-drive, and headlights lit by oil. At the close of the 1912 season the brothers took perhaps their most adventurous step so far, by organising a week-long excursion to London, leaving the resort in late October. Owing to insufficient knowledge of locations where petrol might be obtained, they lashed sufficient petrol cans to the running boards to ensure their return to Blackpool! The first night was spent in Birmingham and the last at Leicester; whilst in London excursions were taken to Windsor, Greenwich and Chelsea. Walter acted as navigator, while Vic drove the 29-seat chara; on their return to Blackpool, Vic was presented by his passengers with an inscribed gold watch commemorating his feat. The excursion was recorded contemporarily as the pioneer long-distance excursion from the North West of England, appearing to pre-date claims made some 20 years later by a Morecambe operator. This view was taken on the commencement of the London tour, showing Vic Standerwick in the white jacket and driving cap at the wheel, with Walter in the bowler hat sitting to his right. Note that this chara had the driver positioned centrally, rather than in the right-hand position. Although there are door-handles fitted on the off-side, the brothers appear to have added a continuous waist-rail that effectively seals off the door openings apart from the driver's door area.

Standerwick's second charabanc had a 29-seat torpedo body fitted to the Alldays and Onions chassis: it entered service in 1912. On Sunday 20th July 1913, the Alldays coach is seen on Adelaide Street, Blackpool, loaded with parishioners from the United Methodist Church about to set off on a trip to visit their opposite numbers in Leicester. This was another example of a distant destination that would involve more than a single day's journey. Once again the driver is placed centrally on the front bench. One wonders whether Walter Standerwick, seen attending the departure in summer attire of straw boater and carnation, had arranged to have his chara examined at Alldays factory, which was situated in Leicester, close by the trip's destination!

Stables were demolished and replaced by the red-brick King Edward VII Hotel, whose first licensee was Herbert Whiteside. Despite the rebuilding, which was proceeding around his private stand on Central Drive, Standerwick successfully operated motor excursions as far afield as Morecambe and Southport and, more locally, St Michaels-on-Wyre via Shard Bridge. Provision had been made at the rear of the new hotel for a smaller Livery Stables and these opened by the year end in the occupation of W. C. Standerwick. The exit from the new stables joined Chapel Street between the new hotel and the bridge carrying the railway out of Central Station.

The pressure for licensed stands for motor charabancs continued through the winter of 1912-13 but the end was now in sight and, on instructions from Blackpool Town Council, the Watch Committee viewed possible sites during May 1913. Their recommendations included all three stands requested by W. C. Standerwick, whose fleet now included a third motor chara: a site off Central Promenade (a tiny cul-de-sac on Central Beach alongside a small mews stable); Bonny Street behind the Central Beach stables and Chapel Street, alongside King Edward Hotel. The Council refused to confirm the Bonny Street stand but, in September 1913, Standerwick successfully secured transfer of his Central Beach licence to Bonny Street, realising he could position his third chara on his Central Beach premises without a licence from the Council!

The Council reviewed its licensing policy after the 1913 season and the Watch Committee, while recommending renewal to almost all existing licensees, decided to defer renewal of specific motor stands. Standerwick was advised that licences for 3 motor charas and one horse chara would be issued for 1914, but the Chief Constable's report on 6th February included recommendation that Standerwick's Bonny Street stand be abolished in favour of a return to the Central Beach cul-de-sac; both a motor- and horse-chara would be approved for Chapel Street stand. Standerwick's protests were in vain and there the matter had to remain – at least until the Great War intervened!

Standerwick's business continued during the four years of hostilities, although Walter rendered service with the Motor Volunteers and the Special Constabulary. With a return to peace-time conditions, Blackpool Watch Committee recommenced its licensing functions, recording in April 1919 that W. C. Standerwick was operating four motor charas from three sites: Chapel Street, Central Beach and – once again – Bonny Street; the horse chara had been retired. Fares in spring 1920 (Aintree Races 9/- Chester Races 10/-, Liverpool 12/6d) would seem exorbitant within a couple of years, but were within a few pence of prevailing rail fares. A well-used facility in Spring involved long-day excursions for the now-defunct Blackpool Tradesman's Holiday: in June 1920 these involved trips to Windermere, and a circular tour to Chester using the Birkenhead Luggage Boat to cross the Mersey on the outward run.

Licensing matters were again coming to a head, with the Watch Committee alarmed at the sheer numbers of

The World War I fleet of Standerwick included at least one Tilling Stevens petrol-electric machine, purchased as a result of this marque remaining available to operators as it was not considered suitable for the military. No photograph has come to hand of any of the Standerwick vehicles at this time, but the view here depicts an almost identical machine operating in Blackpool during the war years. Number FR487 almost certainly took its number from a machine commandeered in 1914, the body retaining the registration number when dropped on to a replacement chassis early in 1915 for the Blackpool operator, S. Owen & Sons, who by 1918 was operating three Tilling charas. The Eagle & Child Inn at Weeton was a popular destination for chara trips and among other horse- and motor-charas parked outside the thatched hostelry is a Commer machine. A detachment of soldiers from the nearby military camp is marched by: some of the squaddies are sufficiently indisciplined to be turning to stare at the camera-man.

Blackpool ex-servicemen returning to open coaching businesses in town and it announced that for 1921 no street stands would be permitted. All operators were to secure off-street sites for standing coaches. The operators considered insufficient time had been given to comply, even assuming that sites could be found and, under the banner of the Commercial Motor Users Association, prepared a proposed listing of stands that omitted the most controversial sites and had approval of 90 per cent of the operators. The dissenters – the larger operators – were concerned that a principle of 'one owner – one stand' was a facet of the scheme, preventing running from several sites with their fleets. The Watch Committee expressed interest and further discussions resulted in a compromise whereby certain operators split their businesses for licensing purposes, enabling two stands to be listed for each.

Standerwick had been among the dissenters and the solution enabled his street stand at Chapel Street to be retained, along with a new site at Bethesda Square off Central Drive some 100 metres south of Chapel Street; the Central Beach site was considered private land, but Bonny Street was finally lost. Bethesda Square was in the name of E. V. Standerwick, who was now, on paper, owner of one of W. C. Standerwick's machines. Curiously, this situation would be maintained until at least 1930, with Vic retaining ownership of one of the W. C. Standerwick fleet even after formation of the limited company of which both brothers were directors. In practice, Walter acted as manager of King Edward Garage as the stables had been renamed, while Vic concerned himself with the fleet of coaches and taxis.

Further alarm was caused when it became known the Watch Committee in a last-minute decision was only prepared to license one chara to stand at each site: the owners had assumed that owners of more than one would be permitted to position their charas in turn on the licensed stand. Council was not prepared to concede this point and matters had, perforce, to remain unresolved for 1921. The motor owners were subsequently to take over the Horse-Chara Owners' Association, which had become moribund, to achieve a local voice in future negotiations: this locally-run Association became a powerful force in the years that followed.

After the bruising battle of 1921, the responsible operators were able to lease or purchase off-street stands at suitable locations, where trading was most brisk. One operator is reputed to have described the morning rush of holiday-makers heading for the sea as akin to a rush of lemmings, experience showing that streets running westwards were excellent sites for touts to accost visitors and persuade them aboard the coaches. Standerwick's two inland sites, at the Central Drive corners of Chapel Street and Bethesda Square, were situated very conveniently for Chapel Street Bridge the first crossing under the railway south of Hounds Hill, and visitors from boarding houses on Reads Road/Reads Avenue, Palatine Road, Ribble Road, Belmont Avenue and Ibbison Street would all be targets as they emerged each day. The Central Beach site had become the sole stand at the Central Station end of the

Post-war purchases included a number of Italian-built Lancia charabancs, of which at least one, AJ9664, was purchased second-hand from Robinsons of Scarborough, who traded as 'Royal Blue' at this time, as successors to the coaching operations of the North Eastern Railway from the Scarborough Railway Station. This Lancia chara is possibly the machine that passed to Standerwicks: note the non-standard and awkward passenger door over the wheel arch, with its associated metal step screwed to the rear mudguard. Number AJ9664 entered the Royal Blue fleet in August 1923, passing from Standerwick to Garlick Burrell & Edwards, (dealers) in 1928 in part exchange for a new Tilling coach. In the meantime it is most likely that a more modern body was fitted or a partial rebuild undertaken while with Standerwicks, as the premier Blackpool operators had eliminated charabancs from their fleets at an early date.

Golden Mile; only S. & J. Wood Ltd – now trading at the Brunswick Street site (previously Stricklands) – were in competition, from a stand alongside Victoria Hotel.

A newspaper report in June 1921 indicated that Standerwick had supplied coaches to transport some 285 local parishioners on a church outing, but it is unlikely that sufficient machines were owned at this time to enable the job to be undertaken without hiring-in machines from other operators. Clearly, however, the undertaking was well-based, and a routine of operation was established. Winter trading was light, with excursions to football matches and race meetings leading up to a busy Easter period. Tradesman's Holiday in May or June saw a series of popular two-day tours: from 1922 to 1925 Standerwick's tour visited North Wales, but in the latter year a second tour was based on Scarborough. A selection of day excursions was also run, continuing throughout the season, being joined by daily short tours to local destinations, some actually within the Borough, that were motorised versions of the original horse chara trips. In September a further round of specials for Blackpool Builders' Week gave a boost to the declining season. The increasing number of excursions by Standerwicks was made possible by steady expansion of the fleet, including a small number of light and fast Italian-built Lancias.

The Tradesmen's Holiday of 1925 was to be the final major work to be undertaken by Standerwick in original form, for arrangements were in hand to form a limited company that was to take over the expanding operation.

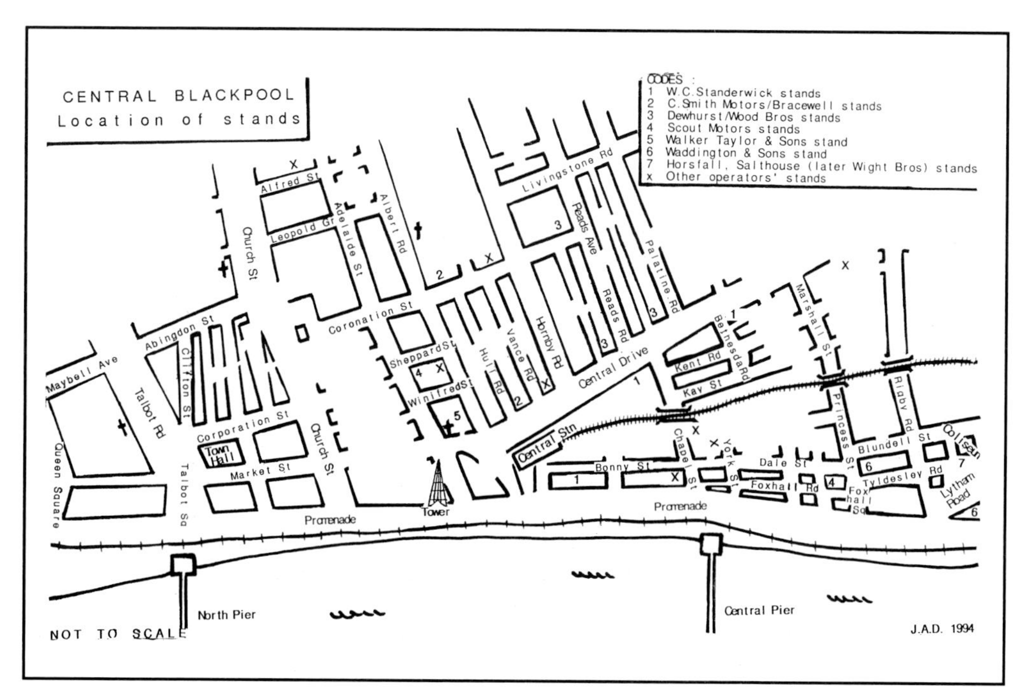

Plan of the Central Drive, Blackpool area, showing stands in operation by various operators

CHAPTER 3

W. C. STANDERWICK LTD
Incorporated 15 May 1925
June 1925-November 1932

W. C. Standerwick Ltd was incorporated to take over the existing business of Walter Clinton Standerwick; its Registered Office was at King Edward Garage, Blackpool. The Standerwick brothers plus Walter's wife Elizabeth Ann Standerwick were directors, with W. C. & E. A. Standerwick controlling 4,200 of the 6,000 £1 shares, the balance being held by E. V. Standerwick. Notwithstanding the clause permitting the company 'to acquire and undertake the whole or any part of the business ...... of any person or company', one vehicle continued to be taxed in Victor's name, perpetuating the myth of the separate ownership of the licensed stand at Bethesda Square.

The company ran seven-day tours to London throughout October 1925 at £2 return; they did not include accommodation and were therefore 'period excursions'. Weekend period excursions to Blackburn, Accrington and Burnley were operated from March 1926, allowing ex-patriot East Lancashire folk to visit their home towns; these ran through spring and resumed in late autumn to Blackburn only. Lancia all-weather coaches now in service ran Tradesmen's two-day tours to Anglesey, plus Harrogate, York and Scarborough and a new four-day Heart of the Welsh Mountains tour. From 11th September 1926 daily trips to Liverpool, initially for Civic Week, and to Manchester, were offered.

Spring 1927 saw resumption of East Lancashire period excursions, now varying between Burnley, Brierfield & Nelson, and Blackburn, Accrington & Darwen trips. From 21st April 1927, a daily Manchester service was offered, it is not clear whether as resumption or continuation of the 1926 operation.The demand for Manchester trips was such that several Blackpool operators were now competing. A resumed series of weekly London excursions throughout October 1927 utilised both Lancia and new Albion coaches; these left Blackpool on Mondays, returning on Saturdays. The fare of £1.17.6d fell further within days to £1.7.6d. Clearly traffic was encouraging, for after a short resumption of East Lancashire weekend runs in January 1928, a weekly London service commenced on Friday 23rd March 1928 – out Monday, returning Friday – at £1.7.6d. The excessive number of coaches in Blackpool was doubtless instrumental in Standerwicks' search for alternative work. The weekly London trip was increasingly popular, continuing throughout the summer, with booked passengers collected by Standerwick taxis.

A single Leyland C9 coach was added to the fleet in 1925: this was a Burlingham 20-seat all-weather machine with an early H. V. Burlingham-built body. The body-builder had quite recently set up on his own, after the break up of the former Burlingham and Richardson partnership. The coach was equipped with entrance doors at front and rear, and seats were generally in pairs with an aisle separating them; the rear row seated five passengers and the driver shared a bench with three passengers.

The stand at the King Edward Garage on Chapel Street was always busy and, despite the stipulation on the licences that only one vehicle was permitted on the stand, the rule was largely ignored. In this view a driver is busy persuading two passers-by to join one of the two coaches loading for evening drives to Great Eccleston & Elswick, and to Cleveleys, Rossall and Fleetwood: both are costed at 1/6d. The photograph reputedly dates from 1928 but the vehicles appear to be the Lancia all-weather coach FR6372 new in 1926 and one of the 1922 Tilling Stevens petrol electric charabancs only one of which survived into 1926. Among the day excursions on the board for the following day are runs to Morecambe Bay, Southport and St Michaels.

Availability of a regular coach to Blackpool from London did not pass unnoticed by established Agents in the capital. By 14th May 1928, northbound bookings were being handled by Lyne, Frank & Wagstaffe, Crescent Place, WC1 and a formal London terminus at Russell Square had been established, departing at 8.30am from either end. From 28th May, however, Standerwicks decided, in the knowledge of Wood Bros. operations, to divert between Preston and Knutsford to serve Blackburn, Darwen and Bolton, rather than Wigan and Warrington. From 2nd July 1928 return fares increased to £1.10.-d; single journeys at £1 or extended return fares at £1.15.-d were also available.

The Manchester excursion, which appears to have ceased during the winter period, was relaunched from Monday 26th March 1928, providing a daily return service, running via Blackburn, Darwen and Bolton; it was also further extended to reach Rochdale via Royton. Departure from King Edward Garage was at 9.30am (Sundays 10am), coaches calling at Central Beach, returning from Rochdale at 5pm with a call outside Lewis's store in Manchester at 5.45pm. The extension to Rochdale was probably prompted by opportunism. Holt Bros. 'Yellow Coaches' had used King Edward Garage as the Blackpool terminal for their Oldham-Rochdale-Blackpool express from November 1927 until their new Central Drive/Westmorland Avenue depot was ready for use in spring 1928, and Standerwicks were attempting to tap Rochdale passengers arriving at Chapel Street! Whatever the reason, Rochdale was a short-lived extension of the Manchester route. A further express – to Liverpool – had also been launched by early April 1928, the precise date not so far having been established.

Competition on both Manchester and Liverpool routes from Blackpool was now severe and, in spring 1928, fare-cutting was rife. Standerwicks' rates to either Manchester or Liverpool were 2/6d single, 3/- day return, 4/6d period return, a far cry from the 1920 rate of 13/6d return. Clearly something had to be done, and Rhodes W. Marshall President of the Motor Coach Owners' Association was successful in securing agreement between all members so that – from 19th April – the Manchester and Liverpool fares rose by 6d single or 1/- return. From 2nd July High Season fares of 4/-, 5/- and 6/- were imposed to Manchester, while Liverpool fares rose even higher: 4/-, 5/6d and 6/6d. The agreement included joint publicity, which showed that in April 1928 Standerwick was competing with four others to Liverpool and no fewer than eleven to Manchester.

Regular interval Ribble services to both Manchester and Liverpool had started running on 23rd May 1928 but the situation was transforrmed from 8th July when Ribble, North Western and Lancashire United commenced a half-hourly joint service to Manchester and subsequently the number of independent operators dwindled in the face of this highly successful service.

A few of the independent Manchester and Liverpool expresses survived by providing a more luxurious service running at specific times and offering guaranteed seats, retaining some traffic that otherwise would have been lost to the Combine Companies' interval service, but Standerwicks' daily services were early casualties, both Manchester and Liverpool routes ceasing in the autumn of 1928, certainly by 24th November. There is evidence, however, that the Manchester route operated intermittently until November 1929, when an arrangement was concluded with M. & H. Motors Ltd, Standerwicks acting as agent for M. & H., allowing them to take on the remaining Standerwick Manchester traffic. In return M. & H. became Agents for the Standerwick London service, with London-bound coaches calling at the M. & H. premises on Lytham Road en route.

In the meantime, Standerwicks had been addressing the question of accommodation for the growing fleet, eventually securing land for a new depot at the south-west corner of Bethesda Road and Kent Road. The building was ready for occupation in the late summer of 1928, the Brunswick Working Men's Club securing a lease of the upper storey. The ground floor was rented to W. C. Standerwick Ltd, ownership of the land and premises remaining with W. C. & Mrs. E. A. Standerwick.

A period of experimentation on the London service heralded autumn operation: from 16th September a daily service for Blackpool Builders' Week and Blackburn September Holiday was in operation and the service was rerouted between Lichfield and Daventry to call at Birmingham. From 23rd September the resumed weekly service returned north on Saturdays rather than Fridays, still at 8.30am. Consternation was caused to Standerwicks when Messrs. Lyne, Frank and Wagstaffe began to act also as London Agent for Wood Bros., who commenced using Central London Coaching Station at Crescent Place; Standerwicks believed that, as their service had been represented for some five months, they had a prior right to use the new Coaching Station. The dispute was further complicated as Wood Bros. also commenced running via Birmingham, poaching end-of-season traffic by offering reduced fares.

On 6th October Standerwicks' winter fares resumed at 15/- single, £1 return and £1.5.-d extended and the service ran southwards on Mondays, returning on both Fridays and Saturdays from Russell Square. From 23rd October a twice-weekly service was in operation: Mondays and Fridays ex-Blackpool, and Fridays and Saturdays ex-London; departure was still 8.30am from each end, but discussions regarding the London problems were reaching fruition. On 6th November Standerwicks' moved into Central London Station, Wood Bros. remaining until fresh arrangements might be concluded; from 20th November they moved to Bush House, Aldwych. Standerwicks' Birmingham diversion was withdrawn, leaving Birmingham and Coventry traffic to Wood Bros. Also from this date Standerwick's Blackpool departure advanced 30 minutes to 8am, matching Wood Bros.

As 1928 drew to a close, Standerwicks began to market the London route as their 'Pullman Lounge Service', whose coaches were 'luxurious in every way; armchair seats under the control of passengers, hat racks, rugs, and central heating by radiators (no exhaust fumes)'. Several experimental timetable changes in early 1929, including, from 2nd May, a return to the Birmingham and Coventry diversion with a thrice-weekly service, concluded with the introduction, from 22nd June 1929, of daily journeys each way, leaving Blackpool at 8am and London (now from MacShanes Motors Ltd, 53, Woburn Place) at 8.30am. Blackpool Coach Owners' fares agreement now extended to London routes and Association pressure brought rate-cutting by Empire and Lansdowne to an end.

A major blow to Standerwicks occurred on Friday 2nd August 1929, with the death, after a period of illness, of the founding director, Walter Standerwick, at the age of 56. Fortunately for the continuing business, the motor coach operation was already managed by Vic, and the company continued without major changes, Walter's widow, Mrs Elizabeth Standerwick, assuming the shares of her late husband and the position of Chairwoman.

From 5th October 1929, a pick-up from Fleetwood for London was advertised and probably effected by Standerwicks' taxi. Vic Standerwick was now attempting to regularise London operation by seeking licences from the many authorities along the line of route, although differing standards were to cause problems. With off-street premises in use, the fleet was already licensed in Blackpool for any coaching purpose, and there were no difficulties at Preston. Blackburn had, to many observers' surprise, granted Standerwicks licences to ply from that town on 23rd September 1929, but Birmingham was to prove more difficult, the company's application first being considered on 25th November 1929, and deferred. Standerwick coaches were noted on 11th December as stopping in New Street near Hen & Chickens Hotel, and although the company had been advised that coaches must use a garage in the city, particulars were still awaited. The company subsequently arranged for The Holiday Bureau Station at Dale End to be utilised, but Birmingham then insisted on examining each of the six coaches for which licences had been requested and – due to service requirements – trips to Birmingham for approval were only being made on an irregular basis. It was to be 24th March 1930 before the fourth was presented, this being a Tilling Stevens 24-seat machine.

Concern was expressed that two of the coaches submitted were equipped with a lavatory and wash-bowl compartment, and it proved necessary for a further examination – by the Medical Officer of Health – to confirm that there was no possible public nuisance. The

Standerwicks were to recommence purchases of Tilling Stevens chassis in 1928 with two B10B2 normal control chassis which received Burlingham all-weather bodies with 26 seat dual-entrance bodies: the first of these, FR9106, is seen here. The seating appears to be quite basic for the length of the journey for the advertised Blackpool-London daily service, with no headrests in evidence, and in fact by 1930 this type of coach had largely been superseded by more luxurious machines on all but the busiest days. This photograph was taken by a Leyland staff photographer on November 21st 1930 when the vehicle was traded in against a new Leyland coach. Note the speed limit of 20mph painted on the side, on delivery the maximum permitted speed had been 12mph.

first Standerwick coach with toilet accommodation had been delivered at the start of 1930 (Leyland TS2 FV720) to respond to Wood Bros., who had pioneered the feature on Blackpool-London expresses. By 26th March 1930, matters had progressed to the extent that they were left in the hands of the Birmingham Chief Constable, but Standerwicks' troubles were still not at an end, as Birmingham – using Midland Red as its standard – still awaited submission of six names for licensing as conductors, and of course – in common with most independents – the company's expresses were manned only by a driver!

In the early part of 1930, Standerwicks, Wood Bros. and C. Smith Motors formed a loose alliance against competing operators, with some joint advertising, and a general agreement on such matters as fares: it is also probable that limited passenger swapping was carried on to achieve more satisfactory loadings, and reduce loss of trade to outsiders. At this time it is likely that Empire and Lansdowne had retired from London to compete only on the Blackpool-Birmingham section, although Holt's Yelloway and James Watkinson's Scout Motors continued to run through to London. From 14th April 1930 the Standerwick/Wood Bros./Smith consortium seasonally increased their London fares to 15/- single, £1.5.-d return.

Meanwhile, during March 1930, Standerwicks' London service was diverted between Preston and Knutsford to run once again via Wigan and Warrington abandoning Blackburn-Darwen-Bolton to Wood Bros. and C. Smith Motors. Possibly Scout's operation via Wigan had a bearing on the change, but another factor was undoubtedly linked to the appointment of James Smith as Wigan Agent. Smith had been advertising a Southport-Wigan-London service, and – although detail is sketchy – it seems that the diverted Standerwick operation carried Smith's traffic on the Wigan-London section, with Smith providing a feeder from and to Southport. Smith was later to suffer financial problems and was rescued by the Webster Brothers, who formed the limited company James Smith & Co (Wigan) Ltd. Standerwicks were creditors, probably for ticket moneys, and they were allotted 500 in shares in the new company in lieu of cash. These arrangements did not preclude, however, an unsuccessful Road Traffic Act application by Smiths to continue an express Southport-London service.

Standerwicks' Birmingham traffic had increased to the stage that a daily Blackpool-Birmingham route was added, commencing post-Easter on 14th April 1930 at 2pm from Blackpool, and from Birmingham at 8.30am on 15th April. Routing was identical to the main London service, the new timings being intended to be more suitable for Birmingham-Blackpool traffic. Through coaches almost crossed in Birmingham at 1.45pm north-bound, 2pm south-bound. Early season traffic had been misjudged, however, and the new timings were discontinued after about a week, but a second attempt – from 1st June 1930 – was more successful, competing with services by C. Smith Motors, Empire and Lansdowne. It was seasonally withdrawn at the end of October, following the end of the Illuminations at Blackpool.

The Birmingham terminus and stage for through journeys was, by June 1930, at Samuelson's Whittall Street Garage, but by late summer it had moved again, and was situated in Digbeth, at Smithfield Garage. In London, the Metropolitan Police were becoming anxious to reduce congestion at Woburn Place and, during September 1930, London journeys were extended to terminate at Clapham (London Terminal Coach Station), this being the only Blackpool route to terminate south of the Thames. Woburn Place continued to be the major pick up/set down stage but, from December, coaches also called en route at Kings Cross Coaching Station. A final diversion saw coaches running between Preston and Wigan via Chorley.

The Road Traffic Act 1930 was now in place and licences were issued by the newly-appointed Traffic Commissioners instead of local authorities. Minor changes imposed included a refusal to permit winter fare reductions and carriage of local traffic to points between Blackpool and Warrington; the Metropolitan Commissioner later imposed similar restrictions between Towcester and the capital. Running times had to be adjusted to conform with the requirements of the Act, extending the 10½-hour journey time to 11 hours.

New business gained in 1931 included a contract to supply coaches for extended tours operated by Edwin F. Parkinson, a Lytham newsagent who had specialised in

A sixth vehicle was taken into stock in 1929 and this normal-control Albion PNC26, numerically the third to be delivered, carried an all-weather dual-entrance body by Burlingham. Twenty-six seats of a much more luxurious design are fitted, and the coach FV47 is depicted as a Standerwick 'Pullman Lounge' vehicle. The company, in common with many of the Blackpool operators, continued to purchase all-weather coaches for some time after the full coach was available. This was due to the fact that a large proportion of their business was connected with excursion traffic, and the public still enjoyed a leisurely drive in an open coach when the weather permitted. The bulk of Standerwicks' express traffic was carried at weekends and even the London coaches, therefore, had a dual-purpose operation. This view, by Leyland, was also taken in November 1930 when the vehicle was part-exchanged for a new coach.

personally-conducted tours over a number of years. Parkinson had acted as Lytham Agent for Standerwicks for several years, but the touring coaches had been supplied by Horsfall, Salthouse & Co up to the end of the 1930 season. Following the loss of this work, Horsfall, Salthouse & Co sold to Wright Bros. (Burnley) Ltd, who already used Coliseum Garage as their Blackpool base. In due course Standerwicks added Parkinson's tours to their own touring programme, gaining pick-up points, for extended tours only, in St Annes and Lytham.

A modification to permit overnight journeys on the London service at 10pm from each terminus was applied for in December 1931: in part this was to correct an oversight on the initial application, for occasional overnight journeys at holiday times had previously operated. The Commissioners allowed these to continue, including a journey at Christmas 1931, but refused an increase up to the nightly basis applied for.

By February 1932, the Robin Hood service from Nottingham to Blackpool commenced to use the King Edward Garage as its Blackpool terminus, moving from the KCR site at Britannia Parking Ground which was otherwise unused in winter-time; Nell Gwynne of Bodenham also used the King Edward Garage for a short period in 1932 in connection with its service from Cardiff. These coaches added stand revenue to Standerwicks' business.

About June 1932 MacShanes Office and Waiting Room at 53 Woburn Place closed suddenly, and Standerwicks, anxious to maintain a main London Control office, made arrangements to open their own office a few doors away, at 57 Woburn Place, henceforth handling their own bookings at both ends. Standerwick and MacShanes offices were situated in the Royal Hotel Buildings.

From 17th June 1932 an extra London stop was introduced at Parnell's, in Victoria, but the grant was subject to an appeal by *inter alia* London Coastal Coaches Ltd who acted for Jos. Bracewell Ltd. Further corrections to the original applications for both London and Birmingham routes were lodged in October 1932, including the feeder from Fleetwood to Blackpool which had probably continued to be operated by taxi and various intermediate pick-ups in Blackpool including the halt at M. & H. Motors Jubilee Garage mentioned above. Both modifications were withdrawn at the hearing in December 1932, but these tidying-up operations had been commenced while the future of the Standerwick company was in some doubt, for Mrs Elizabeth Standerwick had indicated in late summer 1932 that she wished to withdraw from the operation, leaving Vic with little option but to agree that the business should be advertised for sale.

The first of the coaches specially equipped with toilet facilities for the London service was FV720, a Leyland TS1 registered on 29th December 1929 and fitted with a dual-entrance Burlingham 26-seat body with the toilet compartment fitted in the nearside rear corner, as evidenced by the leaded windows in that position. This is shown more clearly in the view on the facing page. Note the Standerwick crest painted on to each side, the quarters bearing the letters W, C, S and L, and the legend beneath carrying the words Pullman Lounge': one imagines that the College of Heralds was little involved in any grant of arms! The lettering for the 'Blackpool and London Regular Service' carefully omits mention of Birmingham: at this date Vic Standerwick was in negotiation with the Birmingham authorities who were insisting on examination of each of the coaches used on the service and doubtless he was anxious to play down the fact that the company's coaches were already carrying traffic to and from that city. This view was taken on the New South Promenade extension, well before the hotels that now line the road were planned or built.

Right: Standerwick's Blackpool to London timetable operative in June 1930.

The Last Word in Road Travel! Experienced & Courteous Drivers

STANDERWICK'S

Pullman Lounge Direct Service

BETWEEN **BLACKPOOL**

BIRMINGHAM AND

LONDON

Saloons leave Blackpool Daily at 8-0 a.m., and arrive in **London** at 53, Woburn Place, W.C.1.

Saloons leave London Daily at 8-30 a.m. from 53, Woburn Place, W.C.1, for **Blackpool.**

FARE: Single 15/-, Return 25/-

Saloons leave Blackpool Daily at 8-0 a.m., for **Birmingham,** arriving at Whithall Street Garage at 1-45.

Saloons leave Birmingham Daily (Whithall Street Garage), at 1-30 p.m. for **Blackpool.** Book at Travel Bureau, 141, Steelhouse Lane.

FARE: Single 12/6, Return 20/-

Passengers booking by letter must pay full fare in advance, and state date of return if possible, otherwise they must notify the Local Agent at least 48 hours before they wish to return.

Outward Journey, Leave			Phone No's
Blackpool	8-0 a.m.	King Edward Garage, Central Drive	627
St. Annes	8-15 a.m.	Moore's, St. Albans Road	1013
Lytham	8-20 a.m.	Parkinson, 44 Clifton Street	113
Preston	9-0 a.m.	Harrison's, 115 Church Street	1967
Wigan	9-30 a.m.	Smith's, Standishgate	568
Ashton-in-Makerfield		Leyland's, 53 Brynn Street	56
Warrington		Gould's, Bridge Foot	1032
Newcastle		Waldron's, 46 Penkhull Street	
Stafford		Swan Hotel, Greengate Street	
Walsall		Rendezvous, Lichfield Road	2673
Birmingham		Whithall Street Garage. Book at Travel Bureau, 141 Steelhouse Lane	6731
Coventry		Market Place	
Daventry		New Arterial Road	
Towcester		Post Office	*Return*
Dunstable		Central Tea Rooms, High Street	10-0 am.
St. Albans		Hansall, 41, London Road	9-30 a.m.
London		McShane, 53 Woburn Place	8-30 a.m. 0042 MUSEUM

LONDON OFFICE: McSHANE'S MOTORS LTD., 53 Woburn Place.

Head Office: STANDERWICK'S King Edward Garage, Blackpool. Tel. 627

STANDERWICK'S
PULLMAN Motor SERVICE
— BETWEEN —

LONDON and BLACKPOOL

LEAVING a.m.
BLACKPOOL every MONDAY at 8-30
(From Standerwick's KING EDWARD GARAGE) and
LONDON · every FRIDAY at 8-30
(From RUSSELL SQUARE).

FARES:		SHORT DATE	LONG DATE
Single 20/-;	Return	25/-	30/-

BOOK at
LONDON OFFICE:
LYNE, FRANK & WAGSTAFF
Crescent Place, Marchmont Street, W.C. 1
and all their authorised Agents.

WIGAN Office: Mr. JAS. GREEN, 76 Wallgate.
DARWEN ,, Mr. CATLOW, 52 Railway Rd.
PRESTON ,, Mr. PETER HARRISON, 115 Church Street.
KIRKHAM ,, Mr. T. FORSHAW, Wireless Engineer, Poulton St.

Head Office:
W. C. STANDERWICK Ltd.
KING EDWARD GARAGE,
Phone 627. BLACKPOOL.

Palatine Press, off 130 Palatine Rd., Blackpool, Tel. 2740

Left: A handbill of the once-weekly express service in July 1928. The bill is produced by the Palatine Press, Blackpool, on WC Standerwick's own in-house printing press, situated in the Standerwick home on Palatine Road, Blackpool. In later years the family home was on East Park Drive, but the printing press was not!

Below: The part of the fleet primarily intended for operation of the London express service was further up-dated in 1930, with two further toilet-equipped coaches on Tilling B10A2 and Leyland TS1 chassis entering the fleet. Early in 1931 five further high-specification vehicles joined the fleet. All were Leyland TS2 machines with Burlingham bodies and toilet washroom compartments: FV1498 was typical of these, with dual-entrance and 26 luxurious seats. The resolution of the licensing negotiations in Birmingham had enabled Standerwicks to include that city's name on the waist panel. The coach has a slightly higher floor than might otherwise have been necessary on a TS2 chassis: this has permitted the inclusion of small luggage lockers along the sides and at the rear, enabling the roof-rack to be of minimal proportions.

CHAPTER 4

W. C. STANDERWICK LTD
November 1932-February 1935

The first indication of a break in the ranks of Blackpool operators reached Ribble in August 1932 in a trade paper advertisement reporting a substantial motor coach business for sale. Major Hickmott was put in touch with Victor Standerwick via W. & A. Blackhurst, solicitors. By 2nd September, Hickmott wrote to his Chairman, W. S. Wreathall, outlining plans to purchase Standerwicks, with 18 coaches, the oldest dating from 1929, including three Leyland Tigers on order to replace Tilling Stevens. He was enthusiastic that the Central Beach site might make an excellent Ribble Enquiry Office, and reported Vic's plan to convert King Edward Garage into a first-class waiting room. The London office lease had a five-year termination clause. Turnover and profits were good, with £4,000 p.a. currently earned; Vic was willing to continue to manage the business.

Hickmott believed Standerwicks ran the best London-Blackpool service, having overtaken John Bull both in efficiency and vehicles, and recommended that the service should not be Ribble-operated in view of co-ordination consequences outside Ribble's sphere of operations, mentioning particularly the recent area agreement with Crosville. He was aware that coaching businesses operated on low wage scales, were largely non-union, and wished to avoid weakening the financial balance and the competitive edge between Standerwick and its competitors by forcing pay and other costs up to rates agreed for Ribble's mainly stage-carriage work. Retention of the Standerwick name would maintain goodwill and also enable other Combine Companies to become shareholders in case of conflict of interest. Wreathall concurred, and conferred with his fellow-chairmen to gauge reaction.

Meanwhile, another Combine Company, Birmingham & Midland Motor Omnibus Co. Ltd.(Midland Red), was conferring with North Western Road Car Co.Ltd., its partner in a Manchester-Birmingham-London service regarding a joint approach to Jos. Bracewell Ltd, whose Blackpool/Colne-Birmingham-London expresses used Midland Red facilities in Birmingham, and competed in part with the larger companies' routes. Mr J. W. Womar, North Western general manager was enthusiastic at the suggestion from O. C. Power of Midland Red and the report from his Chairman, George Cardwell, of Standerwicks' availability was also warmly received. He wrote to Hickmott expressing interest in the

Several coaches for the Standerwick fleet were under construction whilst negotiations for the sale of the business to the Combine companies took place. At the time of completion, a Duple-bodied Leyland Tiger TS4 had been paid for but not delivered. It was to arrive a few days after the transfer of ownership took place on 11th November 1932, and was first registered from 1st December 1932. FV3145, below, had been preceded by four other Duple-bodied machines: an AEC Regal in 1931 had been followed by two Leyland TS4 vehicles and a former Tilling demonstrator. The latest delivery and the earlier TS4s had the now usual toilet compartment for London service coaches and were built to a more rakish design than the earlier Burlingham coaches. See also page 26 for another view of this particular vehicle.

Standerwick purchase, suggesting that Ribble join in an approach to Bracewells, without revealing Midland Red's interest, and also advocated an approach to Yelloway, whose Blackpool-Manchester-London route competed with all the Combine and independent operations.

Hickmott was lukewarm about additional purchases, and, advising Womar that Wood Bros. and Scout would also remain in contention, he felt the Standerwick deal should be completed in isolation. Womar continued to press for an approach to Bracewells but still omitted to disclose the interest of Midland Red; his Chairman, Cardwell, after consulting again with Wreathall, suggested that Bracewells be allowed to lie on the table until the Standerwick deal had been completed and this was conveyed to Power. Surprisingly Womar made no mention of the Standerwick deal. Power's reply on 7th November concluded: 'I know you will appreciate that we are vitally affected by the acquisition of any services running through Birmingham, and I shall be pleased to assist in any way possible when negotiations have progressed a little further. We are greatly concerned with the traffic from Birmingham to the north as we have been associated with Bracewells for 10 years.' Womar became concerned, and on 8th November approached his Chairman and Hickmott at Ribble, to seek their views on advising Midland Red of the Standerwick deal. However, his concern was too late to avoid an inter-company dispute, as will be seen.

By 25th October 1932 a price of £25,500 had been agreed for Standerwicks; Vic was to be retained on a twelve-month service agreement, and Mrs Standerwick confirmed that Kent Road garage would be available for a reasonable period at the rent currently charged. The purchase price was complicated by new vehicle orders, one of the new Leylands having been delivered, and two further chassis paid for that were awaiting new bodies. A fourth Leyland Tiger had been ordered in part-exchange for a Reo, and payment for this chassis and three bodies, one by English Electric and the others by Duple, would be due from the new owners.

THE SALE TO THE COMBINE COMPANIES

Completion on 11th November 1932 brought Standerwicks into the joint and equal ownership of Ribble and North Western: Cardwell and Womar for North Western and Wreathall and Hickmott for Ribble were the new directors. In the flurry of activity, it was 12th November before Womar replied to Power's letter regarding acquisitions, and his letter crossed with a further missive from O. C. Power: 'I have heard rumours that Ribble have purchased Standerwicks, and in view of the persistence of these rumours I shall be much obliged if you will let me have the latest information on this point.' Two days later, having received Womar's letter, Power wrote tersely: 'I note that you are participating with the Ribble Company in the acquisition of Standerwick's service, and I will write you again on this point in the next few days.'

Womar reported to Hickmott, who wrote to Power directly, suggesting Midland Red might take an agency for Standerwicks' service after withdrawing from the existing Bracewell arrangement; he further suggested that a conference might be arranged to consider approaching Bracewells, as indicated by Power. In fact, he was already aware of ripples of alarm among the Blackpool coachmen at the sale of Standerwicks and had been approached by both Bracewells and Wood Bros. as they also wished to sell their businesses: such was their fear of the Combine's power to manipulate matters in the Traffic Courts.

Power was not in a mood to be placated, however, and his letters to Womar and Hickmott on 16th November emphasised his wounded feelings. He referred to the pooling arrangement between North Western and Midland Red, noting that, as the purchase of Standerwicks proceeded while correspondence had been passing between the companies, he had been placed in 'a very awkward situation'. He suggested the Standerwick service should terminate at Birmingham, transferring through passengers on to Midland Red's route to London. In a letter of the same date, Ribble's Chairman, W. S. Wreathall, advised Hickmott that he had visited Power personally, a considerable climb-down, explaining that the failure to notify him had been his (Wreathall's) fault, and was in no way attributable to North Western or Ribble. Power accepted Wreathall's position and wrote to Hickmott to seek details to enable them to decide whether to join in *post-facto*. A week later Midland Red confirmed its intention to take a one-third share in Standerwicks back-dated and a revision of holdings took place on 16th February 1933, when R. J. Howley (chairman) and Power joined the Standerwick Board. Finally 6,000 shares were divided equally between the three companies and their nominees, and Midland Red paid interest at 5 per cent on its late introduction of capital.

Renewal of Standerwick licences was heard on 7th December 1932, when modifications to run a Fleetwood-Blackpool feeder and add extra Blackpool pick-ups were heard. Mr Blackhurst formally withdrew both, revealing that negotiations with Wood Bros. were proceeding and the modifications were no longer appropriate. The Commissioners, accepting the withdrawal, made strong comment that Ribble had not reported its recent investment in Standerwicks. They had received notification from North Western and warned they were reserving their right to refuse renewal unless satisfied as to the transaction. After hasty and apologetic submissions by Ribble, the licences were renewed on 25th February 1933. While this was under scrutiny, the company applied to move its London terminal to Victoria Coach Station, and cease to pick-up at Parnell's; this removed the outstanding objection and the first visit by Standerwicks to Victoria Coach Station took place on 1st March 1933.

Vic Standerwick continued as manager of W. C. Standerwick Ltd, but was not to remain undisturbed for long, as negotiations for the purchase of Wood Bros. and Bracewells by the three Combine operators were well advanced. Fuller details are in Appendices I and II, but, on completion on 1st February 1933, both were placed under Standerwicks' management, and the Birmingham and London expresses were immediately marketed as joint services. By 17th February and 1st March 1933 respectively, Registered Offices of Bracewell and Standerwicks had been transferred to Wood Bros. premises at 124 Coronation Street, Blackpool where there was more room. Vic Standerwick became general manager of the enlarged operation, and Frank Briggs, retained as manager of Bracewells, now acted as assistant manager of Standerwicks. The brothers Wood, who had been retained on monthly salary as managers of Wood Bros., left and Arthur Dinham, the former agent, acted as Blackburn manager.

An initial priority was to arrange for the thorough overhaul of Bracewell and Wood Bros. fleets, this being undertaken at Ribble's Frenchwood, and North Western's Charles Street Stockport works – no part was taken by Midland Red. Bracewells' Daimler coaches were particularly poor and much chassis and body work was carried out to make them available for Easter. Daimler FV454 was found to be suffering from extreme water leakage into the body, while the driver's cab was reported as in danger of falling off entirely; both passenger doors had dropped and could only be closed with great difficulty. The vehicle was accordingly withdrawn.

The three companies were all initially short of liquid funds, and in the lean winter months it became necessary for the new owners to inject substantial loans, not only to meet the cost of re-furbishing coaches, but also to pay for new coaches on order, and meet normal overheads: in due course the loans were to reach a sum of £23,132. No change to licences took place at takeover, the existing services continuing to be operated, at least nominally, by coaches of the three separate companies, albeit under the common management of Standerwicks. Wood Bros. involvement with the Blackpool-Yorkshire joint service continued, but, from June 1933, the Yorkshire route was managed by Armitages, this company controlling Walker Taylors in addition, on behalf of the fledgling Yorkshire-Blackpool Pool. It is not clear whether John Bull coaches continued to operate Blackpool-Leeds, or whether Armitage/Walker Taylor machines were used on hire at this time.

Wood Bros.' daily services Blackpool-Chorley-Bolton-Manchester-Oldham, and Blackpool-Liverpool, and Bracewells' daily services Blackpool-Chorley-Bolton-Manchester, and Blackpool-Wigan-St Helens-Liverpool, all continued, but were subject to revision as the new owners examined operations, under the personal scrutiny of Major Hickmott. Applications in February 1933 to extend Wood Bros.' Manchester and Liverpool routes to commence at Fleetwood were disallowed in May, not least due to objections by joint operators Stephensons and Lansdowne and Parker's Blue Bird of Oldham, but further applications were immediately lodged: (a) to divert Wood Bros.' Manchester Oldham route and Bracewells' Liverpool route via St Annes, (Bracewell's Manchester and Wood Bros.'s Liverpool journeys already ran via St Annes) (b) to use the Fleetwood-Blackpool portions of Wood Bros.' Leeds and London routes as feeders for both Manchester and Liverpool, with through fares, and (c) Wood Bros. to pick up at Vance Road, Blackpool and Bracewell at Coronation Street thus linking the operations of both companies. Bracewell also requested new terminals in Liverpool at Pier Head (ex-Christian Street), and in

The leaded lights on the rear window mark the position of the toilet compartment for London service coaches. The half-cab's windscreen angle was echoed by an extended side-screen continuing the nearside body-line over the mudguard and the extension was hinged to permit access to the engine compartment. The earlier introduction of side luggage lockers had been extended: no fewer than five compartments were fitted under the floor on the nearside including a small one behind the rear passenger door which gave access to the 28 luxurious seats within. Access to the roof-rack was by steps immediately forward of the entrance door, and the off-side of the coach was equipped with a matching set of steps. Two similar machines followed in early 1933: these were FV3446 and FV3447. Both views of FV3145, (here and on page 24), are by Duple, this one being utilised in an advertising card extolling the features on the special body.

Manchester at Aytoun Street (ex-Sharp's Lena Street Garage) with an intermediate call at Fingland's Gt. Bridgwater Street Station: all these matched Wood Bros.' authorisation. A number of objectors persuaded the Commissioners to refuse, however, and all four services were discontinued after operation on Saturday 16th December 1933, with return tickets available on the parent companies' limited stop services for a short period.

LONDON EXPRESS SERVICE CHANGES

On the London services, London Coastal became London agent for all three companies in March 1933; Wood Bros. still started from Bush House, Aldwych, calling at Kings Cross Coaching Station, until 1st October 1933, when Kings Cross became the terminal, but Standerwick coaches ceased to call at Kings Cross from 10th May 1933. Woburn Place office and waiting room remained in use. Bracewells' Southampton Row terminus moved to Victoria Coach Station on 1st October 1933; the Kings Cross call was retained. No plans were made to move the Birmingham stop of Standerwick and Wood Bros. services from Smithfield Garage to the Midland Red terminal at Digbeth thus maintaining the competition with independent Birmingham-London routes. Application by Standerwick and Wood Bros. to move to Ribble's Tithebarn Street Station, Preston, was refused, but the change was implemented after a successful appeal.

After a review of London operations of the three acquired companies, it was decided to seek licences to permit a regular interval service to be run from Blackpool to Birmingham and London as hitherto all three London routes had run at broadly similar times. Application was made to the Commissioners in September 1933 and again in October 1934, but in the face of objections, notably Scout, Yelloway and Imperial of Liverpool, the scheme for London changes was refused, despite inclusion – as a carrot – of some reduction in winter workings. However, revision of the Birmingham shorts was approved in May 1935. These routes had earlier been the subject of much criticism by competitors and the Commissioners had restricted daily vehicle journeys to twelve for Bracewell and six for Standerwick, with no vehicle allowed to operate short journeys.

The other coach on order at the time of sale of the Standerwick company was FV3170, another Leyland TS4. This was built to a broadly similar specification to the Duple examples, including the streamlined front nearside panel and the five under-floor luggage compartments, but was constructed by English Electric at the Dick, Kerr Works in Preston. Detail differences included the fitting of double illuminated boxes on the front for fleet name and destination (the Duple versions had only a single box) and a higher roof profile that merged more closely into the rear roof rack and also allowed more roomy interior luggage racks to be installed. As with the Duple deliveries, a sunshine roof was fitted. Having completed the purchase of Standerwicks and placed the operations of Wood Bros. and Bracewells under the management of Standerwicks after February 1933 no new coaches were purchased for the Standerwick group during the remainder of 1933 or in 1934.

CHANGES TO STANDERWICK GROUP OWNERSHIP

Closure of the Wood Bros. and Bracewell expresses to Liverpool and Manchester reduced vehicle requirements slightly, allowing several of the Bracewell Daimler and Maudslay coaches to be disposed of. Tour operations continued under the separate licences, including the several East Lancashire area licences of Wood Bros.; after appraisal, however, the Blackburn-Blackpool express was discontinued. It may not have run under the new owners, leaving Ribble to provide seasonal limited stop services.

The seasonal excursion business of the three companies was not within the original framework of a joint proprietorship by Ribble, North Western and Midland Red and, during 1934, discussions were undertaken to resolve this problem. Apart from the question of disposal of profits from the excursion businesses, it was also clear that the question of fleet replacement would shortly have to be addressed, and discussions centred on ways of separating excursion and express operations, with North Western and Midland Red retaining an interest only in the latter. The peak weekend vehicle requirement on expresses always drew heavily on coaches used mid-week on excursions, however, and it was agreed by October 1934 that Ribble would purchase the holdings of North Western and Midland Red to become sole owner of the three Blackpool companies. Midland Red had no wish to seek any future interest but North Western intended to purchase from the three Standerwick group companies a one-third interest in the Blackpool/Colne-London and Blackpool-Birmingham express services and an appropriate portion of each of the Blackpool companies' fleets and would apply to run jointly with Standerwick, Wood Bros. and Bracewells on the routes.

Midland Red completed the transfer of its shares to Ribble at the end of October 1934, but it was February 1935 before the transfer from North Western took place: the final formalities took place at Standerwick group Board Meetings held on 6th February 1935. The way was then clear for amalgamation of the three Blackpool businesses into Standerwicks' name: for practical purposes the group had become part of the Ribble organisation. Major Hickmott was most anxious that Vic Standerwick should continue to control operation of the expresses and arranged that, whatever the final plan, all operating companies should make some contribution to his salary. In spring 1935, North Western made formal application for London licences but changes in hand by the Standerwick group overtook North Western's plan, leading to the latter being placed on hold. At the close of 1935 it was decided that expresses should remain solely operated by Standerwicks, North Western's application being formally withdrawn.

PROPOSALS OF W. C. STANDERWICK LTD 'Group' for BIRMINGHAM & LONDON Routes

Timetablesa: Service run as at 1st March 1933`

Operator	Stwk	Brwl	Brwl	Bull	Bull	Brwl	Stwk
Period	Yr	Yr	Yr	Yr	Yr	Yr	Smmr
Days of Op.	Dly	Dly	Dly	Dly	Dly	Dly	Dly
Blackpool	0800	0800	..	0800	0800	0930	1400
Colne......	..	..	0800	..	..	..	..
Blackburn....	..	0920	0920	..	0915	..	..
Wigan	0930			0930	1100	1530	0930
Birmingham	1400	1405	1405	1415	1415	1500	1930
London	1935	1930	1930	1925	1925	..	..

Operator	Brwl	Stwk	Stwk	Brwl	Brwl	Bull	Bull
Period	Yr	Smmr	Yr	Yr	Yr	Yr	Yr
Days of Op.	Dly	Dly	Dly	Dly	Dly	Dly	Dly
London	..	..0800	0800	0800	0830	0830	..
Birmingham	0930	9830	1345	1345	1345	1345	1345
Wigan	1330	1330	1800	..	..	1820	1300
Blackburn	..	..	..	1820	1820	..	1830
Colne......	..	..	..	..	1920	..	..
Blackpool....	1500	1500	1930	1940	..	1940	1940

b: Revision Granted by Commissioners May 1935

Operator	Stwk	Brwl	Brwl	Bull	Bull	Brwl	Brwl	Stwk	Brwl	Stwk
Period	Yr	Yr	Yr	Yr	Yr	Wntr	Smmr	Smmr	Smmr	Smmr
Days of Op.	Dly	Dly	Dly	Dly	Dly	Dly	Su	Su	NSu	NSu
Blackpool	0800	0800	..	0800	0800	0930	1100	1400	1500	1600
Colne......	..	..	0800	..	..	..	..	..	..	..
Blackburn....	..	0920	0920	..	0915	..	..	..	..	..
Wigan				0930	1110	1240	1540	1640	1740	
Birmingham	1400	1405	1405	1415	1415	1545	1700	2100	2000	2200
London	1935	1930	1930	1925	1925	..	..	..	..	..

Operator	Brwl	Stwk	Brwl	Brwl	Stwk	Brwl	Brwl	Bull	Bull
Period	Smmr	Smmr	Wntr	Smmr	Yr	Yr	Yr	Yr	Yr
Days of Op.	NSu	Dly	Dly	Su	Dly	Dly	Dly	Dly	Dly
London	..	..	..	0800	0800	0800	0830	0830	
Birmingham	0830	0930	0930	1030	1345	1345	1345	1345	1345
Wigan	1340	1400	1500	1800	..	..	1820	..	
Blackburn	..	..	1820	1820	..	1830			
Colne......	..	..	..	..	..	..	1920	..	..
Blackpool....	1430	1530	1540	1640	1930	1940	..	1940	1940

c: Proposal: September 1933 refused; October 1934 see May 1935 above for limited approval

Operator	Brwl	Stwk	Brwl	Bull	Bull	Brwl	Stwk	Brwl	Stwk	Brwl
Period	Yr	Yr	Wntr	Yr	Smmr	Smmr	Smmr	Smmr	Smmr	Smmr
Days of Op.	Dly	Dly	Dly	Dly	Dly	Su	Su	NSu	NSu	Dly
Blackpool....	..	0930	0930	1100	1100	1100	1400	1500	1600	2200
Colne......	0800	..	..	..	..	..	..	..	..	..
Blackburn....	0920	..	..	..	1215	..	..	..	..	2315
Wigan........	..	1100	1110	1230	..	1240	1540	1640	1740	..
Birmingham...	1405	1530	1545	1715	1715	1700	2100	2000	2200	..
London.......	1930	2105	..	2225	2225	..	..	..	..	0945

Operator	Brwl	Stwk	Brwl	Brwl	Brwl	Stwk	Bull	Bull	Brwl
Period	Smmr	Smmr	Wntr	Smmr	Yr	Yr	Yr	Smmr	Smmr
Days of Op.	NSu	Dly	Dly	Su	Dly	Dly	Dly	Dly	Dly
London.......	..	..	..	..	0800	0910	1030	1030	2225
Birmingham...	0830	0930	0930	1030	1345	1455	1545	1545	..
Wigan........	1300	1340	1400	1500	..	1910	2020	..	..
Blackburn....	..	..	..	..	1820	..	..	2030	0855
Colne......	..	..	..	..	1920	..	..	..	..
Blackpool....	1430	1530	1540	1640	..	2040	2140	2140	1010

NOTES:-

Brwl: op.by Jos.Bracewell Ltd
Bull: op.by Wood.Br.(Bpl) Ltd
Stwk: op.by W.C.Standerwick Ltd

Yr: op.all year round
Wntr: op.in Winter only
Smmr: op.in Summer only

Dly : Daily Service
Su : Sunday only
NSu : Not Sunday

CHAPTER 5

W. C. STANDERWICK LTD

February 1935-September 1939

With the Standerwick group now owned entirely by Ribble it was not long before thoughts turned to rationalisation of the coaching businesses. Major Hickmott had struck up a friendship with Vic Standerwick, whose efforts to maintain the group's share of London traffic had impressed Ribble's Managing Director, and it was reiterated that Standerwicks should become the retained coach-fleet name within the Ribble group. Further, it was now proposed that excursion work within Ribble's entire area should progressively be taken under Standerwicks' name and it was not long before publicity revealed moves to achieve these changes.

Negotiations in December 1934 saw Ribble agree to purchase the goodwill of M. & H. Motors Ltd, Blackpool, chiefly for two express services between Blackpool, Manchester and Oldham. Acquisition was finally completed on 9th March 1935, the services passing on a revised basis to Ribble, North Western and Lancashire United, Ribble retaining the excursion business. M.& H.'s premises at Jubilee Garage, Lytham Road, were not included, and Ribble applied to move the stand to Britannia Place where a limited licence for the former KCR excursions was based). S. & J. Wood (Seagull) and Marshalls objected to the transfer, arguing that abstraction would seriously affect their traffic, the Commissioners disagreed, and an appeal confirmed their decision. Standerwick coaches were used on hire to operate the new Ribble excursions.

Within Blackpool, a grouping similar to Standerwicks' applied also to W. Armitage & Sons Ltd, chiefly to operate a share of Blackpool-Yorkshire express traffic. Armitage and its subsidiary, Walker Taylor & Sons Ltd were owned jointly by Ribble, West Yorkshire, Yorkshire Woollen District and Yorkshire Traction, but the companies also operated substantial Blackpool excursion work. In February 1935, Ribble purchased sole control of these excursions, leaving only express licences in the jointly-owned Armitage group. In April 1935 Standerwicks applied for Armitage and Walker Taylor excursions: from Lansdowne Crescent (previously Armitage) and Albert Road (ex-Walker Taylor) plus Armitage's Fleetwood and Cleveleys bases. These were granted on 10th August 1935: certain vehicles passed to Standerwicks, but are thought not to have been operated.

EAST & CENTRAL LANCASHIRE ACQUISITIONS

A further series of excursions was applied for in April 1935: these were operated hitherto by East Lancashire Motors Ltd, Blackburn, which had agreed to sell its goodwill, and were from Railway Road, Blackburn and stands at Accrington, Darwen and Clayton-le-Moors. These were the first licences applied for outside the Fylde area and the application was particularly complicated as Ribble had decided that East Lancashire's Extended Tour and express licences would be taken by Ribble itself as the company intended to amalgamate the tours with the former Merseyside Touring licences, which had limited

The first additions to Standerwicks' fleet after sale by the family did not arrive until after the holdings of North Western and Midland Red had passed to Ribble. In 1935, 60 Leyland TS7 coaches with 31-seat English Electric bodies were ordered by Ribble and ten of these were intended for Standerwicks. In 1935 eighteen coaches entered service with Ribble and nine with Standerwick, FV5731-39, while two intended for Ribble – FV5741-42 – were diverted to the newly-acquired subsidiary Salisbury fleet. In 1936, the final Standerwick example, FV5740, plus the balance of 30 coaches for Ribble were supplied, plus two extra Ribble vehicles ordered to replace the two diverted to Salisburys. This English Electric official view shows FV5740, the final 1936-delivered vehicle in Preston. The Ribble examples were delivered in reversed livery, only receiving a mainly cream version on repaint by about 1939. Six Standerwick/Salisbury examples survived until 1947.

The extension of Standerwick operations in East Lancashire during 1935 was part of a deliberate policy by Ribble to contain costs, particularly drivers' wages, by use of the Blackpool subsidiary, which operated under different conditions from those agreed for Ribble's own employees. Ribble had maintained the former tours operation of Kenyons Coleman & Robinson Ltd since the previous year, but in 1935 only retained Extended Tours, transferring day excursions to Standerwick. KCR was licensed to run six coaches, twelve during holiday weeks, from Darwen Street, Blackburn and three other centres. Only two vehicles passed to Ribble: one of these was BV2159, an AEC Regal with Duple 32-seat rear-entrance coachwork, seen here liveried for the Blackburn-Blackpool express, which remained with Ribble.

pick-ups. Simultaneous Ribble applications for these portions of East Lancashire Motors appeared: the separated licences were granted, but vehicle allowances for Standerwicks' excursions were cut by almost half, reflecting the Commissioners' misgivings. Standerwicks appealed; the Minister restored the allowances, but linked Ribble's touring grants to Standerwicks' excursion licences. This reduced the latter's vehicles by the number in use by Ribble, and proved most difficult to administer. After Ribble's later attempt to link its Blackburn Extended Tours with similar licences in Preston and Bolton resulted in even greater erosion of the Standerwick excursion licence, it was decided to pass the former East Lancashire Motors excursions to Ribble to simplify administration, this being approved on 15th April 1939.

Formal approval for the East Lancashire Motors transfer to Standerwicks did not appear until September 1935, but the Commissioners approved in principle and the purchase was completed on 6th June 1935, enabling Standerwicks to operate Blackburn and Darwen Wakes traffic; no coaches were acquired but arrival of the first of twelve new Leyland Tiger coaches enabled many of the excursions to be operated with new machines.

Also in February 1935, Ribble concluded the purchase of Wm. Salisbury & Sons Ltd, a substantial Blackpool operator with about a dozen coaches: its reputation resulted in its retention and it was placed under Standerwicks' control, two of the new Tigers entering service with Salisbury at the year end. Salisburys had been negotiating for acquisition of William Whiteside, a small Cleveleys operator; applications had been lodged but had not been published. The changed ownership of Salisburys resulted in fresh applications being made by Standerwicks. Substantial objections were lodged, and the applications were formally withdrawn in October 1935, Whiteside was to continue for a number of years, subsequently re-launching post-war as Fylde Coaches Ltd.

Two weeks after applications to obtain East Lancashire Motors appeared, Ribble extended its new policy by passing to Standerwicks excursions from the Blackburn area, acquired from Kenyons, Coleman & Robinson Ltd KCR Services in 1934. These were run from Darwen Street, Blackburn, with stands at Accrington, Darwen and Great Harwood, and were also granted on 28th September 1935. Over the succeeding years the former East Lancashire and KCR excursions became partially linked operationally, and transfer in 1939 to Ribble of East Lancashire's excursions was accompanied by return of the four former KCR licences also.

Ribble's excursions from Britannia Place, Blackpool, (also ex- KCR Services) were not transferred: this omission may seem surprising, but Ribble was concerned that, on acquisition in 1934, the resort-based excursions had attracted major objections from many Blackpool operators who felt that KCR had been an interloper in the resort. As a result, the destinations had been severely reduced; annual journeys were now: Morecambe 1, Southport 3, Illuminations tours 215 and local trips 235, the latter limited to destinations with fares of 2/- or less. Retention in Ribble's name in the 1935 changes reflected concern that any fresh transfer might result in further reductions; however, operation was henceforth undertaken by Standerwick coaches on hire.

The East Lancashire operations of Wright Bros. (Burnley) Ltd, a Ribble subsidiary since January 1934 were passed to Standerwicks. Six express services and excursions from Burnley and Colne were approved. As in the case of East Lancashire Motors, extended tours passed to Ribble, restrictions being imposed on the number of vehicles used by Standerwicks on excursions. Wrights' business included excursions from Coliseum Garage, Blackpool; once again Ribble was nervous of transferring a resort licence to Standerwicks. In fact the Blackpool business had been purchased from established local owners, Horsfall & Salthouse, and was unlikely to be subject to any aggressive objection, but Ribble was taking no chances! Expresses acquired were Bacup-Rawtenstall-Accrington-Blackpool and Morecambe; Colne-Burnley-Whalley-Blackpool and Morecambe; Colne-Burnley-Rhyl-Colwyn Bay-Llandudno; and Padiham-Burnley-Colne-Scarborough. Wrights' fleet of 15 coaches passed to Standerwicks in December 1935: operation of Coliseum excursions, still licensed to Wrights' was now by hired Standerwick coaches.

Also in 1935 Standerwick took over the day excursions of East Lancashire Motors Ltd, with period excursions and a seasonal Blackpool express passing to Ribble. The East Lancashire fleet was not acquired, but the licence grant was identical to the KCR figures. This Guy B, CB8345 with East Lancashire triple-entrance body, was operated from August 1928 and later ran in the fleet of Parkinson, Knott End. The allocation of ten new Tiger coaches to Standerwicks in 1935 was intended to expand the fleet to enable that company to operate the former KCR and East Lancashire excursions.

LONDON EXPRESS PROPOSALS – AND MORE ACQUISITIONS

In the meantime applications appeared in August 1935 for a substantially revised series of Standerwick-operated express routes to London and Birmingham, replacing those jointly operated by Standerwick, Bracewell and Wood Bros:

1. Colne-Blackburn-Birmingham-London Victoria, daily replacing Bracewells; may combine with service 2.
2. Blackpool-Blackburn-Birmingham-London Victoria, daily replacing Bracewells; Blackpool terminal to move from Vance Road to Chapel Street. May combine with service 1.
3. Blackpool-Wigan-Birmingham, (via Wolverhampton) re-timed; daily replacing Bracewells.
4. Blackpool-Blackburn-Birmingham-London, daily replacing Wood Bros.; Blackpool terminal to move from Coronation Street to Chapel Street, and London terminal from Kings Cross to Victoria.
5. Fleetwood-Blackpool-Wigan-Birmingham-London, daily combining Wood Bros. & Standerwicks; to call at Pleasant Street (Salisburys), Chapel Street & Coliseum Garage, Blackpool instead of Coronation Street, and London terminal to move from Kings Cross to Victoria. Duplication & additional night journeys at Christmas, Easter & Tradesmans Holiday to be as previous Standerwick service.
6. Blackpool-Wigan-Birmingham (via Walsall), to replace existing Standerwick service. Seasonal 1st June-30th September, but to reduce from daily to Friday, Saturday, Sunday and Monday.

The Commissioners approved the revision in principle, but only from 1st February 1936, after modifying certain aspects. Route 3 must reduce to seasonal operation Easter-31st October; extension of route 4 from Kings Cross to Victoria in London was refused and on route 5, the Chapel Street, Blackpool stop was disallowed, making this the only London service not serving Standerwicks' waiting room. All journeys diverted to use Midland Red Birmingham premises at Digbeth. These services would continue largely unchanged until cessation for World War II, the only notable change taking place on 1st November 1938, when route 2 was withdrawn, leaving Colne-London route 1 'free-standing' in exchange for improved duplication on route 5, including use of special vehicles for conveyance of passengers between Coventry and Birmingham and places in the North Western Traffic Area.

In the meantime, the transfer of Wood Bros. and Bracewell excursion licences to Standerwicks, including the several licences held by Wood Bros. in East Lancashire, was approved in December 1935 and Wood Bros. and Bracewell vehicles were taken into the Standerwick fleet between May and October 1936. Wood Bros. stands were at 124 Coronation Street, Blackpool and Ainsworth Street, Blackburn and at Accrington, Darwen, Great Harwood and Clitheroe; Bracewell's stands were at Vance Road and Royal Garage, Coronation Street, Blackpool.

By the end of 1936, operations by the Standerwick Group, which now controlled (inclusive of the Salisbury subsidiary) some 12 express licences, with 17 excursion licences in Blackpool including the two Ribble stands and the Wright Bros.' Coliseum stand, 5 in North Fylde, 13 in Blackburn and district and 2 in Burnley and district, operated by 93 coaches, were becoming a complicated portion of the Ribble empire, particularly as many operations made use of Ribble facilities. Clearly, the attempt to make Standerwick an area-wide coaching subsidiary had come to a halt, following the problems encountered with the Blackburn transfers, and it was eventually decided that Standerwick should become more closely allied with Ribble.

Having completed the transfer of subsidiary coaching operations to Standerwicks' application being made in December 1936 for Standerwicks to take over the Salisbury business which had absorbed a further Blackpool business, John E. Jenking in July 1936: nine licences were granted in June 1937, and Salisburys was liquidated on 30th June 1937, the fleet and operations passing to Standerwicks. The transferred stands were at Pleasant Street, Blackpool and at Hambleton, plus former Jenking sites at Banks Street, Cheltenham Road, Cocker Street, Warley Road and Carshalton Road, Blackpool and at Fleetwood and Cleveleys.

Ribble and Standerwicks signed a Management Agreement on 29th May 1937, under which the subsidiary was operated as an autonomous part of the Ribble company which accepted all expenses of the Standerwick operation, and paid the subsidiary 10 per cent of its gross receipts, plus £1,050 for use of premises, and a further provisional sum of £17,500, presumably for hire of the fleet, per annum. The existing management of Standerwicks was absorbed.

BLACKPOOL COACHING CHANGES

Meanwhile, in January 1937, Standerwicks acquired the business of Waddington & Son Ltd (Union Jack) with a site on the corner of Crystal Road and Promenade, south of Manchester Square. One coach was taken into stock, but the purchase was chiefly of interest as providing a possible South Promenade site to replace the Ribble ex-KCR stand at Britannia Place which was due to be redeveloped by its landlords. The stand would be lost in a new hotel development and Ribble had already applied to relocate the former M. & H. Motors excursions to a site alongside the Dog & Partridge Hotel at the corner of Lytham Road and Waterloo Road. This resulted in objections to the new site from S. & J. Woods (Seagull) and Marshall, as it was on the Waterloo Road side of the hotel and the M.& H. site had been on the Lytham Road side. It was argued, with some justification, that the new site was directly on the 'lemming route' of holiday-makers to the sea front and was accordingly more detrimental to objectors' stands than the former Lytham Road site; Rhodes Marshall even produced evidence that the owners of the Jubilee Garage were willing to re-let, but the Commissioners granted the transfer, as applied for, in June 1936.

Having relocated its former M. & H. excursions, Ribble attempted in June 1937 to move the former KCR excursions to the Dog & Partridge also, but on this occasion the objectors won the day and the application was refused. Accordingly, Ribble proposed in February 1938 that the ex-KCR excursions be moved to the Crystal Road site now used by Standerwicks. The Commissioners were not impressed that two separate operators, albeit associated, should share one stand and in May 1938 the limited Ribble excursions were added to Standerwicks' licence, enabling Britannia Place to be evacuated.

There was a further change of site during the spring of 1938, when Standerwicks received notice to quit Clarence Garage (formerly Walker Taylors). The hotel and garage were to be demolished to make way for new shops; the present McDonalds Restaurant occupies the site. With no nearby alternative available, the company was forced to move the stand to share a site with its existing licence at 15 Central Promenade. By autumn 1938, Ribble felt that further rationalisation in Blackpool was possible, and sought to transfer to Standerwicks the remaining excursion licence from Coliseum Coach Station of Wright Bros. Following an unopposed hearing, the transfer was approved in January 1939 but, for a reason so far undiscovered, the grant was not taken up by Standerwicks, and the Commissioners withdrew approval two months later. While this matter was proceeding, a further application – to transfer Ribble's last remaining Blackpool stand at the Dog & Partridge to Standerwicks – was approved in August 1939. For practical purposes the change was not to be of use for some time, as the Second War was to result in cessation of excursion work and most express services.

Although Standerwick was not licensed to operate the former excursions of M. & H. Motors Ltd, Blackpool until 1939, in practice the company provided the coaches on hire to Ribble from the time that company acquired the M.& H. business in 1935. M. & H. operated a mixed fleet out of Jubilee Garage in South Shore, including Vulcan, Maudslay, Laffley, Reo and Gilford, plus FR9512, a Leyland Lion PLSC3 with a Morgan fabric body: none were included in the sale. The main attraction of the business had been the thrice-daily express between Blackpool and Oldham via Manchester, and this was taken by Ribble, North Western and Lancashire United jointly in view of its competitive situation vis-a-vis the joint high frequency limited stop service between Blackpool and Manchester.

Above: By 1936 the most recent toilet-equipped London coaches were some three years old and to attend to this Ribble's order for 50 Duple-bodied Leyland Tiger TS7s was increased by four to modernise the Standerwick fleet profile. Number FV6847-FV6850 carried bodies essentially to a standard Duple design, with sloping floor and roof line to permit a more capacious rear boot (and eliminate the roof box) but also had a toilet at the rear, reducing seating to 28. To accommodate structural changes the rear-most three windows were slightly stepped, resulting in all window pillars being painted (Ribble's coaches had alternate painted and plated pillars), and styling differences included a half-canopy and Ribble-style stream-lining. These were to prove long-lived additions to the fleet, surviving until 1961 (receiving new 31-seat Duple bodies in 1951). The change by Ribble to Duple bodies in 1936 is interesting, as the main order was built in an almost identical style to the 1935 English Electric-built fleet (on Ribble's own coaches only the detail of the rear mudguard and roof-box profile were notable). Clearly they were built to Ribble's specification: one wonders whether the extended delivery time for the English Electric examples had a bearing on the change of coachbuilder?

Below: The combined London services appeared from 1935 in a unique composite format, the leaflet opening from the centre and featuring a map. This example was issued on 1st February 1936, and features a new Duple-bodied toilet-equipped coach.

STANDERWICK'S
LUXURY
SERVICES

Main Line Services
"Ribble" Connecting Services

TIME TABLE & FARES LIST CURRENT FROM FEBRUARY 1st, 1936, UNTIL FURTHER NOTICE.

COLNE–
BLACKBURN–
LONDON

FLEETWOOD–
BLACKPOOL–
LONDON

(Connections to and from KENDAL, MORECAMBE, LANCASTER and SOUTHPORT).

Below: The 1937 purchase of the Blackpool excursion business of Waddington & Son Ltd brought a twelve-month-old Albion into the Standerwick fleet. Waddingtons had originated as Waddington, Edwards & England in the Foxhall Road depot that later became the Blackpool headquarters of Scout, moving – as England quit the partnership – to the Union Jack Garage on Princess Street. Earlier examples in the Waddington fleet included this 29-seat charabanc: Princess No. 2 registered FR2045. The radiator is by AEC but seemingly the vehicle was a Daimler, and it bears a livery akin to that carried by F. & C. Smith coaches. Confirmation of this possibility has not yet come to hand. Note the passenger sitting to the driver's right, then quite legal, in this view at Southport's Botanic Gardens.

The 1937 intake of 17 coaches – to replace withdrawn machines – comprised Leyland Tiger TS7s with Duple generally 31-seat front-entrance bodies, of which six were operated briefly in the Salisbury fleet until it was closed and merged with Standerwicks. The eleven delivered to Standerwicks included four with wash-room and toilet: these seated 28. The 17 coaches were numbered 1-17 in the series commenced in October 1936: all except four of the chassis were new to Ribble in 1936 and all were transferred to the subsidiaries after receiving new bodies. Seventeen new chassis, originally intended for Standerwicks and registered FV8027-41 and FV8558/9, were received later in the year and took the bodies removed from the 1936-built ex-Ribble coaches before entering service with Ribble. Number 10, RN7785, is seen by Penrith Castle on private hire in June 1937: it was one of the four toilet-equipped coaches, and stands behind FV6847 – now numbered 87 – allowing a comparison to be made between the Ribble-stylestandard body on 10 and the stepped window variant taken by Standerwicks in 1936.

After the large intake of coaches in 1937 there were no new deliveries in 1938, but no fewer than 28 coaches were taken into stock in 1939. The first six, Nos. 96-101 RN8515-20 were Leyland TS8s with Ribble-style Duple front-entrance bodies seating 31. At least one seated 28 and was equipped with a toilet. All these coaches survived until 1954. Illustrated below is No. 99 RN8518 in a photograph that has been air-brushed for use in Duple's publicity.

Above: The six 1939 Leylands were followed by 22 AEC Regal IIs, Nos. 102-123 RN8521-32 and RN8649-58 which had bodies almost identical to the Duples, but built by Burlingham. Detail differences were chiefly in the radius of the driver's bonnet window and the rear mouldings; again, at least one was toilet-equipped. These were the last coaches to carry the Standerwick crest. Seventeen of the AEC coaches were to be requisitioned by the War Department. Within a year five returned and the ten survivors remained with Standerwicks until 1950-1951. Illustrated is No. 123 RN8658, which was equipped with toilet facilities. The outbreak of World War II meant that no further coaches would join the Standerwick fleet for eight years.

Below: The arrival of a new fleet of coaches in 1939 enabled withdrawal of a number of the older vehicles, and some thought was given to countering competition on the Illuminations tours from Blackpool's open tramcars. It was decided to retain six of the older Leyland Tiger TS2s for this purpose. Three Standerwick coaches, Nos. 63-65: FV1679-81 of 1931 and three ex-Wood Bros, Nos. 50-52: FV1859/60 and FV2385 were refurbished and fitted with new open centre-entrance 32-seat runabout bodies built by Brush of Loughborough. These were used for Promenade Illuminations tours and short Fylde excursions and proved popular with the public despite their wooden seats. Renumbered 1-6, the half-dozen runabouts survived in their new form until 1952, although they were not in use as often as the main fleet coaches. Number 5, FV1860, is seen outside Devonshire Road garage in post-war livery after repainting.

CHAPTER 6

W. C. STANDERWICK LTD

September 1939 – October 1968

The outbreak of World War II brought early cessation of Standerwicks' seasonal operations: many vehicles were impressed by the War Department, but others were retained for use by Ribble. Any licence changes necessary were approved under permit by the wartime Regional Transport Commissioner, to meet often urgent needs in the most practical way possible. Express operations were also curtailed, but the authorities relaxed the new rules to match the situation prevalent in the following year, enabling Standerwicks' seasonal expresses from Colne and Bacup to both Blackpool and Morecambe to operate with a single daily journey on each. These also operated in summer 1941, but the Ministry of War Transport directed that no resumption could be made in 1942. London expresses were also reopened briefly from September 1940, running jointly with Scout Motor Services Ltd and fuller details will be found in Chapter Seven.

In December 1945, the Standerwick board was re-constituted, Horace Bottomley, Ribble's general manager, now acting also as Standerwicks' Managing Director, while Vic Standerwick returned to the Board. His place as manager was taken by Frank Briggs, who retained this position until his retirement in 1971, although Vic Standerwick continued to come into the office regularly during the 'fifties. Briggs was a rather dour man whose moods were influenced by the fortunes of Blackpool FC; although he came to the Ribble group via Bracewells, and hailed from East Lancashire, he had developed an attitude very much in the mould of Blackpool's 'sand-grown' coach operators. He worked hard – seven days a week in the summer and no thought of any days off in lieu. He resented any sign of interference from Ribble, and while F. A. Dickinson was traffic manager, got very little of it.

Briggs had a remarkable ability to be in the unexpected place at the unexpected time. Once, when returning from a late meeting in Birmingham, he had reached Standish on the A49 at about 12.30am when he came up behind a darkened Standerwick coach being driven northwards in a spirited fashion. Knowing of no reason for a coach to be there at that time, he dropped back and followed it to Blackpool where it made its way to the Grange Park housing estate. There the driver, a new seasonal man, unloaded his wife, three children and a considerable quantity of household effects! Controls at Devonshire Road garage were so lax that the man had completed an evening excursion and – instead of returning to the garage – had taken his coach to Wigan to bring his family back to newly-obtained accommodation. On another occasion Briggs had been to a meeting at Scotland Yard where the Metropolitan Police had been assured that suitable action had been taken to prevent illegal setting down of passengers in the London streets. Walking back along Victoria Street, he witnessed a Standerwick coach setting down passengers at the Army and Navy Stores!

Under Briggs' management Standerwicks continued to retain its air of independence from Ribble until well into the 'sixties: before 1939 even vehicle policies had differed, with several AECs entering service. From 1945 that changed and, normally, new Standerwick coaches became parts of larger Ribble orders. Nevertheless, there were still minor differences, such as the fitting of 33 seats into the Duple-rebodied Tiger coaches compared with Ribble's 31.

With the cessation of hostilities in 1945, it was some little time before the Ministry permitted pleasure traffic to recommence, and at first the few coaches that were available were restricted to excursions within 25 miles of their originating point. Private parties might travel by coach within a 35 mile radius but, from 14th April 1946, the distance limits were removed and efforts to restore trade could commence in earnest. Many Standerwick coaches still in stock had of course been used by Ribble but, as matters returned to normal, vehicles returned and operations could be restored.

The nature of Blackpool's coaching trade caused major variations in the level of business and Standerwicks relied very heavily on seasonal drivers. During the winter, when perhaps as few as 17 vehicles would be licensed, the more senior men were employed in Devonshire Road garage on maintenance work but the majority disappeared into the sunset only to reappear as if by magic the following spring. Extra coaches would be licensed for Christmas and the New Year and the Devonshire Road men emerged to man them. Standerwicks could not have functioned without the spare men, part-time PSV drivers who worked at weekends as required and evenings during the Illuminations. Many were driving instructors from the RAF station at Weeton; others were Ribble fitters or Ribble drivers on holiday. There was often much finger-crossing on Friday evenings when a regular, posted up for an early Saturday duty, had still not confirmed his availability.

From 1st October 1947, the Service Agreement completed in 1937 between Standerwick and Ribble, was re-written, mainly to simplify accounting procedures. Road service licensing and publicity continued, however, to be provided by Ribble.

Frank Briggs was appointed Manager in 1946, retaining that position until his retirement in 1971.

Above: Diversion of seven Leyland PS1/1 coaches to Ribble in 1948 left Standerwicks short of coaches for that season: eight elderly Ribble coaches had been hired to Standerwicks but were now formally transferred to the subsidiary. Number 32, WH7577, was a Leyland TS6 with 32-seat Duple coachwork (new in 1936 to Christy of Bolton, becoming Ribble 2025). The vehicle behind is also ex-Christy: one of 28-29, WH6578/ WH6477, Duple 32-seat TS7s of 1935 (later Ribble 2021-2022). These had the standard Duple stepped-window design from which a Ribble-modified version for Standerwick had been evolved in 1936. In this view, taken on a Standerwick excursion, the two are still in Ribble livery, but carry 'on hire' stickers: they ran for Standerwicks until 1950/1951.

Below: Ribble ordered a total of 62 Burlingham-bodied Leyland PS1/1 coaches immediately following the end of World War II, but only took two batches, seven in each of 1948 and 1949 for its own use. The remaining 48 were allocated to Standerwicks, 21 Preston-registered examples arriving in 1947 Nos. 62-79: ARN204-10, the balance following in 1948/49 Nos. 80-109: CFV701-30. Number 80 is typical of both batches and is seen at Devonshire Road garage, Blackpool: it was fitted with 31 seats and half-drop windows, and equipped with a sliding sunshine roof. Seven of the vehicles intended for the CFV-registered deliveries were diverted to become Ribble's 1948 batch, replacement chassis being obtained to make up the Standerwick order during 1949.

The Duple-bodied Bedford OB coaches delivered in 1949 were frequent performers on the Bacup-Blackpool service. Number 113, DFR702, is seen at Bacup St James Street awaiting its departure. The more frequent operation of Yelloway along the Rossendale section was affecting loadings during the 'fifties and the 29-seat Bedfords often had more than sufficient capacity. Eventually Standerwicks' route was merged with Yelloway's in the 1955 Fylde Coast pool changes.

The six coaches rebuilt by Brush as runabouts in 1939 were perhaps most utilised in the early post-war period, when vehicle shortages dictated that almost anything that would move was to be pressed into service. This example, on an original Standerwick Leyland TS2 chassis, is No. 3, FV1681, seen in the summer of 1948 loaded for a short circular excursion, positioned literally across Central Drive in a way that must have created traffic problems even in those relatively car-free days! In fact it was probably backing off the former C. Smith Motors Vance Road stand which remained in use by Standerwicks until the end of the 1948 season. Just visible behind the runabout is No. 20, FV3170, the English Electric-bodied Leyland TS4 in its last working season and, across the road in the middle distance, is one of the 1948 batch of Leyland PS1s.

EXPRESS OPERATIONS

The six expresses run from East Lancashire were able to resume in 1946, with the Bacup-Blackpool route, for example, operating two daily journeys throughout the main season. The route from Padiham to Scarborough terminated at East Yorkshire bus station in the latter town rather than West Pier Garage from 1950, and those from Colne to Blackpool and to Morecambe were diverted in 1956 to serve the new Omnibus Station in Whalley, rather than Harts Garage. Bacup-Blackpool was withdrawn after the close of the 1954 season as a result of the formation of the new Fylde Coast Pool (see below). Colne-Morecambe and Bacup-Morecambe last operated in September 1967; the latter was abandoned but the route ex-Colne was transferred to Ribble, who commenced on 1st June 1968 under route number X75. Colne-Blackpool ceased after Easter 1968 and was replaced from 1st June 1968 by modification of Ribble's X55, which provided extra journeys and extended in Blackpool from the Coliseum to Talbot Road bus station.

In January 1956, a new seasonal daily express was proposed between Skipton and Rhyl, Colwyn Bay and Llandudno via Earby, Colne, Burnley, Blackburn and Preston; this was to be jointly operated with Ribble and Crosville and incorporated the existing Standerwick express and period excursions. The application attracted substantial opposition – and an alternative joint proposal for a Colne-Llandudno express by Bracewells (Colne) Ltd, Ribblesdale Coachways Ltd and J. Wearden & Sons Ltd. Agreement could not be reached between the parties, not least because the major company proposals involved the slotting-in of the route into the Ribble network at Preston, with connections from other routes. The subsequent Traffic Court battle was not resolved until June 1957, when the Commissioners sanctioned services by both groups, specifically restricting both to traffic originating from the English end and granting only period returns to Standerwick, Ribble and Crosville. Even this was too late for the 1957 season, and the Standerwick service continued until the close of that season.

The new daily express (X35) commenced on 14th June 1958, running twice daily to 14th September: 9am and 4.50pm ex-Skipton; 8.20am and 4.40pm ex-Llandudno; connections at Preston brought traffic from Blackpool, Keswick and the Lakes, Glasgow and Edinburgh. Similar services ran each year, but poor loadings caused partly by unsuitable departure times for East Lancashire holidaymakers, brought a reduction to Fridays, Saturdays, Sundays and Mondays in July and early August when special Wakes timings from East Lancashire towns were

Three batches of the Leyland-bodied version of the Leyland Royal Tiger PSU1 15 coaches followed the initial delivery, with ten entering the fleet in 1951 Nos. 126-135: EFV617-26 and 20 in 1952 Nos. 136-145: FFR355-64 and Nos. 146-155: FFR690-99. These were all centre-entrance machines and 138 FFR357 is a member of the second batch. The coach is heading a convoy of traffic returning from Lancaster or the Lake District to Preston along the A6 in the evening sunshine and is operating on hire to Ribble on what appears to be a private trip.

added. The independent service soon lost Weardens: Ribblesdale and Bracewell continued on Saturday, Sunday, Tuesday, Wednesday and Thursday, offering day- and period-return fares.

Not surprisingly both operations suffered and, from 1st June 1963, the rival routes were combined, the revised X35 – being run jointly by Standerwicks, Ribble, Crosville, Ribblesdale and Bracewells. Skipton was now served on Saturdays and Sundays, the daily service leaving from Colne at 8.5am; the return left Llandudno at 2.15pm on Saturdays, 5.30pm Sunday-Friday and day- and period-return fares were now available. A feeder linked in from Darwen; Glasgow and Edinburgh connections were lost due to the revised timings but the remainder continued. Attempts to introduce single fares, and for traffic originating in North Wales to be carried, were rejected by the Commissioner. Bracewells retired from the service and a new joint X45 Saturday service by Standerwick, Ribble, Crosville and Ribblesdale commenced on 20th May 1967, leaving Colne at 6.30am for Pwllheli (Butlins) using similar pick-ups to X35.

In 1967 Midland Red proposed a seasonal Saturday Banbury-Coventry-Nuneaton-Cannock-Stafford-Morecambe express; in view of abstraction from Standerwick, Scout and Ribble services it was decided Ribble and Standerwick should take an interest, and it commenced on 1st June 1968: this was the first such operation excluding Scout as partner.

Applications in April 1968 by Ribble, Standerwick and Southdown sought facilities from Blackpool and Colne via the usual routings to Knutsford thence to Brighton and Eastbourne. These were to resurrect former connectional operations previously run by Standerwicks and Southdown in 1953-55. Through overnight London coaches had continued to Brighton and Worthing, also to Portsmouth and Southsea, on hire to Southdown. The grant came too late for 1968, but the Friday night outward and Saturday return journeys commenced on 23rd May 1969. Inclusion of Ribble on the licence is curious: it may be at this time that the parent company was already considering winding up the Scout business.

Above: Ribble had deliberately refrained from purchasing more front-engined coaches than necessary in the post-war period, preferring to wait for projected new designs that promised innovation and a more modern image; an increase in permitted length and width of psv's was also announced by the Ministry. When the Royal Tiger went into production an initial order for 120 complete vehicles was placed with Leyland by Ribble, but to permit the entry into Standerwicks of some of the new coaches an initial order for six Leyland PSU1 15 chassis with 41-seat front-entrance Roadmaster bodies by Duple was completed in 1951. Number 121, EFV146, is seen on excursion work at Ingleton, parked alongside a Wallace Arnold coach. The six continued with Standerwicks until March 1963 when they passed to Ribble, as its numbers 1054-1059, for two further seasons.

Below: Yelloway had the largest holding in the Fylde Coast pool, with the frequent X79 service providing the greatest traffic to the Fylde Coast. Two of the 1954 delivery of Yelloway AEC Regal IV chassis fitted with Burlingham Seagull 41-seat bodies (one is LDK381) arrive at Blackpool's Coliseum Coach Station after working from Oldham on X9 formerly a service licensed to Ribble, North Western and Lancashire United.

With the arrival of the new Royal Tiger coaches it became possible to release some of the pre-war standard front-engined coaches to be modernised to allow them a further lease of life. The first batch was Nos. 35-38 FV6847-50, 1936-built Leyland TS7s. The chassis were overhauled and modified to take 8ft-wide bodies, while the petrol engines were replaced by 7.4 litre oil engines. Finally new 31-seat Duple bodies were fitted. Number 35, FV6847, is seen above outside Duple's works at Hendon ready for delivery to Blackpool and re-entry into service apart from the fitting of a destination blind. The interior view, right, shows the post-war standards applied. Note the comfortable moquette-covered seats and also the narrow sliding window in the bulkhead behind the driver's seat to permit communication between driver and conductor. These coaches continued in service until 1961 but number 35 was to end in an unusual way, as seen at the foot of the page, working for the British Transport Commission's Rowing Section with frames erected on the roof to facilitate the carriage of the rowing boats.

The heavy Royal Tiger coaches were followed by a lighter-weight design, the Leyland Tiger Cub PSUC1/2, and Standerwicks took delivery of two batches of five carrying examples of the classic Burlingham Seagull coachwork. The first joined the fleet in 1954 and were of the centre-entrance 41-seat variety, number 156, HFR601, is seen at Southport on excursion duty. The 1956 deliveries had the entrance positioned at the front, and detail differences included the fitment of straight glass in the front windows to minimise expense on replacement but at a cost of spoiling the lines of the coach.

Fourteen further Burlingham Seagulls were to join the fleet in 1958, this time on Leyland Tiger Cub PSUC1 2T chassis. Number 3, NFR951, is off-service in this view, which shows the new radiused side-window profiles of the re-vamped body design. Much of the elegance of the earlier design was lost with the revised construction, and the change to forward entrance will be noted.

FYLDE COAST POOL SERVICES

As a result of changes in post-war travel habits in the early 'fifties, there were opportunities to rationalise competitive operations and discussions with Yelloway resulted in the formation of the Fylde Coast Pool from 1st April 1955. Publicity for the pool was handled by Ribble; much benefit was gained from the ability of coaches to return home via another pool route, bearing in mind the large number of towns served with holidays on the Wakes Week principle.

The pool consisted of Yelloway, North Western, Lancashire United, Ribble and Standerwick, each contributing services to the pool, of which the most substantial was Yelloway's Oldham-Rochdale-Bacup-Rawtenstall-Haslingden-Preston-Lytham-Blackpool, with several daily journeys throughout the year, plus weekend extras that served Weeton Camp for servicemen on leave. This became X79, taking over Standerwicks' Bacup-Blackpool express and the Bacup-Blackpool section of Ribble's seasonal X97 Todmorden-Blackpool, Todmorden-Bacup being abandoned. A seasonal variant of X79 was X89 Oldham-Rochdale-Norden-Edenfield-Haslingden-Preston-Lytham-Blackpool, replacing Ribble's X89 which commenced at Rochdale and had run via Belthorn. North Western, Ribble, Lancashire United X9 Oldham-Manchester-Bury-Bolton-Preston-Lytham-Blackpool also joined the pool: this ran three times daily in summer with a single journey (twice on Saturdays) in winter and had earlier been M.& H.Motors Ltd route. Service X79 was extended north of Blackpool seasonally to serve Bispham, Cleveleys and Fleetwood from 9th June 1962.

In February 1956 Yelloway purchased T. H. Parker's Blue Bird Motors and Parker's seasonal Hyde-Dukinfield-Ashton-Oldham-Middleton-Heywood-Blackpool-Cleveleys express was added to the pool from 26th March 1956, becoming X69. This brought an extra service into the pool, for it competed with North Western's Glossop-Stalybridge-Dukinfield-Ashton-Blackpool seasonal route and this was included (as X59) from 19th April 1957. It was not included in Ribble publicity, possibly because interavailability with X69 had been refused. In 1958, an attempt to add a Bury stop on X69 was refused, but a 1963 attempt was more successful, when Bury was included in a package in which X59 and X69 were amalgamated as

In a classic Blackpool view Gay Hostess number18, SFV414, heads south along the Golden Mile to take up service on the motorway route to London, having just passed Standerwicks' busy Promenade excursion stand. In typical Blackpool style, however, this is not quite what it seems, for the shadows suggest that the 1963 view was taken around midday, when no London departure was scheduled; the coach is in reality posed for publicity, to the probable frustration of the queue of motorists waiting behind it.

Ten of the fourteen production Gay Hostess coaches were transferred from Ribble to Standerwicks in 1963 the remaining four going to Scout. Number 46, NRN608, heads for Arpley Bus Station, Warrington in June 1971 on a northbound London-Blackpool timing. The coach is lightly loaded, illustrating the problems of securing a worthwhile load on services using the slower A5 route. It is of interest to note that the fourteen Ribble production models were originally fitted with route number boxes on the left of the destination boxes; the prototype's indicator boxes were the other way round!

Above: Changed fleet numbering after Scout came into the Ribble group saw deliveries to Standerwicks carrying numbers in the Ribble series, but with the suffix 'S'. These Leyland Leopard PSU3 3RT chassis with 49-seat Plaxton Panorama coachwork were the 729-38S TRN729-38 and were the first to carry route number boxes for Standerwicks. In this view, with 731S and 738S missing, the boxes are set up for Keswick, Colne and London – using M1 to denote via Motorway – and for Private or Excursion work. Route numbers were supposed to be used on the Fylde Coast services and North Wales X35, but this had been largely ignored up to this time.

The Leyland Leopard Plaxton Panorama combination continued to be the standard purchase until 1968: two such vehicles are seen in the yard of Devonshire Road garage, Blackpool in April 1973. Both have seen service on the Springfields works route W10, but the newer coach, No. 102 FCK935F, has also been used on an excursion to the Races probably the 1973 Grand National. A chalked sign on the windscreen denotes its unavailability for immediate service as it is scheduled for a steam-clean. Number 24 ARN802C was new in 1965, and appears to have lost one of the twin fog-lamps fitted into the grille.

X49, extending to run Glossop-Hyde-Stalybridge-Dukinfield-Ashton-Oldham-Middleton-Heywood-Bury-Blackpool-Bispham-Cleveleys from 1st June 1963.

EXCURSION & TOURS OPERATIONS

In post-war years, Standerwicks continued to operate from a great many Blackpool stands but, as the years passed most fell into disuse for a variety of reasons. These included changes in passenger demand as holiday habits changed, the growing influence of the motor car and the inability of longer and wider coaches to fit on the sites. The excursion business was controlled from the main office, King Edward Garage, although the garage itself had disappeared many years earlier, having largely been lost to provide extra office space and customer circulating areas. Other sites that were retained included Central Promenade (Golden Mile); Pleasant Street, North Shore (originally Salisburys but now with an office close by on Dickson Road); Dog & Partridge, Waterloo Road, South Shore; and Coliseum Coach Station, which continued to be serviced on hire to Wright Bros until May 1948 when a second attempt to transfer the licence to Standerwick succeeded. Several sites were used only in peak season.

From reopening of the excursions in 1946, the Commissioners allowed use of intermediate pick-up points for coaches leaving Blackpool, to relieve pressure on the bus services still operating on emergency arrangements. Additional points were at Layton Institute and Poulton (Sheaf Street) for northbound excursions and at Preston New Road corner for coaches leaving via Kirkham.

The first sites vacated post-war were the two ex-Bracewells stands, Vance Road and Royal Garage, Coronation Street: these closed at the end of 1948 on expiry of the lease and, with no suitable alternative sites available, both licences were switched to King Edward Garage. One of the ex-Salisbury licences was deleted in April 1953: this originated at Hambleton, Over Wyre, and renewal had been opposed by Birch's Motor Service Ltd on the grounds on non-use over a period of time. Withdrawal of this licence subsequently assisted Birch to expand his operating area out of Knott-End-on-Sea.

Head Office, 124 Coronation Street, was a rabbit-warren of a place inherited from Wood Bros., with a small garage, and dismal offices. An excursion licence covered the forecourt, with subsidiary stands at 1, Reads Avenue and Palatine Road, Central Drive corner; in a historical link with the situation in 1930 the twelve-coach vehicle allowance also included operation from the five ex-Wood Bros stands in East Lancashire. Although still licensed, operation from all three Blackpool stands had ceased by 1950 and, with the lease about to expire, plans were made to vacate the offices and resite the various functions; the Chart Room to Chapel Street and other functions, including Briggs' office, were moved in May 1952 to the newly-opened Travel Corner at the junction of Abingdon Street and Talbot Road.

In late 1955, the empty Coronation Street premises were leased by Frank Standerwick, a member of another branch of the family, who already maintained a limited company Standerwick Motor Co Ltd, incorporated on

The Gay Hostess coaches were subject to high mileages, operating some 450 miles on each round trip from Blackpool to London, and in 1968 thoughts turned to the question of a second generation of high-speed motorway double-deck coach for use on the London service. The result was a prototype Bristol VRL LH6L machine with 60-seat Eastern Coach Works body which joined the fleet in 1968. Although two of the vehicles were the victims of unfortunate accidents in later life, the original concept had seemed inspired. The 36-ft long chassis incorporated its Leyland O.680 engine longitudinally-mounted at the rear, and the coachwork was built to a specification produced by Ribble's Chief Engineer, Harry Tennant in conjunction with ECW's chief designer. This included toilets, luggage compartment and air-conditioning, with a centre-entrance, allowing the staircase to be built towards the rear and thus not intruding on passengers' forward vision. Surprisingly Standerwicks' streak of independence has reasserted itself, the route number box being omitted from the fittings. Number 50S, FCK450G, was displayed at the Commercial Motor Show in 1968 and is seen here whilst undertaking trials on the M6 Motorway.

15th March 1949 and who had purchased the long-established business of Alfred Whiteside of Leopold Grove, Blackpool. This town-centre site was a long way from the sea-front, and no longer viable for excursion work and Frank Standerwick wished to relocate to the Coronation Street site he had leased. Mindful of the proximity of the site to the Chapel Street stand, Briggs declined to assist him, using the Coronation Street licence still held by W. C. Standerwick Ltd as protection against the proposed competition. Great consternation was caused when, a few mornings later, an enormous sign, lettered 'Standerwick Motor Co', was erected on the Coronation Street site, but legal opinion quickly confirmed that there was nothing to prevent the new lessee from using the name of one of his businesses on his garage. After much wrangling, it appeared that the price for taking the sign down was an undertaking by W. C. Standerwick Ltd not to oppose transfer of the Whiteside licence to Coronation Street, and this was eventually agreed, the offending sign being replaced by one with the Alfred Whiteside Ltd name.

Nor was this the end of the matter, for the situation under which Standerwicks were to apply to vacate one of its Originating Points to make way for a rival business must have caused enquiry by the Commissioners, who had the power to cancel any licence that was not being used. In this particular instance, the vehicle link with East Lancashire operations rendered the licence more important than might have been the case elsewhere, and it seems that Standerwicks were obliged to undertake some horse-trading with the Commissioners, cancelling four less-important Blackpool excursion licences – Lansdowne Crescent (ex-Armitage), Cheltenham Road and Warley Road (ex-Jenking), and Crystal Road (ex-Waddington) – which were also not in use, in exchange for the retention of the Coronation Street grant, now amended to originate at the former subsidiary Palatine Road site. At the same time an attempt to switch six coaches (half the allocation) to the Dog & Partridge stand brought a chorus of objections that forced withdrawal of the scheme. Operation from Palatine Road was resumed for a period, but eventually ceased once again.

An unusual excursion licence was granted in May 1953 to permit Standerwicks to provide coaches to run from Warrington to London in connection with a promotion during June by the *Salford City Reporter* newspaper: this of course was linked with Standerwicks' right to carry express passengers between these points.

In May 1958 Standerwicks purchased the business of Geo. Moore & Son (St Annes) Ltd, the only licensed excursion operator in Lytham St Annes. Moores had commenced operating coaches in 1922 and re-formed as a limited company on 18th October 1932. The coaching section of the only competing business – T. Towler (Lytham) Ltd – had been taken over in 1952; Towlers operated coaches from about the same time as Moores, but had existed as carriers and removers since about 1870. Moore's excursions originated at Ashton Gardens, St Annes a congested stand, picking up at Hove Road, Lytham Pier and Queens Garage, Bath Street: four coaches were licensed but none was acquired. The transfer to Standerwicks was completed on 28th June 1958. The Ashton Gardens problem was solved in 1960 when Standerwicks transferred the originating point to St Annes Pier Approach.

Declining traffic eventually forced Blackpool operators to apply for schemes to improve loadings: a 1957 plan to enable operators to share loads with one another took three years to receive the Commissioners' modified approval

Royal Tiger coach No. 144, FFR363, was involved in an accident during 1954, and the Leyland centre entrance body was damaged beyond repair. The chassis was sent to Burlinghams for fitment of a new Seagull -type centre-entrance body seating 41 to enable the vehicle to re-enter service. Here No. 144 sports its new body at the Ribble Coach Station, Tithebarn Street, Preston.

under which the Fylde was split into areas, enabling operators to swap half-loads on one trip with half-loads on another, to secure improved loadings. Later in 1960, certain excursions on a line of route could be combined, permitting for example passengers for Windermere to be carried on Keswick excursions. In practice this had been done for many years as had the combination of Liverpool and New Brighton trips.

In north Fylde, the excursion business continued at Cleveleys and Fleetwood where an attempt in 1948 to add a pick-up point at Thornton Railway Station was refused. The Cleveleys holiday trade altered significantly in the 'fifties, and continued property development on Victoria Road swallowed the coach sites which were largely on waste ground, leading to eventual withdrawal, with Abbott's remaining as the sole excursion provider. Fleetwood excursion licences were transferred to Ribble's name, having been re-located from Poulton Road to a point outside the Birch Street depot in 1948.

The Gay Hostess coaches were used extensively on excursion and private hire work, the stewardess service proving a popular addition to the service. Number 26, VFR368, is the first of the 1961 batch of twelve coaches and is seen in Southport in Eastbank Street opposite the Scarisbrick Hotel on a private hire. Behind the Atlantean stands one of Southport Corporation Transport's Crossley double-deck buses, No. 111, GFY411 at the stop loading for Kew. The apparent similarity in the livery is obvious, but in practice, of course, Southport used a much brighter red than Standerwick or Ribble.

EAST LANCASHIRE EXCURSIONS

The former Wood Bros licences at Blackburn, Darwen, Accrington, Great Harwood and Clitheroe continued post-war as Standerwick licences, although operation was still by Ribble vehicles on hire. Over a period of time the licences were revised to a form that parallelled Ribble's own licences, enabling the Standerwick grants to be used to supplement the Ribble operations. The Ainsworth Street premises were not used post-war and excursions moved to the Ribble point at Foundry Hill; in Darwen the Station Road Garage of Harry Harwood was vacated in May 1951, when Harwood retired, in favour of stands at Church Street for day excursions or Borough Road Parking Ground for period excursions. In June 1958, all five licences were exchanged in a major reorganisation in which Ribble and Standerwick excursions became based on Blackburn with feeders from Darwen, Accrington, Great Harwood and Clitheroe.

In contrast, Burnley and Colne-based excursions continued to be run by Standerwick vehicles, with offices at Burnley and Nelson. Congestion at Boot Street, Burnley resulted in excursions leaving from the Cattle Market Bus Station from resumption in 1946, but Cumberland Street, Colne was used until 1968 when the new bus station opened. The eight permitted coaches were increased to twelve at Wakes Weeks in 1956 and fifteen in 1957.

CHAPTER 7

STANDERWICK & SCOUT
Joint Express Operations
September 1940-October 1968

The London 'blitz' peaked during September 1940 and some coach services to and from the capital were reinstated in reduced form to alleviate the effect of rail disruption. Ribble and Scout's stage carriage services had already been pooled as a result of wartime restrictions and the emergency version of the Fleetwood-Blackpool-London express service, with a feeder between Colne and Knutsford, was also operated jointly. Scout vehicles became the first privately-owned coaches to use Victoria Coach Station in their own right. The service is believed to have ceased during June 1941 when the fuel ration was cancelled.

The Standerwick-Scout London express Agreement was formalised when the Lancashire-London services were reinstated from Friday 15th February 1946 southbound and Saturday 16th northbound. The agreed proportions were Standerwick 75%, Scout 25%, parties being paid out for any excess mileage. The initial Agreement was for five years. South of Knutsford, the three services – 7.20am Fleetwood-Blackpool-Lytham St. Annes-Preston-Wigan-London, 8.0am Blackpool-Kirkham-Preston-Blackburn-Bolton-London, and 8.0am Colne-Blackburn-London – were combined as necessary at Knutsford, returning from London Victoria at 8.0am and Kings Cross, which had only been released after use as a London bus store a week earlier, at 8.30am . The Standerwick picking-up points were generally adopted though at both Blackpool and Preston, calls were made at the Scout garages. Scout's Birmingham stop at Victor Garage, Digbeth gave way to Midland Red's Digbeth garage.

The through fare was fixed at £1.11.3d (£1.56) return; this was increased to £1.13.3d (£1.66) in 1951 and, thereafter, there were regular increases to cover higher costs including weekend fares as adopted by most companies using the facilities of London Coastal Coaches.

The ex-Standerwick Blackpool-Birmingham services resumed jointly, the daily route via Wolverhampton at Easter and the weekend route via Walsall, known internally as the 'Ghost Train' because of its poor loadings, on 5th July. The former Scout seasonal night service recommenced jointly on 7th June 1946 leaving Blackpool at 9.30pm and London (Kings Cross) at 10.15pm; Victoria was not served until the licences were revised in 1948. In recognition of its senior status on the night service, Scout always had the first coach, then the third, fifth, seventh and so on. The demand for all the services was insatiable and extra duplication was allowed in the austere summers of 1947 and 1948; in 1949 the Commissioners sanctioned increased duplication only on the Blackpool-Birmingham via Wolverhampton service and warned that even this would not be granted in 1950.

Each route had a 'service man', whose responsibility was to take charge of the convoy and keep to the time-table. He carried a ticket book and could take cash from casual passengers, receiving a small commission. On the London services, each service driver had his own coach and worked a return trip followed by a day off, so that in some weeks they worked only four days. On the days off, their coaches stood idle in the garage. Supervisors recall being soundly berated by a driver for allocating his vehicle to another driver on an exceptionally busy weekday when every wheel counted. These men were superb drivers, thoroughly reliable and with immaculate accident-free records. They were invariably 'characters'. One service man on the Blackpool-Birmingham via Wolverhampton service used to tell highly unlikely tales about intimate conversations he had had with the 'Chief Constable of Stafford'. The same man missed his way into Digbeth in dense fog and followed a tram into Coventry Road depot.

At the peak of the season, coaches did a quick turnround at both ends, running 450 miles a day – but the service man's coach was sacrosanct for many years. These quick turn-rounds were achieved despite the fact that, on paper, the night coaches arrived at each terminus half an hour after the day service departed! Through loaded duplicates arrived literally hours early and even the service coach was usually well ahead of time. There were many

The resumption of the London and Birmingham services, now operated jointly by Standerwick and Scout, saw a variety of ageing vehicles in use until the arrival of new coaches in 1947 enabled the vehicle profile to be improved. Even then peak demands brought out vehicles that would not have been considered in pre-war days. It is reputed that Standerwicks' open-top runabouts were occasionally pressed into service as far as the Knutsford interchange! Number 34, WH7579, was a Leyland TS7 with 32-seat Duple coachwork that came to Standerwicks from Ribble in 1948 but had been operated on hire previously; it was new to Christy of Bolton in 1936. Here it is seen in London's Victoria Coach Station at the refuelling bay after completing a journey on one of the joint routes.

complaints of overnight passengers from London being set down at Preston coach station as much as two hours early, with no facilities open and long pre-dawn waits for connecting Ribble services. Nevertheless, the staff at Devonshire Road garage and at Samuelson's in London, often worked minor miracles in cleaning and servicing a convoy of coaches in an incredibly short time.

Only rarely before Scout was purchased did Standerwick men drive Scout coaches and vice versa. In such cases, to ensure adequate insurance cover, they were theoretically taken on the payroll of the other company for that day.

The Day Service time-table started at Fleetwood but the Fleetwood-Blackpool section was always worked by the 'Fleetwood feeder'. In the winter this was an Austin 16 car, (AFR 2) or an Austin station-wagon (NTB 859) both of which were licensed as PSVs. At other times, they were used to ferry excursion passengers between stands to make up loads.

Developments in the 'Fifties

Despite rationalisation of licences inherited from the companies acquired in the 'thirties, the Blackpool- London services were not seriously hampered by the Ministry of Transport's 'Industrial Towns' clause limiting accommodation to triplication and on the 'Day Service' from Blackpool to London up to 1,000 passengers each way were booked on busy Saturdays, plus a further eight coaches intermediately between Blackpool and Coventry. When Royal Tigers replaced 31-seaters, the latter automatically rose from 240 to 320 passengers, the margin of error being one seat per coach. The Colne-London route, serving only industrial towns, was seriously restricted but duplicates could be put in at Blackburn, using the Blackpool-Blackburn-Bolton-London licence; these were usually Scout coaches. On the days when the Colne-London service could cope, the Blackpool service via Blackburn was not run.

Charting of southbound bookings and their return trips was done at Blackpool where the Chart Room was responsible for recording the advance bookings, issuing 'Stop Notices' when available accommodation was filled and controlling the agents. Bookings originating in London and its environs was charted by London Coastal Coaches at Victoria to agreed limits while Midland Red bulked their offices' bookings and sent them to Blackpool. All bookings between Coventry and Stafford were normally done by Midland Red offices and agents but there was one exception, at Bloxwich, where Mr Ball, a fiercely independent shopkeeper, was a direct Standerwick agent.

In February 1951, following a rare example of interference from Ribble, a Ribble man was appointed Chart Room Supervisor for the Standerwick-Scout pool. The appointment followed the alleged lack of action on numerous complaints from Scout about gross inaccuracies in the charts on the London services, resulting in serious inconvenience to passengers. It will be readily appreciated that an overload of, say, 14 passengers at a place such as Towcester, where there was no readily obtainable back-up, could have grave consequences. After a preliminary talk with the Assistant Traffic Manager of Ribble, he was interviewed for the job by Charles Watkinson, managing director of Scout. Frank Briggs would not concede that there was a problem and ignored him for over a week after he took over! Eventually, however, they established a reasonable working relationship though it was very difficult to get much-needed changes agreed and on more than one occasion this was only done by discreetly enlisting the aid of Jack Williams, Traffic Manager of Scout, who arranged for pressure to be applied through senior Ribble management. Many of the top level discussions between the Ribble organisation and Scout took place in Preston Conservative Club where both the Watkinsons and Bottomley, the Ribble general manager, were members.

The chart room had been staffed by untrained girls who had little idea of the significance of what they were doing. There was a substantial volume of last-minute booking and these were not all being charted. It did not take long to improve matters and, while there were still occasional overloads, they were usually due to lack of discipline by agents. Much of this was cured by contributing to the cost of telephone calls. In 1952, the Chart Room Supervisor and Joe Jackson, one of Ribble's publicity men, made a tour of all agents, a few of whom said they had not seen anyone from Standerwicks since before the War! On the same trip, they took a model of a Royal Tiger coach, made

Standerwick No. 106, CFV727, heads for Victoria Coach Station through the streets of London: the Burlingham-bodied Leyland PS1 1 is not fully loaded and may have dropped passengers at the towns along the A5. The coaches called in London at Kings Cross Coach Station until 29th September 1947, following which the halt was transferred to the new station at Judd Street off Pentonville Road. Later, this call was changed, and vehicles called at a stop in Euston Square.

Above: The six Standerwick Leyland Royal Tiger PSU1 15s with Duple Roadmaster bodies were regular performers on the London services, and the 41 seats permitted an extra eight passengers per coach to be booked. Here No. 120, EFV145, is seen leaving the BOAC premises on Buckingham Palace Road; some contract work was performed for the airline using coaches already in the capital.

Below: Number 136, FFR355, the first of the second batch of Standerwicks' Leyland-bodied Royal Tiger coaches is seen at Scout's Starchhouse Square, Preston premises, the indicator showing Birmingham.

FCK567, first of a batch of three Leyland Royal Tiger PSU1/15 coaches with Duple Coronation Ambassador style bodies new to Scout in 1953, loads in Victoria Coach Station for a duplicate journey to Preston.

The introduction of motorway journeys on the M1 between London and Coventry enabled journey times to and from the capital to be reduced by about two hours. Standerwicks' Leyland Tiger Cub No. 163, LFR 572, with its front-entrance Burlingham Seagull coachwork, is rostered for the north-bound motorway service to Colne, and is seen arriving at Victoria Coach Station to collect its load.

Standerwick Tiger Cub number 2, NFR950, with front-entrance Burlingham Seagull lightweight body arrives at London's Victoria Coach Station with its load from the north-west. These vehicles, new in 1958, were fairly short-lived by Standerwick standards, remaining in the fleet for only nine or ten years.

Right: The Gay Hostess double-deck coaches brought an improved standard of comfort to passengers at a time when motorway services were in their infancy. Standerwick No. 20, SFV416, has a good load on this London-bound journey in June 1960, seen at speed on the M1 in Northamptonshire. The absence of street furniture on the recently-opened motorway, particularly the lack of a crash barrier, looks curious some 34 years later. From January 1961 it became possible to advertise that all motorway journeys would be operated using the new machines, enabling a return to the pre-war standards of toilet-equipped coaches, but with the added facility of hostess-served buffet services en route.

Below: This photograph from Ribble's publicity department depicts Standerwick No. 37, VFR379, leaving London's Victoria Coach Station and turning into Buckingham Palace Road towards the Victoria Rail Station at the start of a journey to Blackpool via the M1 motorway.

The arrival of the Gay Hostess Ribble coaches brought a revived standard of toilet-equipped coaches for passengers, and Scout responded to the Ribble initiative by adding, in 1961, five toilet-equipped Leopards with Duple Northern 38-seat bodies for work on London routes. PRN149 is seen at Victoria Coach Station, London.

Scout S33 DRN361, a Royal Tiger with Duple Ambassador 41-seat coachwork, waits at Victoria Coach Station in front of several Standerwick Gay Hostess double-deckers. Number S33 has been re-painted with the Ribble-style Scout fleetname used after 1961.

Running long-distance coach services is not always as smooth or simple as the timetable might suggest and, when mechanical difficulties strike, there is a double problem for management – arranging completion of their journey for the passengers and recovering the defective vehicle. Hopefully, the first item will have been attended to long before this view was taken. Number 36, VFR378, is about to return to Devonshire Road garage behind Ribble's BD1 on trade plates 004RN after failing on a London-Blackpool via M1 journey. BD1 was originally a Leyland Tiger PS2/5 with Burlingham 35-seat single-deck body (Ribble 2778, later 228: CRN978) new in 1950 and converted for its new work in December 1964.

by Ribble apprentices, down for display at Victoria Coach Station. For the occasion, the *Ribble* fleet names were replaced by *Standerwick* driver's cap badges. One wonders what became of that model.

In October 1951, the joint operators and Ribble applied for an entirely new service between Keswick, Windermere, Kendal, Lancaster, Preston and London. An existing Ribble Keswick to Liverpool timing was used between Keswick and Preston and, in summer, the London coach was duplicated to Preston by a Ribble vehicle which continued to Liverpool. However, in winter, local traffic was carried on the Standerwick coach and two drivers were trained as conductors to work this section. The afternoon Ribble Preston-Carlisle journey was retimed to act as a connection from London while a new Ribble journey at 7.0am from Carlisle fed the London coach at Kendal and a Ribble feeder from Barrow-in-Furness and Grange-over-Sands met the new service at Lancaster. In summer, these feeders also carried traffic for the West of England via Liverpool.

The background to this venture was an attempt by Blair and Palmer in 1951 to run two services on four days a week between Carlisle and Whitehaven and London via Penrith, for the Festival of Britain. Both were refused on the understanding that the established operators would provide facilities. Western SMT was the first to act, commencing as a duplicate to their day and night Glasgow-London express, through feeders from Whitehaven via Carlisle to London, operated by Cumberland Motor Services from 20th August 1951. The proposed Standerwick-Scout-Ribble service represented a great improvement on the existing connectional facilities from Kendal and Lancaster which were at inconveniently early times. The new service commenced on 10th April 1952, leaving London daily throughout the year at 8.0am and Keswick at 7.45am, with Cumberland express feeders from West Cumberland towns added in late summer. Four coaches were authorised to run south of Preston. A diversion to serve Morecambe followed from 1st February 1953.

The Keswick-London service was superior to the Western SMT operation for passengers from West Cumberland and Carlisle, both in terms of journey times and fares. Whitehaven-Keswick-London's fifteen hours was some 90 minutes less than via Carlisle and the fares were about £1.00 cheaper from either Whitehaven or Carlisle. Consequently, the Western SMT service was progressively undermined by the Keswick-London route. As traffic built up, there were through loads from London to Barrow-in-Furness or Carlisle and senior seasonal drivers could lose themselves on the route for several days, sorting out the feeder passengers and getting a return load from Barrow or Carlisle to London.

In January 1952 an attempt was made to extend overnight operation to all the year round, but only Christmas and Easter periods were added to the existing Whitsuntide to September service. More successful was an application, in common with most other operators serving the capital, to increase duplication on London services during the summer of 1953 for the Coronation of Queen Elizabeth II. Up to an extra 36 vehicles daily ex-Blackpool and fifteen ex-Colne were authorised, an appeal by the Railway Executive, arguing that any extra traffic should be directed to rail, being unsuccessful. A seasonal Colne-London night service, sharing the Blackpool timings south of Knutsford, commenced on 22nd May 1954, with some restrictions on loadings, designed to protect competitive services.

In November 1953, there commenced a long-running battle to obtain a new route between Blackpool and London via Oxford, surrendering the existing ex-Scout Blackpool-London licence as a *quid pro quo*. Although the application was widely supported in the north west, opposition in the Midlands, led by the railways and City of Oxford Motor Services and South Midland, resulted in its refusal. As the main point of contention was the Oxford-London section, a modified scheme was soon presented in which only one vehicle would run through to London, duplication being restricted to the Blackpool-Oxford section but the opposition was only appeased by the further concession that there would be no stops between Oxford and London, the proposed stops at High Wycombe, Beaconsfield and Uxbridge being deleted. After several more days before the Commissioners, in the course of which the applicants conceded that duplicate coaches should run direct between Stafford and Kenilworth, avoiding Birmingham and Coventry, the service was approved in April 1955 and the service started on 28th

One of the four former Ribble Gay Hostess class double-deck coaches transferred to Scout in 1963, S60, NRN611, waits at Victoria Coach Station alongside a Standerwick example. Although the four vehicles transferred to Scout retained their route number boxes they were not always used to indicate to passengers whether the coach was to travel via the M1 motorway or the A5 to Dunstable.

May 1955 with departures at 8.0am from both ends.

The service was not a success and, in April 1957, the operators sought to discontinue the Oxford-London section then decided to amend it to divert via High Wycombe, Beaconsfield, Gerrards Cross, Uxbridge and Ealing. Once again, a chorus of objectors held up progress and it was agreed to curtail the service at Oxford with a connection into West London by the South Midland limited stop service, an arrangement which came into force, seasonally, on 23rd May 1958.

In 1958, the pool partners contracted with 'Gaytours', a Blackpool tour promoter, to ferry passengers to various airports for coach-air holidays to Jersey. A weekly or bi-weekly Blackpool-Preston-Wigan-Warrington-Blackbushe airport service, granted in December 1958, was augmented in February 1960 by a Blackpool-Preston-Bolton-Manchester-Knutsford routing, some flights now leaving from Coventry airport. Blackbushe closed down after 14th May 1960 and all coach journeys were diverted to Southend-on-Sea airport. It is interesting to note that the charge to 'Gaytours' for a return double-deck coach journey between Blackpool and Southend at this time was £60. In 1963, some flights were diverted to leave from Derby airport, resulting in further rerouting and the situation was complicated when North Western, Trent and Lancashire United each claimed a share of the rerouted journeys. Operations continued until the close of the 1965 season after which the licences were not renewed.

Motorway Routes

Britain's first motorway, the Preston by-pass portion of the M6, opened on 8th October 1958. Work was well in hand on the first section of the M1 and it was obvious that these new roads would revolutionise coach travel by reducing journey times substantially. Horace Bottomley, general manager of Ribble and managing director of Standerwicks, applied his mind to devising the best means of maximising the benefits of the new roads on which, of course, no stopping would be permitted. The provision of refreshment and toilet facilities was essential, as service areas were initially few and widely spaced. The 'Gay Hostess' double-deck coach was Bottomley's concept of a fast motorway coach, conveying economic loads in greater comfort with built-in refreshment and toilet facilities. The prototype vehicle on rear-engined Leyland Atlantean chassis (Ribble 1251) was tested in August 1959 on the Blackpool-London service. Its original O.600 engine was replaced by an O.680 and the gear ratios adjusted to permit a motorway speed of 64 mph. Testing and driver tuition continued and on 2nd November 1959 it became the first PSV to enter the M1 from the Luton spur when the first part of the M1 was opened. On this day it also found itself up against the first scheduled trip of the Midland Red C5 motorway coach between Birmingham and London. A welcoming ceremony had been arranged but the waiting dignitaries at Victoria were first treated to the sight of a 'Gay Hostess' coach displaying the legend 'Britain's Most Up-to-date Coach'. D.M. Sinclair, Midland Red's general manager is said not to have been pleased at this turn of events and suggested to his C5 driver that the return journey should arrive in Birmingham ahead of the 'Gay Hostess' which was preparing to return north. Any competitive driving was swiftly ended when the C5 burst

The Preston-Southport-London service was operated at weekends by a Gay Hostess coach but often during the week there was only suffiicient traffic to require a single-deck vehicle. One of the 1963 Plaxton-bodied single-deck Leopards with Plaxton coachwork 732S, TRN732, is seen at Ribble's Southport bus station (earlier Lord Street Railway Station) after working from London.

a tyre at speed but was safely brought to rest by its driver. Happily, tyre technology rapidly improved to meet the new demands of high speed motorway travel.

Motorway services to London officially started on 14th April 1960 as variants of the established A5 routes. The day service coaches from Blackpool and Colne met at Knutsford where passengers were sorted out on to A5 or M1 coaches, the latter reducing the running time by 2hr 10min. The Keswick-London service was diverted on to the M1 with a Saturday and Sunday A5 service from June to September. Southbound night services were treated differently to avoid arrival in London at an unsocial hour, the traditional A5 services from Blackpool and London continuing to leave at 8.30pm with a Blackpool coach leaving two hours later via the M1 arriving in London at the same time as the A5 vehicle. However, from Christmas 1960, all night coaches left Blackpool or Colne around 9.30pm arriving in London officially at 6.50am (via M1) or 9.0am (via A5). Northbound day and night coaches left London two hours later on the M1 service, catching up the A5 coaches at Knutsford to interchange passengers as necessary. A further refinement to the pattern at this time was the introduction of seasonal afternoon journeys from Coventry to Blackpool, using the existing London service duplication allowance. In practice, this regularised the well-established practice of working Blackpool-Coventry returns which required a smart performance and by-passing most of the intermediate points. Even a Blackpool-Birmingham return, which was regularly run, meant commencing the return journey ten minutes before the scheduled arrival time!

In practice, splitting the services into A5 and M1 routes created operating problems as at off-peak times there were very few passengers on the A5 route and London passengers were not prepared to use the slower coaches. From 3rd June 1960, passengers from Manchester and Altrincham to places on the A5 were transferred from North Western or Midland Red coaches to the Standerwick-Scout service at Newcastle-under-Lyme. Passengers from Rugeley, Lichfield and Sutton Coldfield were similarly transferred at Birmingham, allowing the Manchester-London coaches to join the motorway east of Coventry.

The night services were finally authorised to run throughout the year from 23rd March 1964. By this time loaded duplicates on the Blackpool day services were using the M6 between Preston and Newcastle and from 15th May 1964, the Blackpool-Oxford service used the M6 between Warrington and Bloxwich, the by-passed intermediate stops being abandoned, saving 77 minutes on the through journey. From the following day, a new summer Saturday service was licensed to Standerwick, Scout, North Western and Midland Red but operated by Potteries Motor Traction Co Ltd on hire. This left Tunstall at 7.20am, calling at Burslem, Hanley and Newcastle, then direct by M6 and M1 motorways to London, returning at 4.0pm. It was designed to provide an earlier service to the Potteries people who, being part way along routes from further north, had had only late departures. Connections for south coast resorts in both directions were now improved. The permitted vehicle allowance varied from four to six, one third taken from Standerwick-Scout and two-thirds from North Western-Midland Red pools. The service was very successful and, from 1967, tickets were interavailable with other services running through Newcastle.

Number 108, FCK941F, was originally 941S and was one of eight 49-seater Leopards with Plaxton Panorama coachwork delivered in 1968. It is pictured outside the Four-in-Hand cafe at Newcastle-under-Lyme, whilst operating a duplicate motorway short journey between Blackpool and Coventry.

Following the success of the tests with Ribble 1251, ten 'Gay Hostess' coaches were delivered to Standerwicks in 1960 and a further twelve in 1961. In 1963, all the Ribble vehicles were transferred, eleven to Standerwicks and four to Scout and thus all London service workings and much duplication could be covered by this type of vehicle. A complete new organisation had to be set up to deal with the new conditions. Stewardesses had to be recruited and trained; caterers were appointed to supply food at Blackpool, Preston, Burnley and London and routines for servicing the toilets had to be established. Moreover, all these arrangements had to be capable of being done quickly as intensive utilisation of these expensive vehicles was essential. The turnover of stewardesses was considerable as the apparent glamour of an exciting job with nights off in London soon palled. There were problems when stewardesses did not report for duty as 'running without a girl' meant extra stops for refreshments which the timetable did not allow for.

As the motorway network was extended, the timetables needed to be constantly reappraised. In 1965 it was proposed to surrender the Blackpool-Blackburn-London licence if the Commissioners would approve a new seasonal Preston-Southport-Wigan-London service. Southport had been served by an extension of the Crosville Liverpool-London service up to 1939 but this had never been reintroduced and the slow Ribble bus connection to Wigan was unattractive. The traffic potential had been increased by a new Pontin's camp at nearby Ainsdale and the New Town of Skelmersdale which was on the route, would also bring new traffic.

The new service started on 12th April 1965 when various changes were made to the network. These included a new later Blackpool-London timing at 10.15am which shared the Keswick-London timings from Preston. In high season there were non-stop journeys from London to Preston and Blackpool, giving a 4½hour journey time and the various timings were rearranged so that alternate services leap-frogged along the motorway, serving different intermediate towns to avoid losing time for through passengers. The fastest Blackpool-London timing was now 6hr 40min. though fully loaded duplicates improved on that considerably.

As the 'sixties progressed, Ribble's traffic managers began to take more interest in the Standerwick-Scout operations and a number of Ribble men were recruited as inspectors. Standerwick drivers soon put an end to the scheme by 'accidentally' stranding inspectors at places such as Stony Stratford or Dunstable. The two long-serving pool representatives at Victoria, Messrs Richardson and Hughes, also went into uniform. From 7th April 1966, King Edward Garage, Chapel Street, which had become congested by parked cars, was replaced by the Coliseum coach station as the Blackpool terminus. The danger of a double-deck coach attempting to go under the low bridge in Chapel Street was also eliminated by the move.

After resuming on 28th May 1966, the Preston-Southport-London service was continued throughout the year but the seasonal weekend Keswick-London A5 service ceased after 31st October. From 1st November 1967 the Blackpool-M1-London night service diverted to serve the Potteries towns of Tunstall, Burslem and Hanley. Seasonal weekend overnight Keswick-London trips, feeding into the service from Blackpool at Preston commenced on 31st May 1968 but, in practice, running through on most occasions.

On 25th October 1968, Scout Motor Services' operations on the London services were transferred to Standerwicks who became responsible for the whole network.

T.A. 2. W. 11/60

RIBBLE MOTOR SERVICES LTD.
W. C. STANDERWICK LTD.

FOODBILL

BOX No. URN No.
EXTRAS
PACKED BY DATE ISSUED
REFRESHMENT DEPOT

HOSTESS/STEWARD
WAGE LETTER WAGE No.
DEPOT

COMMODITY 1	ISSUED 2	REQUISITIONED 3	TOTAL 4	WRITTEN OFF 5	6	RETURNED 7	SOLD 8	PRICE 9	CASH £ s d. 10	FOR OFFICE USE 11
			2 + 3				4-5-7		8 × 9	
CONFECTIONERY										
Fruit & Nut Chocolate								6d.		
Mars Bar								6d.		
Peppermint Cream Choc.								3d.		
Spangles, assorted								3d.		
Pastilles								3d.		
Cadbury Snack								6d.		
Kit Kat								3d.		
Biscuits Plain/Cream								3d.		
CIGARETTES Players								2/-½		
Senior Service								2/-½		
Woodbines								1/7		
Matches								2d.		
SANDWICHES Ham								10d.		
Salmon								10d.		
Cheese								8d.		
CAKE Fruit								6d.		
FRUIT DRINK Orange								6d.		
CRISPS, POTATO								4d.		
CUPS								6d.		
LEAF TEA PACKETS								—	— — —	
LIQUID TEA GALLONS								—	— — —	
MILK PINTS								—	— — —	

REQUISITION FOR REFRESHMENTS — CLOSING No. / OPENING No. / No. ISSUED

Returns Checked by

CASH TOTAL — CASH OVER / SHOR

FOODBILL MUST BE RETURNED TO REFRESHMENT DEPOT INSIDE CONFECTIONERY BOX

Full Instructions Overleaf

The introduction of Gay Hostess coaches required additional support and one of the new items added by Standerwick – and Ribble – was a foodbill to assist the accounting and stocking of the Hostesses. A typical menu is shown, right.

STANDERWICK DINER-COACH EXCURSIONS

HERE ARE SOME TYPICAL MENUS:—

LUNCH 7/-	LUNCH 8/-
HOT SOUP	HOT SOUP
HAM SALAD	COLD ROAST CHICKEN SALAD
TRIFLE	TRIFLE
COFFEE	COFFEE

HIGH TEA 8/-	AFTERNOON TEA 3/-
FRESH SALMON SALAD	HAM ROLL
MIXED PICKLES	BREAD
FRUIT AND FRESH CREAM	BUTTERED SCONE AND JAM
CHEESE AND BISCUITS	CAKE
TEA	TEA

CHAPTER 8

W. C. STANDERWICK LTD.
October 1968-April 1974

From 25th October 1968, the end of operations by Scout left Standerwicks in sole control of the London, Birmingham and Oxford express services and Ribble also surrendered their Keswick-London licences. In addition, Standerwicks acquired the Scout excursions from York Street and Sheppard Street, Blackpool and Scout's share of the joint excursions from Preston and Kirkham. Ribble excursions from Windy Harbour Caravan Site, Singleton were also taken over. Scout's stage carriage services had all been joint with Ribble who took over operation of all but the works services between Blackpool and Springfields Atomic Energy plant, They were now shared by Ribble and Standerwick, much of Scout's share having been operated by coaches.

In 1972, declining traffic brought about a further rationalisation of Blackburn area excursion facilities, when the separate licences of Ribble, Standerwicks, Ribblesdale and Holdens' Tours were merged to provide for joint operation.

LONDON, OXFORD & SOUTH COAST OPERATIONS

Through services were reduced from 1st November 1968 when the 8.0am Blackpool-Birmingham-London journey was truncated to terminate in Birmingham; the return timing enabled the coach to set off for home from Birmingham at 2.52pm. The London via Coventry service, also leaving Blackpool at 8.0am, continued to provide a service to the capital but the Birmingham 'short' was re-extended seasonally from 3rd April 1969. After a second winter running to Birmingham only in 1969-70, it ran henceforth as a Blackpool-London summer seasonal service only. From 1st November 1970, the 8.0am departures from both Blackpool and Preston (via Southport) called at both Birmingham and Coventry as a winter replacement for this journey.

Increasingly, the network was coming under centralised control as the National Bus Company sought to weld together services which had been provided independently by the various member companies of the BTC and BET Groups. A policy of retiming services to connect at key points was commenced while target areas for promoting express travel – students, commuters, airports, holiday camps, etc – were explored. From 22nd May 1970, a Saturday only diversion of the Preston-Southport-London route served Pontins holiday camp at Ainsdale, extending the running time by 15 minutes. Retiming the Blackpool-Oxford service created connections with Associated Motorways Oxford-Southampton-Bournemouth services.

From 1st November 1971, the three overnight services were reduced to two: 10.30pm Blackpool-A5-London, which had run latterly on Friday and Sunday only, was abandoned in favour of the similarly-timed Motorway service which left the M1 briefly to serve Dunstable. On 17th December 1971 new Friday and Sunday motorway journeys were added, leaving Blackpool at 5.0pm and Burnley at 4.35pm; Colne and Nelson were not served. Loads were combined as necessary at Newcastle after which calls were made only at Birmingham and Coventry. Journeys from London left at 5.0pm.

The winter timetable, which was intended to end on 30th March 1972, was extended until 20th April when only the 9.45am Blackpool-London service resumed to expand the winter schedule; the Southport service now commenced at Ainsdale (Pontins) on Saturdays. Day journeys from Blackpool diverted to call at Wigan and Warrington, extending journey times by almost an hour. Night services called at Luton Airport rather than Dunstable and the Keswick-London night service resumed Friday to Monday only. All day and night services now called at Birmingham Airport.

The revised fleet name style introduced in 1968 was progressively applied to coaches as they fell due for repaint. These views of Leopards with Plaxton Panorama bodies new in 1967 illustrate the changes. Number 881S is one of five delivered with toilets and is seen, above right, in traditional style, with large 'S' and 'K' and line beneath the other letters; on the front panel the fleetname is on a raised metal plaque. Number 879S, one of five without toilets, now renumbered 93 and seen right, carries the lower case lettering style. This is also painted onto the front panel, in lieu of the metal plate.

Right: The Gay Hostess double-deck coaches were regular performers on the Birmingham expresses and this view shows one of the former Ribble examples, heading away from Coliseum Coach Station along Lytham Road in September 1970. Number 44, NRN606, is working the afternoon Blackpool-Birmingham journey, the driver having omitted to turn the indicator before leaving the coach station. The vehicle carries the new-style lettering along the sides and below the front windows, but the old-style name still appears in the indicator aperture.

Below: The prototype Bristol VRL LH6L ECW-bodied double-deck coach was joined by a further eleven examples in 1970, numbers 51-61, LRN51-61J. The first of these is seen on Tyldesley Road, Blackpool, arriving at the Coliseum Station in this August 1972 view, when it was running on the 9.15am Fleetwood-London journey. This being a Saturday a number of passengers are already on board. The two-year testing period had not by any means solved all the mechanical problems of the VRL and the class continued to be dogged by unreliability problems throughout their lives. One fitter recalled the regularity of gear-box failures, commenting that due to poor design it was very difficult to gain access to the the gearbox. The coaches also operated through the Lake District, and Devonshire Road garage gossip attributed at least part of the problems to a hump-backed bridge near Grasmere.

Above: Three Plaxton Panorama Elite-bodied Leopards were transferred in 1972 from Ribble: number 117, NCK102J, leaves Preston Bus Station on a duplicate Keswick-Coventry short working on Good Friday 31st March 1972. These coaches were new in 1971 and were not fitted with toilets; they seated 43 passengers.

Below: Number 87, CRN851D, an ex-Scout Leopard with Plaxton Panorama toilet-equipped body, is seen in Park Road, Preston. It is operating the London-Blackpool via the A5 route in April 1972. On this particular Wednesday there do not appear to be any passengers aboard at this stage of the journey!

Service changes, particularly in weekend operation brought about while Standerwick was a subsidiary of North Western, revealed a need for some input of coaches from the southern end. This set in motion the operational changes that would lead to the massive contracting of coaches by National Express in subsequent years. Ford SGF482L, with Plaxton coachwork owned by Samuelsons London, operated on London-Blackpool expresses licensed to Standerwicks during 1973. In this August view it is in St Annes, having almost completed a journey on the 11am ex-London, and carries window stickers for both London and Blackpool as well as an on hire sticker. A 'Standerwick' name-plate is also displayed on the side.

Additional services commenced from 16th May 1972. Blackpool-Oxford was resumed but was reduced to operate Friday-Monday only and the former connection at Knutsford from Colne was now a through journey at identical timings to the Blackpool service. The Associated Motorways connections had ceased, the Oxford-South Midland connections to and from West London again being advertised. Ribble's X99 Barrow-Lancaster connection from London was now a Friday-Monday Standerwick through service leaving Barrow at 8.06am, returning from London at 11.0am; it no longer linked into Keswick-London timings as the X99 had been transformed into a North-Western operated Manchester-Grange express service. A new 8.55am Keswick-London Friday-Monday motorway service, returning from London at 10.0am, served stops to Kendal and then ran direct to Luton Airport and London. All these facilities ended seasonally after 25th September 1972. From 18th August 1972, all journeys commencing at Colne and Burnley were diverted to call at Atherton and Leigh; this applied to the Birmingham, London and Oxford services and the Friday night joint service to Brighton and Eastbourne.

From 25th May 1973, former connections by Cumberland from Whitehaven and Workington were replaced by the extension of Standerwicks' Keswick-London route to commence at Whitehaven at 6.45am and 7.0pm; the motorway express left Whitehaven at 7.40am. New Friday-Monday motorway journeys left Blackpool at 9.0am, calling at Preston, or from Burnley via Blackburn and a new route via Chorley and Horwich to Bolton, Atherton and Leigh, then via M6/M1 to Luton and London. Both returned from London at 10.00am.

The former Scout Harrington-bodied Leopards became regular performers on the Fylde Coast pool routes. Number 2, TCK64, is seen below in Oldham in July 1971 after working as a duplicate from the coast to Rochdale. It is possibly about to operate the 1.30pm Hollinwood-Blackpool X49 although the indicator – showing W60 – displays a typical Standerwick disdain for route numbers.

NEW DOUBLE DECK COACHES

A successor was sought for the 'Gay Hostess' double-deck coaches and a striking new vehicle on a 36ft long Bristol VRL/LH chassis with 60-seat Eastern Coach Works bodywork, was exhibited at the 1968 Commercial Motor Show. The engine was mounted longitudinally behind the off-side rear wheel with the staircase above it. The centre-

Above: A coach from the 1971 delivery of Bristol VRL coaches No. 69, OCK69K, off-loads passengers at Moor Lane Bus Station, Bolton on a duplicate journey from London to Blackburn. The outward-opening passenger doors can be clearly seen. The luggage hold was situated at the rear, and provided sufficient accommodation for the normal needs of the 60 passengers accommodated.

Below: The third and final batch of Bristol VRLs arrived in 1972. Number 75, PRN75K, leaves Preston Bus Station on the 9.15am Fleetwood-London service in May 1973. This view shows the offside emergency exit fitted immediately behind the front wheel. Only 55 of these ECW-bodied VRL-type Bristol coaches were constructed. The 30 purchased by Standerwicks represented the entire UK sales, the remaining 25 going to South Africa apart from the prototype.

The final delivery of coaches to Standerwicks was in 1973, when nine Leopards with Duple Dominant 49-seat coachwork were taken into stock, being part of an order shared with North Western. They arrived in all-over white livery with National fleetname and a grey Standerwick owner name. The third of these was No. 34, XTF817L, pictured in August 1973 arriving at Warrington on a London-Keswick express journey.

entrance layout avoided obstructing the forward view which made lower deck travel on the Atlanteans unpopular. The body was of all-aluminium construction with insulating features designed to minimise noise and vibration and retain heat in winter. Toilet facilities included such refinements as an illuminated mirror and shaving point. The engine was the well-tried Leyland O.680 as used in the Atlantean coaches.

After extensive testing, both on the M6 and M1 motorways and the MIRA proving ground at Nuneaton, the new coach (numbered 50S) went into service between Blackpool and London on 14th December 1968, subsequently having trials on the Keswick, Colne and Southport-London services.

With 24-hour refreshment facilities on the motorways, there was no need of on-board catering and the service was discontinued on the Gay Hostesses, relieving the company of many logistic problems.

It was 1971-72 before all 29 production vehicles were in service. Unfortunately the lengthwise-mounted engine and its transmission were not fully tested, and proved unreliable. The failure rate was unacceptably high and there were often problems of moving stranded passengers as the 60-seaters were unique and, if fully loaded, two replacement vehicles were needed. It was unfortunate that these vehicles were produced whilst Bristol was embarking on a steep learning curve with the technology of the VR generally and the engineering demands of high speed rear-engined double-deck coaches was so little understood. Coach 50S was a Mark 1 VR built with little attention to cooling, and incorporated mechanical components including a transfer box and rear axle which could scarcely undertake local service work satisfactorily.

Although both it and the 29 production vehicles were modified to meet the standards of the Mark 2 VRT, no extra allowance was made for their actual role. This meant

Bristol VRL ECW double-deck coach No. 78, PRN78K, appeared in a hybrid livery in 1972 as the change-over to the country-wide National Express livery commenced. In this October 1972 view No. 78 approaches Preston Bus Station in Standerwick colours, but with the National title displayed between decks and a minuscule Standerwick owner name above a grey line. By June 1973 it had been repainted into the full National livery and was operating in all-over white, a scheme which completely destroyed the striking appearance which Ribble and ECW had created and which had made the vehicles instantly recognisable on the motorways.

that although improved reliability was experienced this was quite insufficient to class the vehicles as acceptable for service. The absence of an oil cooler on the gearbox led to that unit running too hot with limited seal and gear band life, whilst the power input to the transfer box and axle was still too great for long life. A further problem which dogged both these vehicles and the VRT bus variant was the poor life of the fluid flywheel seals in the hot environment – failure would be quite sudden and incapacitated the vehicle immediately. A roadside repair was certainly not practical – needing a gear box removal for ease! These problems were resolved on late Mark 2 and the Mark 3 variant of the VRT. For the VRL coaches, patience was at an end. The final blow was the inadequacy of the engine power output. Although they were praised for their ability to cruise all day at 70 mph, a calculation shows that to drive a fully laden vehicle up the maximum gradients in the long term would actually require nearer 300 bhp than the 205 bhp possible in the O.680 Power Plus engine fitted. Bristol and Ribble/Standerwick cannot be criticised for their efforts. PSV technology was struggling to keep up with fast changing demands and the VRLs represented a valiant attempt to apply their respective past experience and foresight in building rear-engined coaches (the RE) and running the Gay Hostess Atlanteans. Unfortunately the vastly changing roads where cruising at 70 mph was the normal routine imposed a very different demand to the Gay Hostesses which rolled along (sometimes literally) at a maximum geared speed of 64 mph. The change of ownership and the new ability to run 53/57 seat single-deck coaches within the 12 metre overall length introduced in 1971 sounded their death knell. Scarcely twelve years later their successors took to the same roads.

These machines were to achieve a perhaps unjustified notoriety for instability after two incidents received wide publicity. In the first, a VRL narrowly avoided plunging into Birmingham's Bull Ring market after skidding on black ice on the elevated roundabout; it slid sideways into the kerb and was precariously held by the crash barrier after falling on to its side. The second, under National Travel auspices in July 1974, provoked questions in the House of Commons after No. 72, travelling at speed on the M1 south of Northampton, was forced to swerve to avoid a jack-knifing lorry. Its off-side wheels sank into newly turned over soil on the central reservation, causing it to overturn. Both vehicles later returned to service.

FYLDE COAST POOL SERVICES

From 24th May 1969, X49 Glossop-Hyde-Oldham-Bury-Blackpool-Cleveleys was extended to Fleetwood and some journeys split in peak season to run on alternative routes between Ashton and Blackpool to reduce journey times. The morning departure from Glossop and evening return were diverted to serve Hollinwood and then go directly to Blackpool, while a separate vehicle started at Oldham to serve the remaining stops to Bury. From 26th May 1973, X49 journeys originating at Glossop called, after Hollinwood, at Moston and Higher Blackley before joining the motorway.

Acquisition by Yelloway of North Manchester Coaches Ltd. in 1968 brought an additional service into the pool; after transfer of the route into Yelloway's name from 23rd March 1970 Middleton-Higher Blackley-Moston-Harpurhey-Cheetham Hill-Lytham-Blackpool operated in the pool as X19; it was, however, altered to X29 when North Western pointed out that X19 clashed with their Barnsley limited stop service. From 23rd May 1970, X89 Oldham-Rochdale-Haslingden-Blackpool ran direct between Preston and Blackpool, as it had done in pre-pool days.

Winter extension of X79, Oldham-Rochdale-Blackpool, to Fleetwood was planned for 26th October 1970 but it did not take place; from 9th April 1971, the Fleetwood terminus moved from London Street South to Queen's Terrace. Winter extension north of Blackpool finally commenced on Saturdays and Sundays from 29th October 1973, reaching only as far as Cleveleys.

From 26th October 1970, X9, Oldham-Manchester-Bury-Bolton-Blackpool, had ceased to call at Chorley and, commencing 30th October 1972, this service was withdrawn from the Oldham-Manchester section and started instead at Middleton, running via Blackley, Harpurhey and Collyhurst to Manchester then on to Blackpool. From 19th April 1973, the Manchester stop was moved from Lower Mosley Street to Chorlton Street station. X9 was also extended in Blackpool from Coliseum to Talbot Road bus station. X29 no longer served Middleton, starting at Hollinwood and serving Newton Heath; in part replacement for X9, it ran to Moston where it picked up the previous routing to Blackpool. By this time, National Travel was increasingly controlling express operations and Lancashire United disposed of its tiny share in the Fylde Coast pool to Ribble as part of a larger rearrangement of interests.

THE FINAL REORGANISATION

During May 1968, Standerwicks' offices moved from Travel Corner and King Edward Garage to premises on the Rigby Road side of the Coliseum coach station, bringing the Chart Room back into the same offices as the other functions. Frank Briggs retired as manager in 1971, having worked for Standerwicks and its Bracewell predecessor for 43 years, and Robert (Bob) MacKay was appointed manager in his place.

The growing centralisation of operational management under the National Bus Company brought about a number of changes, these being linked with similar events at the North Western Road Car Co. Ltd. which had become solely an express- and excursion-operating company in 1972 after sale of its stage carriage routes to SELNEC PTE, Crosville and Trent. North Western moved its head office first to Wilmslow then to Frenchwood, Preston. NBCs Central Activities Group was taking a direct interest in coaching operations and Standerwick and North Western as specialist coach companies were linked in the CAG proposals. From 31st December 1972, W.C. Standerwick Ltd. became a subsidiary of North Western to increase co-operation between the companies.

From 1st October 1973, when responsibility for express operations passed to National Travel, services were operated by the licence holding companies as contractors; this included all services worked by Standerwick and North Western. Vehicles used on express and touring activities had begun to appear in a corporate white livery in 1972, a 'National' title appearing in alternate red and blue letters; vehicle owners' fleet names appeared in small grey letters. From 6th February 1974, responsibility for operations was devolved to five area subsidiaries; North Western was renamed National Travel (North West) Ltd. as one of these local companies. Responsibility for the express services of Ribble and Crosville as well as Standerwicks passed to the newly-renamed company which also acquired the entire Standerwick fleet.

For a time, NT North West continued to trade variously as Standerwick and North Western with vehicles registered in its own name, but a subsequent reorganisation brought part of the National Travel (Midlands) Ltd. company under NT North West control and the 'North West' name was changed to National Travel (West) Ltd. to reflect the enlarged sphere of operation; the Standerwick and North Western trading names were then dropped in favour of a National Travel West identity. As the technicalities were sorted out, licences remained in Standerwicks' name and, indeed, changes continued to be made including such applications as a proposed tour licence for National Holidays jointly with Ribble and NT West from Caernarfon! Despite this, the Standerwick company had effectively ceased to trade with effect from the April 1974 transfer of its assets, bringing to an end a period of some 70 years of continuous operation.

One of the 1971 Leopards acquired from Ribble in 1972 No. 118, NCK103J, is shown here. It is leaving Preston Bus Station, empty, on Good Friday 20th April 1973. The coach has been repainted into the National livery but without any 'Standerwick' fleet name added. Within a year the Standerwick company had ceased to trade, although the fleet-name was kept alive for a time on some of the vehicles owned by National Travel (North West) Ltd.

Fleet of W. C. STANDERWICK LTD Part One: Commencement to 1939

Including fleet of predecessor business :-

Walter Clinton STANDERWICK (to 1925)

Fleet Number 1936	1939	1946	Registration No.	Manufacturer Type	Aqrd	New	Prev.Owner	Coachwork	Type	Sold	Notes
-	-	-	FR 530	Karrier	1910	1910		?	Ch23	c1915	
-	-	-	FR 621	Alldays & Onions	1911	1911		?	Ch29	c1915	
-	-	-	??	??	1911	1911		?	Ch—	c1920	
-	-	-	FR1416	Tilling Stevens	1915	1915		?	Ch—	c1920	
-	-	-	FR2613-FR2615	Tilling Stevens	??	??		?	Ch—	c1925	
-	-	-	FR4731/FR4751	Tilling Stevens	1922	1922		?	Ch—	1925-6	
-	-	-	NB3503	Leyland	??	1920	??	?	Ch—	c1925	
-	-	-	AJ9664	Lancia	c1924	1923	Rbnsn,Scbro	?	Ch23	1925	
-	-	-	FR6372	Lancia	1925	1925		?	Ch—	c1929	
-	-	-	FR6525	Leyland C9	1925	1925		Burlingham	C20D	c1929	
-	-	-	FR7329	Albion PN26	1926	1926		?	C—	c1932	
-	-	-	FR8015-FR8016	Albion PFB26	1927	1927		?	C24-	1930	EVS
-	-	-	FR8973	Leyland PLC1	1928	1928		?	C26-	1929	
-	-	-	FR9106-FR9107	Tilling B10B2	1928	1928		Burlingham	C26D	1931	
-	-	-	FR9827/FR9916	Tilling B10B2	1929	1929		?	C26-	1932	
-	-	-	FV 47	Albion PNC26	1929	1929		Burlingham	C26D	1932	
-	-	-	FV/115/328/374	Tilling B10B2	1929	1929		?	C26-	1932/3	EVS
59	-	-	FV 720	Leyland TS1	1930	1930		Burlingham	C26DT	1938	
-	-	-	FV 993	Reo GE	1930	1930		?	C20-	1932	
-	-	-	FV1060	Tilling B10A2	1930	1930		?	C24DT	1935	
60	-	-	FV1071	Leyland TS1	1930	1930		Burlingham	C26DT	1938	
61-62	-	-	FV1498-FV1499	Leyland TS2	1931	1931		Burlingham	C26DT	1938	
63-65	1-3	1- 3	FV1679-FV1681	Leyland TS2	1931	1931		?	C26DT	1952	a
-	-	-	FR7896	Reo	1931	1927	Thomson	?	C26-	1931	
66	-	-	FV2041	AEC Regal	1931	1931		Duple	C28R	1939	
67	67	7	FV2512	Leyland TS4	1932	1932		Burlingham	C28RT	1949	
68- 69	68- 69	8- 9	FV2513-FV2514	Leyland TS4	1932	1932		Duple	C28RT	1949	
70	-	-	KJ2911	Tilling C60A7	1932	1931	Tilling	Duple	C—	1938	b
71	71	19	FV3145	Leyland TS4	1932	1932		Duple	C28RT	1949	
72	72	20	FV3170	Leyland TS4	1933	1933		Eng.Electric	C28RT	1949	
73-74	73- 74	21- 22	FV3446-FV3447	Leyland TS4	1933	1933		Duple	C28R	1949	
75- 84	75- 84	28- 33	FV5731-FV5740	Leyland TS7	1935	1935		Eng.Electric	C31F	1940/7	c
9	-	-	CW7102	Leyland LC1	1936	1926	Wright Br	Burlingham	C26R	1937	
10	-	-	CW7206	Leyland LC1	1936	1927	Wright Br	Burlingham	C28R	1937	
-	-	-	CW7496	Leyland LC1	1936	1927	Wright Br	Burlingham	C26-	1936	
11	-	-	TD8897	Leyland LC1	1936	1927	Wright Br	?	C—R	1937	
12	-	-	CK3841	Leyland PLC1	1936	1927	Wright Br	Burlingham	C—R	1937	
14	-	-	CW8442	Leyland PLC1	1936	1928	Wright Br	Burlingham	C29-	1937	
-	-	-	CW9144	Leyland PLC1	1936	1928	Wright Br	Burlingham	C26-	1936	
16/15/17	-	-	HG 608-HG 610	AEC Regal	1936	1931	Wright Br	Burlingham	C32R	1937	
18	18	11	HG 995	AEC Regal	1936	1932	Wright Br	Burlingham	C32R	1947	
19	-	-	HG1760	Bedford WLB	1936	1933	Wright Br	Duple	C20F	1937	
20	-	-	HG2368	Bedford WLB	1936	1934	Wright Br	Duple (?)	C20F	1937	d
21- 22	21- 22	25	HG2758-HG2759	Leyland TS6	1936	1934	Wright Br	Eng Electric	C31R	1941/48	d,e
87- 90	87- 90	35- 38	FV6847-FV6850	Leyland TS7	1936	1936		Duple	C28FT	1961	f
91	-	-	LV2311	Leyland TS4	1936	1933	Ribble	Duple	C25C	1938	g
23-24	-	-	FR9794 FV 360	Leyland TS2	1936	1929	Bracewell	?	C30/1-	1937	
25	-	-	FV1550	Leyland TS2	1936	1931	Bracewell	?	C25-T	1938	
26- 27	-	-	FV1837-FV1838	Leyland TS2	1936	1931	Bracewell	?	C26-T	1938	
28	-	-	FV2358	Maudslay ML6	1936	1931	Bracewell	Burlingham	C26RT	1937	
41	-	-	FV 678	Leyland TS2	1936	1929	Wood Bros	Burlingham	C26DT	1938	
42	-	-	FV 925	Leyland TS2	1936	1930	Wood Bros	Burlingham	C26-T	1938	
43	-	-	FV1125	Leyland TS2	1936	1930	Wood Bros	?	C26-T	1938	
44-45	-	-	FV1500-FV1501	AEC Regal	1936	1930	Wood Bros	Burlingham	C25-T	1937	
46	-	-	FV1689	Leyland TS2	1936	1931	Wood Bros	Burlingham	C25DT	1937	
47- 48	-	-	FV1690-FV1691	AEC Regal	1936	1931	Wood Bros	?	C32-	1938	
49	-	-	FV1840	AEC Regal	1936	1931	Wood Bros	Burlingham	C27-	1938	h
50- 51	4- 5	4- 5	FV1859-FV1860	Leyland TS2	1936	1931	Wood Bros	?	C25RT	1952	a
52-53	6	6	FV2385-FV2386	Leyland TS2	1936	1931	Wood Bros	?	C26RT	1937/52	i, j
54	54	13	FV3093	AEC Regal	1936	1932	Wood Bros	Duple	C28RT	1947	
55	55	14	FV3167	AEC Regal	1936	1932	Wood Bros	Burlingham	C28RT	1947	
56- 57	56- 57	17-18	FV3394-FV3395	Leyland TS4	1936	1933	Wood Bros	Burlingham	C28FT	1947	
58	58	15	FV3396	AEC Regal	1936	1933	Wood Bros	Burlingham	C28FT	1948	
95	95	39	FV7606	Albion Victor	1937	1936	Waddington	Plaxton	C26C	1951	
1- 2	1- 2	-	RN7775-RN7776	Leyland TS7	1937	1936	Ribble	Duple	C31F	1940	k
4	4	40	RN7778	Leyland TS7	1937	1936	Ribble	Duple	C28FT	1961	k, l
6- 7	6- 7	-	RN7781-RN7782	Leyland TS7	1937	1936	Ribble	Duple	C31F	1940	k
8/10	8/10	41/43	RN7783/RN7785	Leyland TS7	1937	1936	Ribble	Duple	C28FT	1956/61	k, l
11/013	11/013	-	RN7786/RN7996	Leyland TS7	1937	1936	Ribble	Duple	C31F	1940	k
12	12	44	RN7787	Leyland TS7	1937	1936	Ribble	Duple	C28FT	1961	k, l
16	16	-	RN7999	Leyland TS7	1937	1937	Ribble	Duple	C31F	1940	k
29- 34	29- 34	-	FV1662-FV1667	AEC Regal	1937	1931	Salisbury	Burlingham	C26R	1939/41	
35	35	10	FV2681	Leyland TS4	1937	1932	Salisbury	Burlingham	C28R	1947	
36	36	12	FV2920	AEC Regal	1937	1932	Salisbury	Burlingham	C32R	1947	

Fleet Number 1936	1939	1946	Registration No.	Manufacturer Type	Aqrd	New	Prev.Owner	Coachwork	Type	Sold	Notes
37	37	16	FV3455	Leyland TS4	1937	1933	Salisbury	Burlingham	C28R	1947	
38- 40	38- 40	24	FV4483 4548-4549	AEC Regal	1937	1934	Salisbury	Beadle	C32R	1941/48	m
92	92	23	FV3655	Albion Valiant	1937	1933	Salisbury	Burlingham	C32R	1946	
93- 94	93- 94	26- 27	FV4910-FV4911	Albion PK115	1937	1934	Salisbury	Burlingham	C24R	1946	
85-86	85- 86	34	FV5741-FV5742	Leyland TS7	1937	1936	Salisbury	Eng.Electric	C31F	1940/7	n
3	3	-	RN7777	Leyland TS7	1937	1936	Salisbury	Duple	C31F	1940	k
5	5	-	RN7779	Leyland TS7	1937	1936	Salisbury	Duple	C31F	1940	k
9	9	42	RN7784	Leyland TS7	1937	1936	Salisbury	Duple	C31F	1961	k, l, o
14-15	14-15	-	RN7997-RN7998	Leyland TS7	1937	1937	Salisbury	Duple	C31F	1940	k
17	17	45	RN8000	Leyland TS7	1937	1937	Salisbury	Duple	C31F	1961	k, l, o
-	96-101	46- 51	RN8515-RN8520	Leyland TS8	1939	1939		Duple	C31F	1954	p, q
-	102-113	52- 54	RN8521-RN8532	AEC Regal II	1939	1939		Burlingham	C31F	1940-51	q, r
-	114-123	55- 61	RN8649-RN8658	AEC Regal II	1939	1939		Burlingham	C31F	1940-51	q, s

NOTES :

No detail of fleet numbering (if any) in the period prior to 1936 has survived. The business of W. C. Standerwick Ltd became a subsidiary of Ribble, North Western and Midland Red (jointly) from November 1932, becoming solely owned by Ribble in October 1934. Over a period of time other coaching businesses owned by Ribble were amalgamated with Standerwick, with vehicles of Wright Bros. (Burnley) Ltd entering the Standerwick fleet in December 1935, followed by J.Bracewell Ltd in May 1936 and Wood Bros. (Blackpool) Ltd in October 1936. At that date (by which time new vehicles were being allocated a number in the Ribble series), a Standerwick Salisbury series in the 1-200 range was introduced. Wm.Salisbury & Sons Ltd fleet merged with Standerwick in July 1937. A single coach from the Waddington & Son Ltd fleet was taken into stock in August 1937, but no vehicles from other businesses acquired (including W. Armitage & Sons Ltd., Walker Taylor & Sons Ltd., or J E. Jenking) survived to be added to the Standerwick fleet.
In 1939 a renumbering of six vehicles rebuilt with Brush open bodies (for Illuminations Tours) took place, and after the war-time loss of many fleet vehicles for the needs of the military, the 61 remaining coaches were allocated fresh numbers.
The following 18 vehicles were owned (or on order) by W. C. Standerwick Ltd on purchase by Ribble, North Western & Midland Red) on 11th November 1932:

Tilling : FV328/1060/KJ2911 (3)
Leyland : FV720/1071/1498-9/1679/1780/1681/2512-4/3145/3170/3446-7 (14)
AEC. : FV2041 (1)

EVS Vehicles registered FR8016 and FV 374 showed Ernest Victor Standerwick as legal owner (rather than W.C.Standerwick Ltd).
a - Rebodied Brush OC32C in 1939 for use in connection with Illuminations Tours. Allocated (but did not carry) Ribble numbers 2283-2285 (FV1679- FV1681), 2286-2287 (FV1859-FV1860).
b - Former Tilling demonstrator.
c - FV5740 was delivered in 1936. FV5731-FV5740 were allocated (but did not carry) Ribble numbers 1455-1464. FV5735 6 8 40 passed to War Dept in 1940; the remaining six received the new fleet numbers 28-34 in 1946.
d - Allocated (but did not carry) Ribble numbers 1491 (HG2368), 1492-1493 (HG2758-HG2759).
e - HG2758 passed to RAF in 7/1941, returning to Ribble (NOT Standerwick) in 1948; allocated (but did not carry) Ribble number 2565. Fitted with a 1938 Duple C31F, body, it entered service with Ribble (as 1464) in 1949. HG2759 survived with Standerwick to 1948 (becoming 25 in 1946), then passed to Ribble, receiving a 1939 Burlingham C31F body and entering service as 1460.
f - Allocated (but did not carry) Ribble numbers 1544-1547. New Duple C31F bodie3s fitted in 1951.
g - Originally Pearson 'Happy Days', Liverpool. Seating increased to C28C.
h - Reseated to C26- in 3.1937.
i - Reseated to C31R at unknown date.
j - In 1939 FV2385 rebodied Brush OC32C for use in connection with Illuminations Tours. Allocated (but did not carry) Ribble number 2288.
k - 17 Leyland TS7 chassis (FV8027-FV8041/FV8558-FV8559) were ordered for Standerwick & Salisbury but delivered to Ribble: Ribble 1525-1529/1531-1537 (new 1936) and 1652-1656 (new 1937) were transferred to Standerwick/Salisbury, but the 1936 chassis had new (1937) bodies fitted (the twelve-month old bodies were placed on the 1937 FV-registered chassis).
l - Fitted with new Duple C31F bodies in 1950; 43 was scrapped in 1956, but the new Duple body was fitted to RN8788 (ex-Ribble), which assumed the number 43.
m - FV4483/FV4548 passed to War Dept in 1941; FV 4549 survived to be re-numbered 24 in 1946.
n - Allocated (but did not carry) Ribble numbers 1465-1466. FV5741 passed to War Dept in 1940; FV5742 received the 1946 fleet number 34.
o - Requisitioned by War Department in 1940, but returned in 1943.
p - Allocated (but did not carry) Ribble numbers 2001-2006.
q - Some, including at least RN8518 and RN8658, were equipped with C28FT bodies. RN8523 was definately C31F.
r - Allocated (but did not carry) Ribble numbers 2007-2018. RN8521-RN8525/7/9/31/2 passed to War Dept in 1940. RN8526/8/30 passed to War Dept in 1940, but later returned: these became 52-54 in 1946.
s - Allocated (but did not carry) Ribble numbers 2084-2093. RN8651-RN8653 passed to War Dept in 1940. RN8649-RN8650 passed to War Dept in 1940, but later returned: these became 55/61 in 1946. RN8654-RN8658 became 56-60 in 1946.

Fleet of W.C.STANDERWICK LTD Part Two: 1940 - 1974

Fleet Number			Registration No.	Manufacturer			Prev.Owner	Coachwork	Type	Sold	Notes
1946	1968	1971		Type	Agrd	New					
62-79	-	-	ARN204-ARN221	Leyland PS1/1	1947	1947		Burlingham	C31F	1960-1	
26	-	-	WH7684	AEC Regal	1948	1936	Ribble	Watson	C32C	1950	a
27	-	-	KMG593	AEC Regal	1948	1939	Ribble	Burlingham	C31F	1953	b
28-29	-	-	WH6578/WH6477	Leyland TS6	1948	1935	Ribble	Duple	C32F	1950	c
30- 32	-	-	WH7575-WH7577	Leyland TS7	1948	1936	Ribble	Duple	C32F	1950-1	c
33-34	-	-	WH7578-WH7579	Leyland TS7	1948	1936	Ribble	Duple	C32F	1951	c
80-109	-	-	CFV701-CFV730	Leyland PS1/1	1948/9	1948/9		Burlingham	C31F	1960-1	d
110-119	-	-	DFR699-DFR708	Bedford OB	1949	1949		Duple	C29F	1955	
120-125	-	-	EFV145-EFV150	Leyland PSU1/15	1951	1951		Duple	C41F	1963	
126-135	-	-	EFV617-EFV626	Leyland PSU1/15	1951	1951		Leyland	C41C	1963-6	
136-145	-	-	FFR355-FFR364	Leyland PSU1/15	1952	1952		Leyland	C41C	1963-5	e
146-155	-	-	FFR690-FFR699	Leyland PSU1/15	1952	1952		Leyland	C41C	1963-5	
156-160	-	-	HFR601-HFR605	Leyland PSUC1/2	1954	1954		Burlingham	C41C	1967-8	
161-165	-	-	LFR570-LFR574	Leyland PSUC1/2	1956	1956		Burlingham	C41F	1968	
43	-	-	RN8788	Leyland TS8	1956	1939	Ribble	Duple	C31F	1961	f
1-12/4-5	-	-	NFR949-NFR962	Leyland PSUC1/2T	1958	1958		Burlingham	C41F	1967-8	
16-25	16-25	-	SFV412-SFV421	Leyland PDR1/1	1960	1960		Weymann	CH34/16FT	1970-1	
26-37	26-37	-	VFR368-VFR379	Leyland PDR1/1	1961	1961		Weymann	CH34/16FT	1971-2	
38	38	-	MCK812	Leyland PDR1/1	1963	1959	Ribble	MCCW/Weymann	CH34/16FT	1969	
39-48	39-48	-	NRN601-NRN610	Leyland PDR1/1	1963	1960	Ribble	Weymann	CH34/16FT	1970-1	
729s-730s	-	-	TRN729-TRN730	Leyland PSU3/3RT	1963	1963		Plaxton	C49F	1968	j
731s-738s	4-11	4-11	TRN731-TRN738	Leyland PSU3/3RT	1963	1963		Plaxton	C49F	1974	o
795s-796s	65-66	17-18	ARN795C-ARN796C	Leyland PSU3/3RT	1965	1965		Plaxton	C49F	1972	m
797s-803s	67-73	19- 25	ARN797C-ARN803C	Leyland PSU3/3RT	1965	1965		Plaxton	C49F	1974	g
842s-843s	78- 79	30- 31	CRN842D-CRN843D	Leyland PSU3/4R	1966	1966		Plaxton	C44FT	1974	g
844s-849s	80-85	80- 85	CRN844D-CRN849D	Leyland PSU3/4R	1966	1966		Plaxton	C44FT	1974	g
950s	-	-	GCK285	Leyland PSUC1/2	1966	1954	Ribble	Burlingham	C41C	1967	
876s-880s	90-94	90- 94	ECK876E-ECK880E	Leyland PSU3/4R	1967	1967		Plaxton	C49F	1972/4	l
881s-885s	95- 99	95- 99	ECK881E-ECK885E	Leyland PSU3/4R	1967	1967		Plaxton	C44FT	1974	g
934s-941s	101-108	101-108	FCK934F-FCK941F	Leyland PSU3/4R	1968	1968		Plaxton	C49F	1974	g
50s	50	50	FCK450G	Bristol VRL/LH6L	1968	1968		ECW	CH42/18CT	1974	g
-	1-3	1-3	TCK 63-TCK 65	Leyland PSU3/3R	1968	1963	Scout	Harrington	C49F	1972-4	i
-	12/4/5/49	-	NRN611-NRN614	Leyland PDR1/1	1968	1960	Scout	Weymann	CH34/16FT	1970-1	k
-	61-64	12/4-6	TRN739-TRN742	Leyland PSU3/3RT	1968	1963	Scout	Plaxton	C49F	1974	n
-	74-77	26-29	ARN804C-ARN807C	Leyland PSU3/3RT	1968	1965	Scout	Plaxton	C49F	1974	g
-	86-89	86-89	CRN850D-CRN853D	Leyland PSU3/4R	1968	1966	Scout	Plaxton	C44FT	1974	g
-	100	100	ECK889E	Leyland PSU3/4R	1968	1967	Scout	Plaxton	C44FT	1974	g
-	109-112	109-112	FCK942F-FCK945F	Leyland PSU3 4R	1968	1968	Scout	Plaxton	C44F	1974	g
-	113-116	113-116	SCK866/868-870	Leyland PSU3/3RT	1970	1962	Ribble	Duple Nthrn	C40FT	1971	
-	51-61	51-61	LRN51J-LRN61J	Bristol VRL/LH6L	1970	1970		ECW	CH42/18CT	1974	g
-	62-71	62-71	OCK62K-OCK71K	Bristol VRL/LH6L	1971	1971		ECW	CH42/18CT	1974	g
-	117-119	117-119	NCK102J-NCK104J	Leyland PSU4B/4R	1972	1971	Ribble	Plaxton	C43F	1974	g
-	72-79	72-79	PRN72K-PRN79K	Bristol VRL/LH6L	1972	1972		ECW	CH42/18CT	1974	g
-	32-40	32-40	XTF815L-XTF823L	Leyland PSU3B/4R	1973	1973		Duple	C49F	1974	g

NOTES:

In addition to the vehicles listed, two small vehicles (but registered as PSVs) were used to ferry excursion passengers between stands to make up loads, and to run theFleetwood Feeder to the London coach at Chapel Street office at quiet times. These were AFR2, an Austin 16 car and NTB859, an Austin station-wagon. From 1963, new deliveries carried numbers that were within the Ribble series (albeit with an S suffix to identify the Standerwick allocation), but from October 1968, when the Scout Motor Services Ltd coaching fleet was passed to Standerwick, the former policy of allocating fleet numbers within the 1-200 band was resumed, with appropriate re-numbering where necessary. A further re-numbering exercise took place in 1971 to provide a more rational series for the current vehicles. The majority of the Standerwick fleet of coaches passed in April 1974 into the ownership of National Travel (North West) Ltd, the area subsidiary of the coaching division of the National Bus Company, and the few remaining vehicles passed to Ribble, ending some seventy years of trading under the Standerwick name.

a – New to Snaylam, Bolton.
b – Formerly an AEC demonstrator.
c – New to Christy, Bolton.
d – 92/3/7/8, 102/3/7 new 1949 (original chassis diverted to Ribble: 2548-2554).
e – 144 (FFR363) received a new Burlingham C41C body in 1954, following an accident.
f – Chassis only transferred: fitted with body ex-43 (RN7785).
g – Passed to National Travel (North West) Ltd in February 1974.
h – ECK879E-ECK880E passed to National Travel (North West) Ltd in February 1974.
i – TCK 64 passed to National Travel (North West) Ltd in February 1974.
j – TRN729/30 transferred to Ribble as its 729/30 in January 1968.
k – NRN612/3 transferred to Ribble as its 1286/7 in March 1970.
l – ECK 876-8E transferred to Ribble as its 876-8 in January 1972.
m – ARN795/6C transferred to Ribble as its 795/6 in December 1972.
n – TRN 739-42 transferred to Ribble as its 739-42 in March 1974.

STANDERWICK VEHICLES PRESERVED

Two Standerwick vehicles are known to have been preserved subsequent to sale by the company.
FV 4548 operated by the Ministry of Supply between 1941 and 1948. Received second-hand body when returned believed to be English Electric C26R from HG 2759 Leyland Tiger TS6 originally new to Wright Bros. Vehicle passed to Ribble as driver training vehicle DS1. Later to Colin Shears, Exeter then to the Welsh Historic Vehicle Trust, Swansea and now with Screaton, Warrington from August 1981. Reseated to C18R and relicensed as a PSV in July 1992.
FV 5737 passed to Ribble as its number 1461 in 1948 fitted with Leyland 7.4-litre oil engine and rebodied Duple C31F in 1950. Renumbered 753 in 1951, withdrawn 1960. Passed through various dealers and eventually restored and seen at rallies. Sold to Clavewer, Antwerp, Belgium by October 1992.

One of the second batch of Bristol VRL coaches, No. 65, OCK65K, approaches Southport's Lord Street Bus Station in August 1973 after travelling from London on the 11am journey. The ten vehicles were delivered in 1971 and were equipped with ECW bodies to the same design as the earlier examples. The narrow front door, marked No Entrance, was intended to be an emergency exit, but, in practice, became used as the driver's door.

CHAPTER 9

SCOUT MOTOR SERVICES LTD

Incorporated 24th December 1932

1919-September 1939.

Includes predecessor business:
James WATKINSON

Fleet Name: SCOUT MOTORS 1919-1933

The transport business of James Watkinson, farm produce merchant, Preston commenced in 1919. Two lorries were initially fitted with convertible lorry-chara bodies to enable coaching to be carried out at weekends and in the Annual Wakes Week. A removals business with premises at Eldon Street was also operated. At first the pattern of operation was similar to the vast majority of small inland town operators, with excursions and private hire coaching in the summer season and trips to race meetings and football matches in winter. In common with most such operators, Watkinson was unable to provide sufficient machines for the annual Holiday week and he became a customer of F. & C. Smith of Blackpool who hired him additional coaches at peak times. In 1923, when F. & C. Smith Ltd was in course of reorganisation, at least two coaches were purchased from Charles Smith Jnr, and this relationship continued throughout the decade.

Watkinson's business (trading as Scout) expanded in spring 1927 when a lease was taken of Foxhall Garage in Blackpool, and used for the removals business. Some twelve months later a couple of coaches worked from the Blackpool premises and, in May 1928, Blackpool Tradesman's Holiday saw two extended tours operated from Foxhall Road by Scout Motors' new Leyland Lioness all-weather coaches. To the annoyance of local operators, Scout continued to operate day excursions throughout the Blackpool season and in the years that followed. Although the premises were tiny, vehicles could run through, coaches entering from Foxhall Road and departing on to Dale Street via a narrow entry. The Lionesses and a Leyland Lion vehicle were in use later in 1928 to provide extended tours from Preston, Accrington, Blackburn and Great Harwood to Scotland, English Lakes and the Vale of Avon. Despite extensive publicity, it appears the programme was unsuccessful, and no trace of any repeat operation in subsequent years has come to light.

Whether it was the poor revenue from the touring programme, or a growing interest in recently established Blackpool-London expresses (Watkinson was agent for C. Smith Motors London service), the decision was made to open a Scout express to London, and from mid-November 1928 Smith's agency was hastily removed. Scout's service opened on Monday 3rd December 1928, using 'Excursion Safety Coaches' leaving Preston at 9am, running via

After the unsuccessful attempt at Christmas 1928 to inaugurate a London express with unheated Leyland Lionness touring coaches, Charles Watkinson re-launched the service with two Leyland-bodied Leyland Tigers in July 1929. These were also soon replaced, the service being operated from1930 with half-a-dozen Tigers fitted with distinctive Spicer coachwork. Number 5, CK4336, was numerically the first but two earlier registered chassis CK4255/59, numbered 9-10, also carried Spicer bodies and may have been rebodied by the Southport-based builder in late 1930. An illuminated raised destination box was fitted on the roof of the driver's cab, and illuminated panels carrying the name Scout or Scout Motors were installed in the front panel above the headlight and on the roof mounted luggage box. Outward-opening passenger doors at front and rear gave access to the passenger compartment, which was fitted with 29 seats and luxuriously appointed, including fitment of curtains. The interior specification was, however, upstaged by the new Wood Brothers' machines for their London service, for these were fitted with toilet compartments. Note that the front window on the passenger compartment is fitted with a fully opening top section identical to the mandatory opening section on the driver's window; this would certainly circulate fresh air to the passengers on the long inter urban sections of the London journey! These photographs were taken by Leyland Motors' photographer in the main street at Leyland immediately prior to delivery on March 31st 1930.

Two further Spicer-bodied coaches on Leyland Lion LT2 chassis were taken into stock in 1931, but later in that year no less than five additional coaches on Leyland Tiger TS2 chassis were purchased 26-30: CK4575 4571-4574. These were clearly intended to resemble the Spicer bodied machines, but were in fact built by Leyland, using frames based on the omnibus body then current, but suitably adapted for coaching. The distinctive Spicer roof, with its sloping forward section, was copied, but a squarer sectioned roof indicator box was fitted; the roof-mounted luggage box was of a lower profile, but retained Scout Motors illuminated panels. The two opening passenger doors had given way to a single entrance with sliding door, still positioned towards the front to permit a double seat to be placed forward of the steps. The outward-opening front passenger window had been retained, but now four louvred opening side windows were fitted behind the entrance door – only three were fitted on Spicer bodies, but the rear corner profile was now clearly related to Leyland's standard single-deck bus body as was the door entrance profile. The words Pullman Road Travel appeared above the side windows, and lettering on the waist-panel publicised theDaily Service Blackpool, Birmingham and London. This illustration was utilised by Leyland for publicity purposes.

Stafford, Wolverhampton, Birmingham and Coventry. Two feeders linked in at Preston: from Blackpool (Foxhall Road) at 8am and from Darwen (Duckworth Street) at 8am, and Blackburn at 8.15am; arrangements were said to be in place to pick up from any part of Lancashire. Heavy advertising continued in all centres, but loadings were poor and the operation ceased after 9th January 1929.

After an approach by Charles Smith Jnr. to Joseph Bracewell, Watkinson was allowed to take up his agency for C. Smith Motors' express once again for probably every booking was vitally required in the depths of that winter, but thoughts of a Scout Motors service had not left James Watkinson's mind. The arrival of two Leyland Tigers in 1929 brought matters to a head and Watkinson withdrew from Smith's agency again to open a modified London service from Blackpool and Preston to Stafford, Birmingham, Coventry and London (Rymers, Southampton Row), running daily from Saturday 20th July 1929 with overnight journeys south each Saturday from 10th August until the end of the Blackpool season. The new coaches were equipped with rugs, and passengers were allocated numbered seats, perhaps resolving some of the problems encountered earlier. The fares undercut existing operators and, of course, Scout was barred from membership of the Blackpool Coach Owner's Association, which had established common fares for its members. Perhaps as a result of Wood Bros test case, no feeder from Blackburn was run and although Watkinson applied for licences he was refused. With the arrival of additional Leyland Tiger coaches Scout was in a position to expand, and night services recommenced from Easter, running Friday southwards and Saturday northwards through the season. A limited touring programme for the Blackpool Tradesmans' Holiday was also re-introduced.

PRESTON BLACKPOOL OMNIBUS SERVICES

By early May 1930, the Preston office and Headquarters had moved to Starchhouse Square Garage in a chain of circumstances that was to bring even greater change to the Scout business. These reached back to October 1926, when Ribble had purchased the omnibus business of Pilot Motors Ltd, leading to dismissal of most employees. A new business, Empress Motors (later re-formed as Preston & Longridge Motor Co Ltd), was commenced by ex-Pilot employees to run buses between Preston and Longridge; others were employed by Councillor Matthew Wade's Majestic Motors, which expanded to run from Preston to Garstang and Lancaster with proposals to extend to Morecambe, Walton-le-Dale and Blackburn, Kirkham and Blackpool, and Walmer Bridge. The resultant bus war with Ribble was intensive and the circumstances of the setting-up of these independents precluded negotiations between the combatants. In spring 1929 Ribble used its subsidiary, County Motors Ltd, to launch an attack with drastic fare cutting against Majestic and Empress, who formed a partnership to fight back, but were obliged to withdraw the Walmer Bridge route.

With the independents still unwilling to treat with Ribble, approaches were made, probably through a nominee, by LM&S Railway, a major shareholder in Ribble. The railway purchased control of Majestic & Empress omnibus routes on 10th April 1930, withdrawing

Numbers 28-29, CK4603-4, completed the 1931 delivery of Scout's double-deck buses, and No. 29 is seen outside Leyland's South Works on completion. The front and rear indicator blinds had not then been installed. As on the initial deliveries, drop sliding side windows were fitted for ventilation. The louvres indicate that two windows on each side of the lower-deck could be lowered, but on the upper-deck only three nearside windows were so equipped. The interior-illuminated fleetname is clearly visible in both front and rear views. This vehicle is equipped with an extra lamp, apparently identical to the side-lights, and seen above the driver's compartment beneath the route indicator box. This was used as an additional night-time identifier in the manner common at the time in many Lancashire fleets, and was subsequently fitted to all double-deckers operated at least until 1935. All five double-deckers were equipped with 49 seats, 27 on bench seats upstairs and 24 on double seats below. The bodies were of the lowbridge type, with a lowered side gangway running along the offside of the upper-deck, and intruding into the lower-saloon, resulting in reduced headroom above the offside seats. The rear seats on the lower-deck were side-mounted over the wheel arches. One further, similar, double-deck bus on a TD2 chassis would follow in 1932.

all but the Longridge route which was to be handed to Rishton & Antley, putting about 100 employees out of work. Once again local feeling ran high, and at least some routes were reopened to enable the crews to be re-employed. Matthew Wade's base was at Starchhouse Square Garage in Preston, and Scout Motors moved into these premises as a new and larger headquarters.

Both James Watkinson and Charles Smith Jnr. made application to run buses between Preston and Blackpool; to assist his application in Preston, Smith purchased control of the coach business of James Davis Ltd, Pole Street, Preston. Blackpool Watch Committee refused all three applicants in June 1930, but the decisions were referred back by the full Council. The applications were again considered by the Watch Committee on 25th July: James Davis Ltd was again refused and only Watkinson's application was initially granted. Smith's application was deferred, pending information on routes and number of

Deliveries to Scout in 1931 concluded with a smaller coach, used in the main for touring work. This was a Leyland Cub type KP3, registered CK4612, and it was fitted with H. V. Burlingham, Blackpool, coachwork. It had a mock clerestory roof and a sliding front entrance. Internally, 20 leather and moquette seats with headrests were fitted, four pairs on each side of the aisle, plus a single seat on near and offside to allow circulating space by the doorway. There was also a double seat forward of the door, alongside the driver. A small compartment was fitted behind the rearmost offside seats, adjacent to the rear mounted emergency exit where passengers' luggage could be stowed. Metal bars were fitted over adjacent windows to prevent damage should suitcases slip in transit. Overhead luggage racks were also fitted to accommodate smaller items. Note the patterned linoleum-covered floor.

vehicles to be used; this angered the full Council on 6th August when the Watch Committee's decision was overruled and granted unconditionally. It was suggested that Smith, a Blackpool ratepayer, had received poor consideration in the resort because he had been fortunate enough to make money by selling one business; he had been granted licences, through James Davis Ltd, to ply in both Preston and Kirkham.

Charles Smith Jnr. intended to operate between Blackpool and Preston by three routes: (i) Wrea Green and Kirkham; (ii) St Annes, Lytham and Warton; and (iii) Singleton, Weeton and Kirkham. Once again his relationship with Watkinson was such that he had no desire to compete against his fellow independent and Scout Motors alone operated on the Preston-Kirkham-Wrea Green-Blackpool route. This commenced half-hourly in mid-August 1930, while the vehicles gathered together by Smith/James Davis Ltd passed to Scout for use on the new operation. Later in the year, five new Leyland Lion buses, three bodied by Leyland and two by Spicer, and the first of three Leyland Titan double-deckers were placed in service on the route, enabling the headway to be increased to 20 minutes. In a letter to the Minister of Transport, Ribble had immediately expressed its anger at the action of the local authorities in licensing new independent services, and correspondence ensued during September without the formality of an Appeal.

LOCAL AND EXPRESS DEVELOPMENTS

Meanwhile, expansion of the London route had been possible on delivery of six Leyland Tiger coaches with Spicer bodies and, on Saturday 14th June 1930, a thrice-daily service commenced, leaving Blackpool at 8am, 11am and 9pm (Preston one hour later) and returning from London at 8.30am, 12 noon and 10pm. A new Lake District feeder from Keswick (8am) Ambleside, Windermere, Kendal, Morecambe and Lancaster met up with the 1pm departure ex-Preston with a break for lunch at Law's Cafe in Starchhouse Square; the 8.30am ex London served the northbound feeder to Keswick. Overnight journeys did not have timed stages south of Knutsford or north of Dunstable, although traffic was not refused.

The expanded London express was not successful and it is possible the simultaneous efforts expended on the new bus service had an adverse effect upon promotion of the express facilities. After only six weeks operation, the London route was sharply cut back and, from Saturday 2nd August, the service reverted to a daily journey 8am ex-Blackpool, 8.30am ex-London, with nightly journeys Preston-London and London-Preston at 10pm; extension from/to Blackpool was on Friday nights only. Overnight journeys ceased seasonally after the end of September.

On the assumption of powers by the North Western Traffic Commissioners, Scout Motors made application to continue the bus route, the London express and excursions from Preston and Blackpool. During the early part of 1931 the position of the London Agency and Terminal was in doubt, following collapse of Rymer's and amalgamation with Imperial: by May 1931, coaches terminated at Central London Coaching Station, Crescent Place. All licences were approved by the year end except Preston-Blackpool, which had seen strenuous objection from Ribble who argued that their service was adequate and wasteful competition would result if Scout were granted a licence.

The provision of toilet facilities on long distance coaches was a major improvement but it has not been possible to trace with certainty the first Scout coach to be so equipped. Two 28-seat TS2 coaches, CK4594-5, built and bodied by Leyland and delivered in 1931, might have been the first, but even at this date Scout was lagging behind the standard set by all the Blackpool-based London express operators, all of whom offered toilet facilities on their services by summer 1930. Scout's repeat order for complete vehicles to be supplied by Leyland on TS4 chassis for 1932 delivery, however, included toilet compartments, CK4655/6, CK4667/8 carried only 24 passengers, with seven double seats on the offside plus five on the nearside. The toilet compartments were fitted on the nearside, behind the rear-entrance door; the emergency door was at front offside, adjacent to the driver's door. All side windows except the small ones at the rear had sliding upper portions for ventilation, and a sliding roof panel could also be opened in warm weather. Suspended luggage racks over the seats were supplemented by a large roof-mounted box, which continued the tradition of an illuminated fleetname display on each side. There was also an illuminated front display panel with fleetname and destination boxes. The first pair carried single destination boxes, but the second pair had twin destination screens. Vehicle number CK4667 is seen with the words Coventry and Contract displayed in the two apertures.

The Commissioner was swayed by the argument and approved operation as an express service only, stopping only at Preston, Blackpool and Swan Hotel, Kirkham. Watkinson continued to operate and appealed, while Ribble lodged Appeal against the Express Licence for the route.

The Appeal hearing took place in Preston on Tuesday 5th January 1932, with Mr J. Lustgarten representing Ribble; Scout was represented by Mr Norman Birkett KC; it is believed this was the only Road Traffic Act Appeal in which the latter appeared. Mr Birkett presented a 9,000-strong petition and reported that loss of the route would place 38 Scout employees at risk of redundancy. He referred to the fact that Scout was replacing facilities earlier provided by Majestic which had not been offered by Ribble, and revealed that, in the summer of 1930, when Scout commenced running, there had been an increase of over 200,000 passengers (or 58 per cent) on statistics for 1929. Mr Lustgarten's response was that there was capacity on the Ribble buses to accommodate all Scout traffic. The Minister reported on 13th February 1932 that he had found in favour of Scout, and instructed the Commissioners to issue a licence for a stage carriage service at the reduced frequency of half-hourly, co-ordinating with Ribble's fifteen minute frequency. From 28th May 1932, co-ordination was implemented, and a correction to the Scout licence included a single limited stop journey that had been omitted from the original grant.

A sixth double-decker was added to the fleet in 1934. This had been a Leyland TD2 demonstrator and arrived with 48 seats, but was subsequently converted to 51 seats (27 on the top-deck and 24 below) in line with the standard Scout configuration. The year 1935 saw the arrival of a seventh double-decker, shown here at Leyland prior to despatch to Scout. Number 26, RN7576, a Titan TD4, was equipped with a Leyland all-metal body to a more modern design containing 53 seats (27 on top, 26 below). The back indicator box, rear-mounted on earlier buses, has been repositioned over the entrance step. This petrol-engined vehicle, subsequently converted to diesel, was the last to be equipped with the extra front identifier lamp. In post-war days it was rebodied by Duple as a 33-seat coach before eventual sale in 1948.

The 1934 season saw no less than seven new coaches delivered, replacing a number of earlier vehicles. Four Leylands with Burlingham 30-seat bodies were taken into stock, two TS6 Tigers and two LT5A Lions. A 26-seater Leyland SKP Cub with Weymann coachwork replaced the three-year-old Burlingham-bodied Cub, while two further Lions carried Weymann 30-seat bodies. This view, in Avenham Square, Preston, shows one of the latter vehicles, numbered 6 or 7, CK4902/3, with rear sliding door. Particularly capacious roof boxes were carried, and most windows had sliding glass frames. None of the 1934 coaches had toilets; they were purchased chiefly for excursions although, of course, peak demand on the London service would see almost any of the Scout coaches pressed into service.

Above: An unusual event on 30th April 1935 was the photography of the current Scout all-Leyland fleet for the maker's publicity department. The photographer must have undertaken his task early, for the date in question was a Tuesday, and operations would have commenced about 6am! The fleet is posed outside the Starchhouse Square headquarters, and from left to right are Nos. 4/3, CK4901/0, Burlingham-bodied Lions; Nos. 26, RN7576; 28, CK4603; 30, CK4654; 22, CK4386; 29, CK4604; 24, CK4569; the former demonstrator, 25, TF9462 and 23, CK4568 – all Leyland-bodied Titans. Numbers 2/1, CK4898/9, Burlingham-bodied Tiger; Nos. 7/6, CK4903/2, Weymann-bodied Lion; No. 31, CK4655; and CK4668, toilet equipped Leyland-bodied Tiger. Note the different types of indicators. In fact, the fleet is not quite complete, and four vehicles are missing: number 32, CK4656, and CK4667 – the sisters of Nos. CK4655/68 – No. 5, CK4904, Weymann-bodied Cub; and RN7577, the latest Burlingham-bodied Tiger. The last two would probably be at the Blackpool depot, where early-season excursions would already require a couple of machines, and the Leyland-bodied toilet-equipped coaches would be away in service on the London express – one at Blackpool and the other in the capital. It is of interest to note that none of the coaches is more than two years old, and the oldest Titan double-decker was purchased in 1931.

Below: Only one further double-decker was to enter the fleet prior to the outbreak of war. This was number 27, RN8038, a 53-seat Titan TD4 delivered in January 1937, which carried the new Leyland 'Bailey' body. It was equipped with yet another refinement, a folding door fitted to the entrance platform. This necessitated the inclusion of a front offside emergency exit to meet the safety regulations. The identifier lamp from previous double-deckers has been replaced by a small illuminated box above the main destination screen, marked with a letter S to improve recognition. This view was taken on July 18th, 1937, at Avenham Square, Preston prior to entry into service .

London expresses were sanctioned on 14th December 1931, with night journeys restricted to Whitsuntide-30th September: early season and Christmas night journeys were thereafter lost. However, application was made on 17th December 1932 to operate the entire winter period service overnight, Scout proposing that henceforth day-time journeys would only run in the summer period. The application, opposed by LM&S Railway, Yelloway and Finglands, was heard on 3rd February 1933, when Scout reported that the application had already been heard by the Metropolitan Commissioner, who was in favour, subject to the decision of the North Western Commissioners because it would move one operator away from the present competitive daytime situation. The North Western Commissioners, however, refused to grant the modification.

DEVELOPMENTS UNDER THE LIMITED COMPANY

James Watkinson was now taking steps to transfer his business into a limited company – Scout Motor Services Ltd – which was incorporated on 24th December 1932, with James Watkinson and sons Ernest and James Charles Watkinson as shareholders.

The sale of three major members of the Blackpool Coach Owners' Association to the Combine Companies by March 1933 had seriously weakened the Association and in view of the licensing – and therefore legitamising – of out-of-town operators by the Commissioners, the Association sought to regain strength by admitting these former opponents. Accordingly, Scout was able to become a member and join in the May 1933 Association blanket application for reinstatement of the former one shilling tours from the resort, and for special reductions for Guest Week holidaymakers; both requests were granted in time for the 1933 season.

With time-honoured tradition, Scout added James Smith & Co (Wigan) Ltd to its list of London express service agents by May 1933: Smiths had lost Standerwicks' agency in the rearrangements following sale to the Combine Companies and Scout correctly anticipated that bookings would still flow to the Standishgate office of Smiths. Scout now made much of the fact that it was the only non-combine firm operating Blackpool-London via Birmingham (thus eliminating Yelloway's Blackpool-Manchester-Leicester-London route from the equation). The London terminus was revised on closure of Central London Station: from 25th May 1934 Scout expresses

One of the tasks that was regularly carried out by Scout vehicles was the supply of coaches to perform such duties as carrying the victorious Preston North End football team to welcoming ceremonies in the town centre. The views below and on the following page show a convoy of three coaches with police escort conveying the team from Preston station on its return from Wembley with the FA Cup in May 1937. The vehicles seen turning from the station approach (below) are RN8138, a 1937 Leyland Tiger TS7 equipped with Duple 28-seat coachwork, RN7908, a similar Tiger new in 1937 but carrying Burlingham 28-seat coachwork and CK4903, one of the 1934 Weymann-bodied Lions. The two leading vehicles are lettered for the London express, but the older coach was chiefly used for excursion work and merely carries the legend Scout Services.

commenced using Kings Cross Motor Station, Euston Road, the new agency promoting the route as 'The Lancashire Express'. Restrictions on duplication, part of a nationwide policy in 1934 to reduce licensed capacity, were the subject of an Appeal by Scout, resulting in fine tuning that defined duplication for each departure from a minimum of four extra coaches in winter to 21 during August. By late summer 1935, the Birmingham stop switched from Smithfield Garage, Digbeth to Victor Garage, Moor Street.

Meanwhile the Preston-Blackpool service had been threatened in September 1933 by a Ribble application to revise fares on its limited stop services between the towns: existing fares of 2/3d single, 3/3d return, set to protect stage carriage services, were to be replaced by a single fare of 1/6d. Scout viewed the proposal with alarm and its objection was upheld. However, eventually the two operators agreed to replace their stage carriage return fare of 2/3d by a 1/1d single. This was a sensible practical measure, as at busy times both firms had difficulty in accommodating their own return ticket holders. A further attack came in April 1936, when Ribble applied to divert one journey per hour to run via Garstang Road and Blackpool Road (the route used by Scout's buses) rather than via Fylde Road. Once again Scout, now running under the control of the founder's sons, objected and reported that, in a previous experiment by Ribble, Scout's business had lost £27 per week. They also drew attention to alleged operation of a 7½ minute service by Ribble buses during the previous Illuminations, apparently spacing out duplicates on the scheduled 15-minute headway to the detriment of Scout's 30-minute service which was also duplicated. The Commissioner refused Ribble's application.

In June 1938, Scout and Ribble both applied for new licences to run short journeys between Preston and Lea, Kirkham and Wrea Green at times when through Blackpool buses could not cope. After a protracted hearing both withdrew, and an uneasy peace was to survive until the outbreak of World War II, when circumstances would bring drastic changes.

In the rear view of the football team's procession (see previous page), note how steps are built in to the rear panels of CK4903 to enable the driver to reach a small platform from which he could load or unload the roof box. The box has a rolled tarpaulin to protect passengers' property from the weather. On this short journey the roof sections of all three coaches have been rolled back to allow the players to stand on the seats and receive the accolades of their waiting fans as the procession nears the awaiting dignitaries.

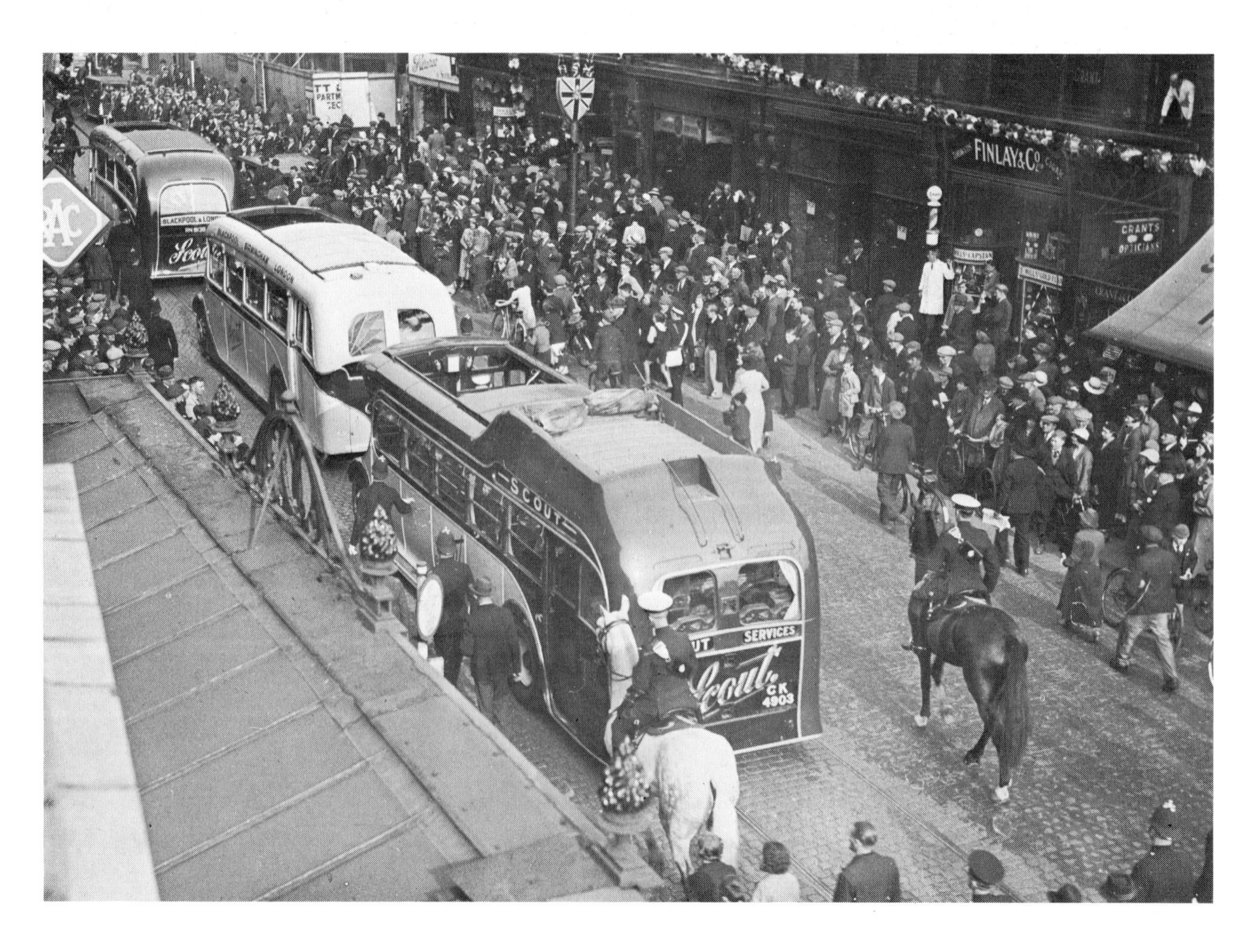

CHAPTER 10

SCOUT MOTOR SERVICES LTD
September 1939 1968

As the inevitability of the Second World War became apparent, thoughts turned to the arrangements required to maintain bus services under the changed circumstances and the Commissioner, who would assume virtually absolute powers during the war years, ordered operators to prepare plans for reducing fuel used on stage carriage services. Competing services were to be examined with a view to introducing co-ordination, thus reducing waste and ensuring maximum efficiency. Ribble already had joint working agreements with several independents, some of which provided support services such as licensing and publicity for its partners on specific routes. From 20th September 1939, Ribble and Scout commenced a formal working arrangement creating a pool on the Preston-Blackpool road with receipts and mileage shared in the proportions Ribble 60 per cent and Scout 40 per cent. Supervision, publicity and road service licensing services were provided by Ribble in return for a management fee.

Both operators issued Ribble tickets and Scout conductors drew their equipment and paid cash into Ribble offices, statistics for the pool being prepared by Ribble who made regular payments to Scout. A later enhancement saw Ribble conductors working peak hour journeys on Scout buses at overtime rates, saving Scout from having to pay its conductors for eight hours to cover two or three hours work.

Scout buses were extended from Starchhouse Square to Ribble's Tithebarn Street station while Ribble buses diverted to call at Starchhouse Square. The overall headway was reduced to 20 minutes with two journeys an hour via Wrea Green and one via Weeton and Scout buses now participated on both routes as necessary. These routes were very busy during the war as the Fylde had several large military camps including sites at Kirkham and Weeton which required special services. In addition, many military personnel were billeted in Blackpool boarding houses. The increase in traffic resulted in Scout being allocated three new double-deck buses (an unfrozen Leyland TD7, a Daimler CWA6 and a Guy Arab) and, in 1945, two coaches were rebodied as double-deckers. Despite these measures, some operation by Blackpool Corporation buses to the camps was necessary during the war.

The reopening of the Blackpool-London express service in 1940 brought agreement for joint operation on this route also and details will be found in Chapter Seven. Scout also provided vehicles for the pool coaching operations of the Passenger Vehicle Operators' Association, liaising with the wartime Regional Transport Commissioner to provide, among other tasks, emergency

Typical of Scout's early post war fleet coaches was BRN474, a 33-seat Duple-bodied Leyland PS1 new in 1947. Ten of these attractive vehicles entered service between 1946 and 1949, plus other examples bodied by Bellhouse Hartwell and Burlingham. The chalk marks on the front nearside wheel of BRN474 appear to relate to a form of coaching roulette in which the passenger whose number is touching the floor when the coach stops receives a jackpot prize.

Thirty-five Bedford OB 29-seat coaches were placed in service in the period from 1946 to 1950. Most of these had Duple coachwork, including BRN791 seen passing through Talbot Square, Blackpool, but four carried the almost identical SMT variant. Two Blackpool centre entrance double-deckers wait at the centre island, one working on route 23 South Pier. A Vambac railcoach stands at the Marton route terminus and, in the distance, a Blackpool standard car is about to turn out of Clifton Street into Abingdon Street. Note that in those days all traffic passed to the north side of the centre island, with the south side restricted to tramcars and a narrow lane alongside the Town Hall and Clifton Hotel.

Above: Four DupleAmbassador-bodied Leyland Royal Tigers entered service in 1951. These centre-entrance coaches seated 41, and DRN361 is seen outside the former BOAC terminal in Buckingham Palace Road, London.

Right: Deliveries during 1952 included six further Duple Ambassador-bodied Royal Tigers. These were also 41-seat coaches with a centre-entrance and ECK872 is seen in August 1956 on Safari Service in Knowsley Park.

road services in both Manchester and Liverpool following the heavy air raids.

With the return of peace, Scout enjoyed a period of prosperity with substantial vehicle replacements and considerable expansion of stage carriage, express and excursion activities. As the 'fifties progressed, traffic requirements changed and passenger figures gradually declined as motor car ownership increased leading to the directors deciding in 1961 to retire from the road passenger transport industry. Sale to Ribble had been considered on two previous occasions as the five-year agreements came up for renewal. Ownership of Scout passed to Ribble on 5th December 1961 for a sum in excess of £300,000 though the new owners were to continue to operate Scout as a subsidiary for several years. The fleet was accommodated, with difficulty, in the Ribble garages at Selborne Street, Preston and Devonshire Road, Blackpool, both of which were nominally full.

The Scout livery of cream with plum and black relief gave way to a version of the Ribble livery with the Scout fleetname applied to the vehicles in Ribble-style lettering. When time-expired, the older Scout buses were replaced by transferring double-deckers from the Ribble fleet but, apart from a couple of elderly Tiger Cubs transferred in 1966, the coach fleet continued to be updated with new vehicles, usually forming a part of orders for the Ribble and Standerwick fleets. The Scout registered office moved to Frenchwood Avenue, Preston and the small administrative staff moved to 30 Lancaster Road, Preston.

STAGE CARRIAGE OPERATIONS 1945-68

The success of the pool operation may have surprised the Watkinson brothers and they had no wish to resume competitive running when hostilities ceased in 1945. When the quarter-hourly Preston-Blackpool frequency

Above: The Ambassador body was revamped by Duple in 1953, becoming the Coronation Ambassador but retaining the centre-entrance and 41 seat configuration. Scout received three of these, registered FCK567-69. The second is seen in this Duple official view, taken before delivery to the company.

Below: Bus deliveries recommenced in 1946 with two all-Leyland PD1s. These lowbridge vehicles seated 53 passengers, and had the radiator shells painted cream, rather then the customary chrome-plated finish. They were numbered 28-29 ARN950-1, and the first is seen here in a Leyland official view. The indicators are set for route 158, Preston-Blackpool via Weeton, which had been a Ribble only route prior to the 1939 Agreement.

resumed, Scout buses left both termini at 5 minutes past the hour (via Wrea Green) and 35 (via Weeton) while Ribble operated at 20 (through to and from Burnley) and 50 (to and from Bolton). Proposals in 1947 for Scout to take a share in the 126 service to Bolton were abandoned though the necessary legend had been added to the destination blinds of the new PD1s.

On 1st January 1948, Ribble and Preston Corporation introduced a network of joint cross-town services one of which (P1) ran out to Victoria Park Drive, Lea to which point a few short trips had run on the Blackpool service. Scout took an 8 per cent share but never actively participated. In 1955, it was extended two ways, to Aldfield Avenue, Lea and Larches Estate, the latter later becoming P3. At the Blackpool end, there were also short workings between Blackpool and Peel Corner which were the subject of several applications to the Traffic Commissioners, Blackpool Corporation resenting the fact that they were precluded from running along Preston New Road. These culminated in a new all day service (B1) between Blackpool (Talbot Road), Clifton Arms and Peel, running via Park Road instead of Whitegate Drive, as followed by the Preston buses. This service, which commenced in December 1951, was generally worked by Ribble's Blackpool depot but Scout buses participated on occasions. It was a white elephant, persistently incurring losses but was continued as a political gesture to give Blackpool Corporation no excuse to run along Preston New Road. Another contentious application, also in 1951, covered a special service between Blackpool (Coliseum) and a proposed new stadium in Mythop Road, on the Weeton route but the plan for the stadium was abandoned.

An Atomic Energy plant had been built at Springfields, near Salwick, in the immediate post-war years, services having been provided by Ribble on wartime permits until September 1949 when they were formally jointly licensed.

Top of page: Scout number 3, BRN 153, one of the six vehicles mentioned below, had only a year left to serve with Scout when seen in Starchhouse Square, Preston, in 1960. It is waiting between turns on service 155, Preston-Blackpool via Wrea Green, with Atlantean No. 1, OCK500, in the background. In the following year the PD1 would be replaced by a further Atlantean.

Lower view: Six further Leyland-bodied PD1s, numbered 1-6, BRN151-6, arrived in 1947, and formed the mainstay of the post-war bus fleet for a number of years. Although Scout vehicles did not operate regularly on service B1, (Blackpool-Peel), when demands on Ribble's Blackpool garage were excessive it was not unusual for a Scout vehicle to stand in. Number 2 is seen on Talbot Road, Blackpool, passing the former North railway station on such an occasion.

Above: Another view of number 3, BRN153, this time a 1950s scene in Starchhouse Square, Preston. The PD1 stands between turns on service 167 (Preston-Lytham). The lining out applied to Scout's PD1 Leyland-bodied buses at this time can be clearly seen.

Below: An evocative view of what is believed to be number 7, CRN244, a 1949-built Leyland bodied PD2/3. It is operating on service 158, Preston-Blackpool via Weeton, which ran along Whitegate Drive, Blackpool, approaching Devonshire Square. The cars include a Ford Anglia, an Austin A35, two Vauxhalls and a Standard Vanguard. Number 7 was fitted with platform doors in 1956 and two similar vehicles, Nos. 8-9, DRN364-5 and one PD2/1, No. 10, DRN366, were added to the fleet in 1950/1.

Ribble style indicator displays were fitted to Nos. 21-22, LRN62-63, Leyland PD3/3 buses with Burlingham 74-seat forward-entrance bodies delivered in 1958. In that year Ribble took delivery of a number of basically similar Burlingham-bodied PD3s, but to a full fronted design. Number 22 is seen leaving Starchhouse Square on a peak-period short journey to Kirkham on route 158.

The labour force was drawn mainly from Blackpool but also from Preston and Chorley and a substantial amount of work was created for Ribble and Scout, a significant proportion being for shift workers outside the peak hours. Buses ran from Blackpool via Wrea Green and direct and eventually also via Lytham St. Annes, via Poulton and via Staining and Weeton.

A reduction of frequency on the Preston-Blackpool services to 20-minutes in the winter of 1950 resulted in difficulty in achieving the correct pool proportions and, to rectify the imbalance, Scout buses participated on the Preston-Lytham (167) service on Sundays carrying 'on hire to Ribble' labels, until the quarter-hourly frequency was restored in 1951. From 5th April 1952, the Preston-Lytham (167), Blackpool-Bolton (126) and Blackpool-Burnley (154) services were rerouted in Preston via Addison Road (now Blackpool Road) and Garstang Road to facilitate the use of highbridge double-deckers which, at that time, the low bridge in Fylde Road precluded. There was thus a half-hourly service by each route, both of which were used by Scout buses. In 1953, Ribble was actively engaged in linking together stage carriage services to form long routes and wanted to include the two Preston-Blackpool hourly journeys usually worked by Scout in through services from Wigan and Rochdale. From the start of the summer timetable on 27th June 1953, Scout took over two bus duties on the Blackpool-Burnley (154) service and one on a new link up formed by joining Blackpool-Weeton-Preston (158), Preston-Feniscowles-Blackburn (1) and Blackburn-Rochdale (244) with a round trip time of six hours. Scout also started regular operation on the Preston-Lytham (167) service from the same day.

Use of three route numbers on the Rochdale workings was cumbersome and the problem was solved when, following the grant of a through licence, the entire route was renumbered 158. Through working across Preston was further extended to include hourly journeys between Burnley and Lytham by combining the 152 Burnley-Preston and 167 services and one Scout bus was used on this route from the 28th June 1958.

Scout was licensed for services which impinged on the pool area but were always run by Ribble. These included an infrequent Great Eccleston-Kirkham (168) service which ran 1951-65, but was truncated to terminate at Wharles in 1959, and Blackpool-Warton via Wrea Green and Bryning (W80), a workers' service for English Electric which started on 24th June 1961 but was withdrawn after a short time for lack of support. From 13th October 1956, a few journeys on 155 were rerouted, between Wrea Green and Peel, as 156, through the hamlets of Westby and Ballam and there was some Scout participation.

The cross-Preston services encountered punctuality problems as road traffic increased and it was decided to split them at Preston both to improve reliability and to enable frequencies to be attuned to altered traffic demands. From 26th June 1965, therefore, all Scout operation east of Preston ceased, the company retaining its share of Preston-Kirkham-Blackpool traffic on routes 154 via Garstang Road and Wrea Green, 155 via Fylde Road and Wrea Green and 158 via Fylde Road and Weeton, each hourly. The infrequent 156 via Ballam remained and there were a few peak hour limited stop trips from Preston to Blackpool, originally intended to be numbered X54, but eventually they became 153; these were run by Scout vehicles, usually coaches. Through running between Burnley and Lytham also ceased and Scout reverted to running on the Preston-Lytham section (166 via Fylde Road and 167 via Garstang Road).

EXCURSION DEVELOPMENTS

In the post-war period, coaching had been developed, with Scout active in the purchase of new machines to restore operations. In September 1949, a new excursion licence was approved for Kirkham, to be operated jointly by Scout and Ribble; although only two vehicles per day were initially sanctioned, the allowance was doubled at weekends and holidays in 1952. In May of that year, a major move in Blackpool was the purchase of the goodwill of the six-vehicle excursion licence of Whittaker Brothers (Blackpool) Ltd, whose stand was on Sheppard Street. The office was located on the corner, at 42 Adelaide Street and was subsequently modernised as Scout progressively transferred its main Blackpool efforts to this centrally-located site. Whittakers had been founded in 1914 by George Whittaker, trading variously as G. Whittaker & Sons and Lady Winifred Motors from premises at the corner of Albert Road and Winifred Street, but from 1921 the site was relocated at the Adelaide Street end of Winifred Street. From July 1927 the business was conducted by Edgar and J. I. Whittaker, who retained the Lady Winifred title but, after trading for a period with the Whittaker & Sons name, changed it to Whittaker Bros . A garage was leased on Back Winifred Street. The limited company was incorporated on 5th October 1933 with G., J. I. and E.Whittaker as directors but neither the Whittaker company nor its vehicles was included in the purchase by Scout. The licence included a number of extended tours, chiefly operated at Tradesmans Holiday and at the end of the long Blackpool season.

In April 1954 a further coaching acquisition was the goodwill of Preston Embee Motors Ltd, which had been incorporated on 14th May 1914, with Frederick W., A.E. and W.E. Merigold as directors. Once again, neither company nor vehicles were acquired: the licence authorised two coaches, and the originating point was transferred from The Old Vicarage Works, Avenham Street, Preston to Starchhouse Square.

A feature of Scout operations was the intensive use of its coaches around the clock: a vehicle might operate morning journeys on Preston-Blackpool or Springfield works journeys, then run from Blackpool to London, returning on the overnight service. After cleaning, there would be excursion work throughout the day before a further journey to London on the overnight service commenced a new cycle of workings. The Blackpool coach fleet was utilised for evening workpeople's services between afternoon and evening excursion.

The purchase by Ribble of the Scout company was followed by a change in the Blackpool arrangements for excursions when, at the end of 1962, those operating from Foxhall Road Garage were moved to a new site at nearby

continued on page 92

One double-decker was purchased in 1960, this being Scout's first rear-engined bus. A Leyland Atlantean PDR1/1, number 1, registered OCK500, it carried a 77-seat body with frames by Metro-Cammell but finished by Willowbrook. It is seen in pristine condition at the Ribble bus station in Preston, working on the 152 Blackpool-Burnley service soon after being delivered from the maker's.

A second Atlantean joined the Scout fleet in 1961. Number 2, 398JTB, was a further Leyland demonstrator, new in 1959, and carried 78-seat Metro-Cammell bodywork. It is seen at Blackburn Boulevard while working a journey on service 158 from Rochdale to Blackpool.

Number S18, CCK823, was originally purchased by Ribble in 1949 and was transferred into the Scout fleet in 1963. It carried a 56-seat Leyland-built body on a PD2/3 chassis. It was photographed in Starchhouse Square, Preston on a 155 (Preston Blackpool via Wrea Green) working in July 1963, looking smart in its cherry-red and cream Ribble-style livery.

The existing Scout vehicles were repainted into Ribble style livery over a period of time. Number S20, STC887, is seen in its revised livery on Preston New Road Blackpool working on a Salwick Blackpool works service. At that time the fleet number appeared on a metal plate attached to the front panel. Despite its Scout ownership the bus advertises 'Ribble – a Service at your Service'.

Gleaming in its newly painted Ribble-type livery is number S22, LRN63, the Burlingham-bodied Leyland PD3/3 double-decker. It is seen parked outside Blackpool's Talbot Road bus station in between trips on service 155, Preston Blackpool via Wrea Green, in April 1967.

The former Atlantean demonstrator, number S2, 398JTB, had lost its distintive appearance when pictured in Ribble-style cherry-red and cream livery passing Blackpool Corporation's Marton depot on Whitegate Drive. It was working on service 154, Blackpool Preston Burnley. Once again the fleet number appears on a metal plate attached to the front panel.

The white-coated drivers posed in front of their Leyland Tiger Cub coaches give a poignant reminder of the way things used to be – when a uniform was something to proud of, or to denote status acheived from long service perhaps.

Above: Six Duple Elizabethan-bodied Leyland Tiger Cub PSUC1/2 coaches were purchased in 1954. A line-up photograph was arranged and FRN985 and colleagues are seen when new. All had centre entrances and seated 37. The first of the batch carried only 35 initially, but was later up-seated to match the others.

Right: Number S43, FRN981, is shown as it appeared after Scout was taken over by Ribble. It carries modified livery and restyled front end, including the fitment of more effective trafficators and without the Scout and maker's badges on the front panel.

Four additional Tiger Cubs arrived in 1956, carrying the last centre-entrance bodies to be purchased. They were of Duple Brittannia 41-seat design and JCK686 is seen on a private hire, wearing its original, chiefly cream, livery.

Above: The last of the 1956-built Duple Britannia coaches was JCK691, seen here on the left, in revised livery with maroon lower panels in Starchhouse Square, Preston. To its right is KRN193, one of the 1957 Britannias built to a front-entrance design seating 41. Two examples of this model were added to the fleet.

Below: In 1960 Scout purchased four Tiger Cubs with Duple Northern 41-seat coachwork. This was built at the former Burlingham factory at Blackpool, after Duple moved from Loughborough following their earlier move from Hendon. NRN166 was the first of the four, and is seen in Starchhouse Square.

The first new coaches added under Ribble ownership were three Harrington-bodied 49-seat Leyland Leopards purchased in 1963. A rear view of the third vehicle No. S64, TCK64, is shown here.

Left: Also in 1963 four Plaxton Panorama-bodied 49-seaters on Leopard chassis were delivered to Scout as numbers S739-42, TRN739-42. Number S739 is pictured at Llandudno coach park at Easter 1967. These coaches were part of an order for 22 vehicles, eight joining Ribble and ten going to Standerwicks.

Below: Four Plaxton Panorama-bodied Leopards, numbers S804-7, ARN804-7C, came to Scout in 1965. These were 49-seaters and again formed part of larger orders placed by Ribble. Similar deliveries followed each year thereafter. Number S804 is seen outside the Scout stand, (previously Whittakers), at Adelaide Street, Blackpool. Note the wooden step to assist passengers boarding the vehicle.

York Street: this site had originally been the depot of the Blackpool pioneer motor charabanc operator, Edward Butterworth, and his successors J. G. Warburton Ltd, but it had not subsequently been used for motor coaching. The site was now used as the Blackpool park for visiting Preston-based Scout excursions, although the Saturday evening incoming excursions unloaded and stood at the more centrally located Sheppard Street stand in the winter. Scout coaches were included in the combining of departure stands and destinations referred to in Chapter Six.

The joint Kirkham licence was strengthened from 1965 by addition of new pick-ups at Freckleton and Warton, and links with the Standerwick licences at Lytham and St Annes to enable loads to be combined. Excursions in Preston were also revised for the 1965 season, with the main licence transferred to the Ribble coach station The subsidiary ex-Preston Embee stand was left at Starchhouse Square (soon to disappear under new road works), but was now also authorised to call at the Ribble coach station. The 1966 season saw the grant of new joint Ribble Scout excursions from Ribble coach station, with a series of suburban pick-ups, replacing Ribble's own excursions (including the former Viking licences from the town centre and Woodplumpton Road) and both of Scout's Preston-based licences.

CLOSURE OF SCOUT OPERATIONS

In the run up to the integration of Ribble and Standerwick into the National Bus Company on 1st January 1969, it was decided that Scout should be wound up. The decision to close Scout down took effect on 25th October 1968, and four Preston-Blackpool and two Preston-Lytham routes passed to Ribble from that date; Scout's nominal interest in Blackpool-Peel and Larches/Lea Frenchwood ceased.

Expresses and Blackpool excursions, plus Scout's share of the Preston and Kirkham joint excursions (together with Scout's Springfield workers operations) were transferred to Standerwicks, bringing to an end 49 years of road transport operations under the Scout title. Vehicles were transferred to Ribble or Standerwick as appropriate. The necessary relicensing was undertaken *post facto* and after completing its final road transport accounts the Scout company became dormant; it was, however, later reactivated in a new guise, and, renamed Scout Computer Services Ltd, provided computer facilities for Ribble, and later Crosville and Cumberland, for a number of years. In 1977, it was further renamed NBC Computer Services Ltd. As National Bus Company was being wound down, corporate services were, of necessity, transferred into the soon-to-be-privatised operating companies. This was to be no exception although the parts of the computer business were transferred to the company's employees as Warwick Computer Systems Ltd. This venture did not last long but the renamed Scout Company was formally wound up on 31st December 1985 by Northern Bus Company.

Left: Ribble Burlingham-bodied Tiger Cub number GCK281 was transferred to Scout in 1966, with whom it became S946. The centre-entrance coach is seen in Blackpool's Devonshire Road garage after working a journey on Salwick service W10. The coach was withdrawn in April 1967.

Below: S63/S65 TCK63/65 are seen posed for the publicity department when new in a livery that matches 22 similar machines delivered to Ribble in that year. Note the uniforms now worn by Scout drivers.

Fleet of SCOUT MOTOR SERVICES LTD Part One : Commencement to 1939.
Including fleet of James WATKINSON SCOUT MOTORS

Fleet No.	Registration No.	Manufacturer Type	Aqrd	New	Prev.Owner	Coachwork	Type	Sold	Notes
-	CK3113	Daimler CK	1920	1919	Ainsworth	Buckingham?	Ch24	?	
-	CK3273/CK3301	Daimler CK	1920	1920		Buckingham?	Ch24	c1929	
-	CK3420	Daimler CK	1921	1921		Buckingham?	Ch24	c1929	a
-	FR1925	Leyland	1921	1920	Lucas, Bpl	?	Ch30	1923	
-	CK3390	Daimler CK	1922	1920	Kellett	Buckingham?	Ch28	c1929	a
-	FR2992	Leyland	1923	1921	C. Smith, Bpl	?	Ch33 ?		
-	FR4281	Leyland	1923	1921	C. Smith, Bpl	?	Ch	1931	b
-	CK3578	Leyland	1924	1924		Buckingham?	Ch28	1928	
-	?	Guy	1924	?	?	?	Ch	1925	
-	CK4031	Leyland PLSC	1928	1928		Leyland	B32R	c1933	
1-2	CK4032 CK4040	Leyland PLC	1928	1928		Burlingham	C28	c1929	
3-4	CK4147 CK4146	Leyland TS2	1929	1929		Leyland	C32F	1931	
9-10	CK4255 CK4259	Leyland TS2	1930	1930		Spicer	C29D	1931/2	
5-6	CK4336/CK4337	Leyland TS2	1930	1930		Spicer	C29D	1932	
7-8	CK4348/CK4349	Leyland TS2	1930	1930		Spicer	C29D	1932	
(Note d)	FR8950	Leyland PLC1	1930	1928	C. Smith, Bpl	Burlingham	C26	1930	c
17-19	CK4380/4381/4383	Leyland LT2	1930	1930		Leyland	B30F	1931/2	
20-21	CK4384/CK4385	Leyland LT2	1931	1931		Spicer	B32R	1931/2	
22	CK4386	Leyland TD1	1931	1931		Leyland	L27/24R	1946	
23-24	CK4568/CK4569	Leyland TD1	1931	1931		Leyland	L27/24R	1947/50	
27-30/26	CK4571/CK4575	Leyland TS2	1931	1931		Leyland	C29F	1934	
25	CK4593	Leyland TS2	1931	1931		Leyland	B32-	1933	d
-	CK4594-CK4595	Leyland TS2	1931	1931		Leyland	C28R	1933	e
28-29	CK4603-CK4604	Leyland TD1	1931	1931		Leyland	L24/24R	1946/7	f
-	CK4612	Leyland KP3	1931	1931		Burlingham	C20F	1934	
30	CK4654	Leyland TD2	1932	1932		Leyland	L27/24R	1948	
31 32	CK4655-CK4656	Leyland TS4	1932	1932		Leyland	C24RT	1937	g
-	CK4667-CK4668	Leyland TS4	1932	1932		Leyland	C24RT	1939	
2/1	CK4898/CK4899	Leyland TS6	1934	1934		Burlingham	C30R	1949	h
3-4	CK4900-CK4901	Leyland LT5A	1934	1934		Burlingham	C30R	1940/8	i
6-7	CK4902-CK4903	Leyland LT5A	1934	1934		Weymann	C30R	1940	
5	CK4904	Leyland SKP	1934	1934		Weymann	C26F	c1946	
25	TF9462	Leyland TD2	1934	1932	Leyland Mtrs	Leyland	L24 24R	?	j
26	RN7576	Leyland TD4	1935	1935		Leyland	L27 26R	c1948	k
-	RN7577	Leyland TS7	1935	1935		Burlingham	C31R	c1948	l
-	RN7908-RN7909	Leyland TS7	1936	1936		Burlingham	C28RT	c1946	
27	RN8038	Leyland TD4	1937	1937		Leyland	L27 26RD	1949	
-	RN8138	Leyland TS7	1937	1937		Duple	C28FT	1947	
-	RN8537	Leyland TS8	1938	1938		Burlingham	C31F	1947	
-	RN8857-RN8858	Leyland LT8	1939	1939		Duple	C35F	1947	
-	RN8859-RN8860	Leyland TS8	1939	1939		Duple	C28F	1947	

NOTES :

- a Rebodied by Buckingham (CK3420: B24F in 1924; CK3390: C26F in 1926)
- b Converted to lorry of Watkinson.
- c 11-16 are believed to have come from C. Smith Jnr James Davis Ltd, and this coach (new to S. & J. Wood Ltd) is thought to have come via C. Smith Jnr.
- d Coachwork also quoted as by Weymann.
- e May have been equipped as C28FT
- f Later reseated as L27/24R
- g Later reseated to C30R.
- h Re bodied NCB L27/24R and re numbered 17/18, in 1945
- i 3 (CK4900) was rebodied Duple C33F and renumbered 44, in 1946.
- j ex-Demonstrator; later altered to seat L27/24R
- k Rebodied Duple C33F c1946.
- l Seating later altered to C28R.

Fleet of SCOUT MOTOR SERVICES LTD Part Two : 1940 1961

Fleet Number. 1946	1961	Registration No.	Manufacturer Type	Aqr	New	Prev.Owner	Coachwork	Type	Sold	Notes
21		ACK529	Leyland TD7	1941	1941		Leyland	L27/26R	?	
20		ACK740	Guy Arab II	1943	1943		Duple	L2728R	1952	a
19		ACK790	Daimler CWA6	1944	1944		Duple	L27/28R	1951	b
40		ARN889	Leyland PS1	1946	1946		Duple	C33F	c1951	b
28-29		ARN950-ARN951	Leyland PD1	1946	1946		Leyland	L27/26R	c1959	
31-34		BCK328-BCK329	Bedford OB	1947	1947		Duple	C26F	1948	
35-37		BCK535/551-552	Bedford OB	1947	1947		Duple	C26F	1948	
41		BCK753	Daimler CVD6	1947	1947		Duple	C33F	1948	
38-39		BCK799-BCK800	Bedford OB	1947	1947		Duple	C29F	c1949	
-		BCK982/BRN62	Bedford OB	1947	1947		S.M.T.	C29F	c1949	
-		BRN 61	Bedford OB	1947	1947		Duple	C29F	c1949	
-		BRN 63	Leyland PS1	1947	1947		Duple	C33F	c1950	
1-6		BRN151-BRN156	Leyland PD1	1947	1947		Leyland	L27 26R	?	
-		BRN175-BRN176	Leyland PS1	1947	1947		Duple	C33F	1951	
-		BRN361-BRN362	Bedford OB	1947	1947		S.M.T.	C29F	1950	
-		BRN425/474-475	Leyland PS1	1947	1947		Duple	C33F/C31F	1951	
-		BRN690	Leyland PS1	1947	1947		B'hse Hrtwl	C33F	?	
-		BRN494-BRN495	Bedford OB	1948	1948		S.M.T.	C29F	1949	
-		BRN497-BRN500	Bedford OB	1948	1948		Duple	C29F	1949	
-		BRN686-689/691	Leyland PS1	1948	1948		Duple	C33F	?	
-		BRN791	Bedford OB	1948	1948		Duple	C29F	c1950	
-		CCK 30-CCK 32	Bedford OB	1948	1948		Duple	C29F	1950	
-		CCK589-CCK591	Bedford OB	1948	1948		Duple	C29F	1950	
-		BRN864-BRN866	Leyland PS1	1949	1949		Burlingham	C33F	1952	e
-		CCK927	Bedford OB	1949	1949		Duple	C29F	c1951	
-		CRN158-CRN159	Bedford OB	1949	1949		Duple	C29F	c1951	
-		AFR564	Leyland TS8	1949	1938	Jcksn Hol Tr	Duple	C33F	1954	f
7	s 7	CRN244	Leyland PD2/3	1949	1949		Leyland	L27 26R	1963	g
-		CRN417	Bedford OB	1949	1949		Duple	C29F	1951	
-		CRN501-CRN506	Bedford OB	1950	1950		Duple	C29F	c1954	
8-9	s 8-s 9	DRN364-DRN365	Leyland PD2/3	1950	1950		Leyland	L27/26R	?	
-	s 31	DRN355-DRN357	Leyland PSU/11	1951	1951		Duple	C41F	1959-6x	h, i
-	32-s 33	DRN358-DRN362	Leyland PSU1/15	1951	1951		Duple	C41C	1960-3	j
-		DRN363	Leyland PSU1/15	1951	1951		B'hse Hrtwl	C41C	1956	
10	s10	DRN366	Leyland PD2/1	1951	1951		Leyland	L27/26R	?	
-		DRN367	Bedford SB	1951	1951		Duple	C33F	1954	
-		DRN926-DRN930	Leyland PSU1/15	1951	1951		B'hse Hrtwl	C41C	1956	
-		ECK315-ECK316	Bedford SB	1951	1951		Duple	C33F	1954	
11-12	s 11 s 12	ECK869-ECK870	Leyland PD2/12	1951	1951		Leyland	L27/28R	?	k
-	s 34-s 38	ECK871-ECK876	Leyland PSU1/15	1952	1952		Duple	C41C	?	l
19	s 19	BCK100	Leyland PD1	1953	1946	Viking Prstn	Leyland	L27/26R	1959	
-	s 39-s 41	FCK567-FCK569	Leyland PSU1/15	1953	1953		Duple	C41C	?	
20	S 20	STC887	Leyland PD2/20	1954	1953	Leyland	Leyland	H30/26R	1968	m
-	s 42-s 47	FRN980-FRN985	Leyland PSUC1/2	1954	1954		Duple	C37C	?	n
-	s 48-s 51	JCK686-688/691	Leyland PSUC1/2	1956	1956		Duple	C41C	1965-6	
-	s 52-s 53	KRN192-KRN193	Leyland PSUC1/2	1957	1957		Duple	C41F	1966?	
21-22	s 21-s 22	LRN62-LRN63	Leyland PD3/3	1958	1958		Burlingham	FH41/31F	+	
23-25	s 23-s 25	MCK369-MCK371	Leyland PD3 3	1959	1959		Burlingham	FH41/31F	+	
-	s 54 s 57	NRN166-NRN169	Leyland PSUC1 2T	1960	1960		Duple	C41F	1968	
1	s 1	OCK500	Leyland PDR1/1	1960	1960		MCCW /W'brk	H44 33F	+	
2	s 2	398JTB	Leyland PDR1/1	1961	1959	Leyland	MCCW	H44/34F	+	o
3-5	s 3 s 5	PRN143/PRN145	LeylandPDR1/1	1961	1961		MCCW	H44/33F	+	
58	s 62	PRN146/PRN150	Leyland L2	1961	1961		Duple	C38FT		

NOTES :

a - Later reseated as L27/26R.
b - Later reseated as C31F.
c - Reseated to B31F by 4/1949, and back to C33F by -/1951.
d - LBRN475 entered service in 1948; BRN 425/474 (delivered as C33F) were subsequently re seated to C31F.
e - Diverted from Ribble (were to have been 2562-2564), in exchange for CRN218-CRN220 (Leyland PD2/3 with Leyland L27/26R bodies), which arrived at Ribble with Scout style indicator boxes.
-f - Chassis ex Jackson Hol Tours Ltd, Blackpool: re bodied as shown on purchase. Fitted with doors, 1956: L27/26RD.
h - DRN355 later ran as C24F on contract to Preston North End F.C.; numbered S31 in 1961.
i - DRN356 was a Leyland PSU1/15.
j - DRN359/DRN361 survived to receive numbers s32/s33 in 1961.
k - Fitted with doors, 1956: L27/28RD.
l - LECK871/ECK873/ECK875/ECK876 survived to receive numbers s34/s38 in 1961.
m - Ex-Demonstrator; fitted with doors, -/1956: H30/26RD.
n - FRN980 was delivered with C35C body; later increased to C37C.
-o - Ex-Demonstrator.
\+ - Transferred to Ribble Mtr Svces Ltd. in 10.1968.

Fleet of SCOUT MOTOR SERVICES LTD Part Three : 1962 1968

Fleet No.	Registration No.	Manufacturer Type	Aqrd	New	Prev.Owner	Coachwork	Type	Sold	Notes
s13-s 15	CCK611/612/622	Leyland PD2/3	1963	1948	Ribble	Leyland	H30/26R	1965	
s16-s 17	CCK630/632	Leyland PD2/3	1963	1948	Ribble	Leyland	H30/26R	1964/5	
s 18	CCK823	Leyland PD3	1963	1949	Ribble	Leyland	H30/26R	1964	
s 63-s 65	TCK 63 TCK 65	Leyland PSU3/3RT	1963	1963		Harrington	C49F	*	
s 66-s 69	NRN611 NRN614	Leyland PDR1/1	1963	1960	Ribble	Weymann	CH34/16FT	*	
s 70-s 73	DRN705/17/18/31	Leyland PSU1/15	1963	1951	Ribble	Leyland	C41C	1964	
s 739-s 742	TRN739-TRN742	Leyland PSU3/3RT	1963	1963		Plaxton	C49F	*	
s 903	FCK403	Leyland PSU1/15	1963	1953	Ribble	Leyland	C41C	1965	
s 804-s 807	ARN804C ARN807C	Leyland PSU3/3RT	1965	1965		Plaxton	C49F	*	
s 1396	HRN36	Leyland PD2/13	1965	1955	Ribble	MCCW	H33/28RD	+	
s 1446-s1447	JCK521-JCK522	Leyland PD2/12	1965	1956	Ribble	Burlingham	H33/28RD	+	
s 1456	JCK531	Leyland PD2/12	1965	1956	Ribble	Burlingham	H33/28RD	+	
s 850-s 853	CRN850D-CRN853D	Leyland PSU3 4R	1966	1966		Plaxton	C44FT	*	
s 946	GCK281	Leyland PSUC1/2	1966	1954	Ribble	Burlingham	C41F	1967	
s 961	JRN 27	Leyland PSUC1/2	1966	1956	Ribble	Burlingham	C41F	1967	
s 886-s 887	ECK886E-ECK887E	Leyland PSU3/4R	1967	1967		Plaxton	C49F	*	
s 888-s 889	ECK888E-ECK889E	Leyland PSU3/4R	1967	1967		Plaxton	C44FT	+*	a
s 942-s 945	FCK942F-FCK945F	Leyland PSU3/4R	1968	1968		Plaxton	C49F	*	

NOTES :-

a - ECK888E was converted to C36F in 1967.
* - Transferred to W. C. Standerwick Ltd in 10.1968.
+ - Transferred to Ribble Motor Services Ltd in 10.1968.
+* - ECK888E transferred to Ribble Mtr Svces Ltd; ECK889E transferred to W. C. Standerwick Ltd; in 10.1968.

C. Smiths Motor's Blackpool stand was at 2-6 Vance Road off Central Drive, by Central Railway Station. The ground floor, seen right, had been converted to a covered Loading Station where the coaches were positioned ready for the day's trippers. Long-distance excursions left at 8.0am (or even before) and were joined by the London expresses, then middle-distance trips left at 8.30am and 9.0am. The Liverpool and Manchester expresses departed at 9.30am, but the premises were transformed by 10.0am, for Charles Smith's Lancia Bar took up the floor-space throughout the day, serving tea and light refreshments to passers-by who had not been persuaded to join the excursions. After the sale of the coaches to Joseph Bracewell, the cafe continued in Smith's care. To enable Frank Briggs to settle into Blackpool, the house at 8 Vance Road was purchased for his occupation but part of the ground floor was converted to an office and a tiny (2-vehicle) dormy shed, enabling parked vehicles to be withdrawn from the forecourt of 2-6 to create much needed additional space.

Use of toilet-equipped coaches on London services by John Bull and Standerwick left Bracewell in a difficult position, and from mid-February 1929 the latter commenced a campaign to draw attention to his 'Hygienic Saloon Coaches', reflecting concern in some quarters as to the suitability of toilet compartments on coaches. Despite this, Bracewell was soon obliged to introduce toilets on its own London coaches. A number of Maudslay machines operated from both Blackpool and Colne, and FR2358 (right) was an ML6-type chassis equipped with a Burlingham 26-seat rear-entrance body. Purchased in 1931, this was one of the vehicles equipped with a toilet and was used extensively on the London route. It was taken over by Standerwicks in 1936, but was sold the following year, passing to Hubert Hackett, Manchester.

APPENDIX 1 : Jos. BRACEWELL LTD Incorporated 7th April 1931

Fleet Name: C.SMITH MOTORS

Including predecessor businesses :-
Francis (Frank) SMITH (by June 1897-c1907)
Charles SMITH (by April 1899-c1907)
Francis (Frank) SMITH & Charles SMITH Fleet Name: 'F.& C. SMITH' (c1907-1921)
Charles SMITH & Charles SMITH Jnr Fleet Name: 'F.& C.SMITH & CO' (1921)
F.& C.SMITH LTD Incorporated 17th November 1921. In Receivership by January 1923.
Charles SMITH Jnr Fleet Name: 'C. SMITH MOTORS' (January 1923-July 1928)
Joseph BRACEWELL Jnr Fleet Name: 'C. SMITH MOTORS' (July 1929-cJune 1931)

The portion of the Standerwick business with the longest 'pedigree' is clearly that acquired from Jos. Bracewell Ltd: Francis (Frank) Smith was operating a horse omnibus in Blackpool by June 1897, and his brother Charles Smith was one of the horse omnibus proprietors on the Marton route by April 1899. Both were displaced by electric tramways, turning to horse charabancs by 1901. Charles Smith was leasing the stables at 124 Coronation Street, Blackpool by 1904: these were later used by Wood Bros (Blackpool) Ltd, becoming Standerwick's headquarters from 1933. At the May 1907 Licensing Meeting, the brothers (now in partnership as F. & C. Smith) were allotted four chara routes : to Thornton-le-Fylde, St. Michaels-on-Wyre, Singleton and Wrea Green. The business acquired a reputation for aggressive tactics, with the Watch Committee ordering suspension of licences at various times, particularly during the busy period of the Blackpool Aviation Meeting in August 1910.

The partnership first turned to motor traction in July 1913, but failed to secure a street stand for the new charabanc and was obliged to run it from the stable forecourt until the following season, when a street stand at Charnley Road (Coronation Street junction) was approved; horse charabancs were plying from street stands at Victoria Street (Promenade junction) and Hull Road (Central Drive junction). By February 1914, however, the Smiths had vacated Coronation Street stables and taken a stables and garage on Hornby Road, Blackpool. A second motor chara arrived in March 1915, and the motor chara stands for that season became: Vance Road (Central Drive junction) in place of Charnley Road, and Victoria Street (alongside horse-charabanc stand). A third motor charabanc (delivered August 1915 to replace one of the horse charabancs) was allocated a stand on Hornby Road, opposite Smith's garage premises, in June 1916. A second garage – Back Livingstone Road – was added in April 1918, principally to house and maintain the chara fleet, which had risen to five (completely replacing horse charas) by March 1919. Hornby Road Garage was now used for a car dealership and was the base for a fleet of motor landaulettes and hire cars.

Charles Smith's son (also Charles) was now active in the business, and in 1920 he added several Leyland charas to the fleet, expanding to offer a hire facility to other operators: in August 1920, for example, several coaches were sent to Ramsbottom to augment local fleets during the Wakes Week. Francis Smith left the partnership during the winter of 1920-1921, and a new partnership – styled F. & C. Smith & Company – was established by Charles Smith Snr & Charles Smith Jnr to continue the business. The 1921 season was marred for the Smiths by loss of the Victoria Street stand and the limiting of operations to Vance Road stand under the arrangements concluded by the Operators Association. Some recovery was attempted by nominal transfer of certain vehicles to the individual names of the partners who sought additional stands, but henceforth operation was largely conducted from off-street sites: a lease of 2-6 Vance Road and use of Hornby Road Garage enabled the growing fleet to be displayed to prospective customers.

1920 saw a great expansion of the Blackpool operators' fleets as former military vehicles became readily available for sale to hauliers and coach operators. The formation of F. & C. Smith Ltd at the end of 1921 brought about a formidable fleet able to carry up to 600 passengers at one time. It is not clear how many vehicles in the 1922 fleet were contributed by Josiah Street Ltd and Hilton & Sharpe & Co Ltd but (assuming a seating capacity of about 30) there would have been some twenty charabancs in service during that season. Much depended on work outside Blackpool and this view shows a large contract arranged by Crawshawbooth agent T. Hoyle, some eight machines being posed on Hud Hey Road, Haslingden for a publicity photograph. From the left are CW2493, a Daimler bus owned by Hoyle, plus seven F. & C. Smith Ltd machines: Daimlers FR2079 and FR2005, Maudslay FR2007, and four 29-seat Leylands (FR2486, FR2001, FR2002 and FR2006). The party (numbering about 240) was probably on an outing from one of the Haslingden mills. Charles Smith Jnr. is standing between the two coaches on the right, supervising operations.

AMALGAMATION – AND BREAK-UP

Use of the fleet to hire to other operators had proved successful, and mindful of the apparently successful enterprise of Salford-based Swift Fleet Motors Ltd, the Smiths interested a number of Blackpool operators in setting up a rival company to exploit this side of the operation: on 17th November 1921 F. & C. Smith Ltd was incorporated, amalgamating operations of (at least) F. & C. Smith & Co, Josiah Street Ltd and Hilton, Sharpe & Co. Ltd. The new business was based at Hornby Road Garage, and an East Lancashire base was established in Crawshawbooth, Rossendale, under managership of a local operator (Thomas Hoyle); in addition to charabancs, hire-cars and taxis were also operated. The operation quickly degenerated into discord, and the company was placed into Receivership at the end of 1922.

Only Charles Smith Jnr appears to have continued to operate charas, supplemented by furniture removals and haulage (probably utilising chassis from spare charas). Smith worked initially from Hornby Road Garage, running a twice-weekly coach service to Manchester from January 1923, linked with extensions to Audenshaw Trotting Course, and utilising chiefly pneumatic-tyred Lancias that were the property of the troubled Limited Company. The F. & C. Smith Ltd Receiver proceeded with his work, and in May 1923 transferred the Hornby Road Garage premises to Josiah Street; in anticipation, Smith had taken possession of the 2-6 Vance Road premises and established a stand and office at the corner of Hornby Road and Coronation St. He also purchased many charas from the limited company, particularly the speedy Lancias, most being pneumatic-tyred, and began to use the style Chas Smith's Lancia Cream Motor Service .

One of the arrangements that had been under negotiation in 1922 had been a venture with Birmingham & Midland Motor Omnibus Co Ltd, a combine company wishing to establish holiday services to a number of resorts. A return journey from Birmingham to Blackpool could

not be achieved in a single day and the company had reached agreement for a kiss-and-turn operation that brought passengers from Birmingham, Wolverhampton and Stafford to Knutsford, where transfer to Smith's charas took place while the passengers lunched; Smith of course brought returning passengers from Blackpool to the interchange. Charles Smith concluded the arrangements and the service commenced on 19th May 1923, running seasonally each Saturday in succeeding years; the service became so popular that attempts were later made to offer journeys on other days between Thursday and Sunday, the experiment being largely unsuccessful.

Meanwhile hiring of coaches to inland operators continued, with daily trips offered to Blackburn, Accrington, Haslingden and Rawtenstall during appropriate holiday periods; a period excursion for Manchester holiday-makers was also available in 1923. C. Smith Motors Lancias were hired to Blackpool-based Batty-Holt Touring Services to operate extended tours, from 28th September 1923.

Provision for the growing fleet was made in May 1924, when Havelock St Garage for three coaches was purchased; three months later a garage for six coaches in Boothley Road was taken over additionally. In April 1925 Royal Garage, Coronation Street, was purchased from coachman Richard Blackhurst (who had moved to new premises on Albert Road) as both a depot for six coaches and a three-vehicle stand, to replace Hornby Road stand (which later became a stand for Spencer's Motors).

The Manchester service had continued, usually twice weekly with some experimental changes; by autumn 1925 operations were calling at Chorley, Bolton, Manchester and Audenshaw. Attempts to inaugurate a regular service to Liverpool (commencing 28th June 1924) had been less successful, but from 26th June 1926 both Manchester (now omitting Audenshaw) and Liverpool services operated daily. The Liverpool service was to cease seasonally at the end of October, but Chorley, Bolton and Manchester continued to be served daily throughout the winter.

The hiring arrangements in East Lancashire had not persisted, but in February 1927 an announcement by Thomas Hoyle in Rossendale revealed that Charles Smith Motors coaches would again be made available for hire inland; the re-opened arrangement was in conjunction with North Shore-based William Salisbury & Sons, who had expanded their fleet by purchase of a number of Charles Smith Lancia machines.

Increasing competition to Manchester saw prices fall drastically as the 1926/27 Winter commenced, the 6/- fare dropping to 4/- by 27th November. Prior to Christmas 1926 Smiths ran a special positioning journey to the city and provided a special Christmas weekend return to Blackpool for Manchester-based passengers; services now terminated in St. Peters Square in the City. Single fares were introduced from January 1927, but by 29th March, Smith had linked his Manchester service with that of Buck of Swinton (founder of the pioneer Swift Fleet Motors business) and was terminating in the City at Buck's Lancashire & Yorkshire Motor Coach Station in Sackville Street. As part of this joint service some coaches on the Chorley, Bolton & Manchester service ran via St Annes and Lytham, but Smith stressed that this indirect service was augmented by through direct coaches. To improve the potential of his inward traffic to the resort, Smith began to seek licences to ply in en-route towns: Bolton was unable to reach a decision, and his application to Manchester 'to load in St. Peter's Square' had been overtaken by events when it was considered and given a direct refusal.

From 4th June 1927 the joint service left Blackpool at 9.30am, 1.30pm and 7pm; and Manchester at 9am, 1.30pm and 6pm, but was not to survive for more than a few weeks due to withdrawal by Bucks, and by 2nd July Smith was again operating solely, with the usual departure time of 9.30am ex-Blackpool and 6pm ex-Manchester (services via St Annes and Lytham, which ran for Bucks' benefit, had been discontinued). From 2nd October 1927 coaches resumed via St. Annes and Lytham; once again direct coaches from Blackpool were featured in publicity, but this time there were two separate routes. Direct coaches called at Blackburn (expanding former Wednesday Market excursions) en route to Bolton and Manchester, and journeys via St. Annes followed the original route via Chorley to Bolton and Manchester; return journeys left Manchester at 5.30pm (via Chorley and St. Annes) or 6pm (via Blackburn and direct). The service terminated in the city at the Red Garage, Sackville Street (the same site as the Lancashire & Yorkshire Station, now under management of a co-operative headed by Adam King, a Stretford-based operator). This site lay south of Whitworth Street and in order to provide a more convenient terminal point for his passengers Smith transferred his terminus in mid-January 1928 to John Sharp's Lena Street garage (off Piccadilly). Continuing competition caused fares to fall to a new low in February 1928, with Manchester Bolton 2/6d single, 3/- return, 4/6d extended, and Chorley Blackburn 2/6d day return. Charles Smith was not willing to be beaten, and maintained both routes daily, the Blackburn variant finally being withdrawn during late Summer 1929.

Meanwhile, Liverpool expresses had re-commenced thrice-weekly from 25th April 1927 but from 28th May a daily service operated. Sunday operations ceased from 11th September, and after 28th October thrice-weekly services were re-introduced, but seasonal withdrawal followed by mid-November. Daily resumption was from 14th April 1928.

A fourth depot – Coleridge Road, Blackpool – opened in April 1928, to provide stabling for seven coaches, but the hire contract with Batty-Holt Touring Services finally ended in 1928 when the touring company decided to operate its own coaches: a number of Smith's Lancias was purchased by Batty Holt to inaugurate the new arrangement. Meanwhile, from mid-June 1928, additional stages on the Birmingham seasonal route were established at Wigan and Warrington.

SALE TO JOSEPH BRACEWELL

Blackpool coaching fraternity was surprised to find in July 1928 that the resort's largest coaching business had passed into new hands: control of the 22-strong C.Smith Motors fleet was now with Colne-based Joseph Bracewell (who also controlled the Nelson Carriage & Taxi Co, and had earlier been a Director of Rishton & Antley Motor Co Ltd). Bracewell operated the Smith business from 1st July 1928, although formal agreement was not signed until early August; he placed his future son-in-law (Frank Briggs) in charge of the Blackpool operation. Bracewell's policy was to maintain Trading Names (to minimise licensing problems) and the Charles Smith Motors name was accordingly retained for the Blackpool operation.

Briggs arrived in Blackpool charged with the task of joining the Blackpool-London operators, and he achieved his objective in little over a fortnight: Bracewell's service commenced Monday 16th July 1928, running south on Mondays and Fridays, and returning (from Russell Square) on Tuesdays and Saturdays. Operation was via Lytham, Preston, Blackburn, Bolton and Manchester (Sharp's, Lena Street: and later from St. Peters Square additionally), and coaches called at Birmingham (where Smith's Birmingham partner – Midland Red – acted as Agent) then via Coventry and Fenny Stratford.

Smith remained on hand to offer advice and guidance to the new Manager, a situation that continued for some time after ownership passed to Joseph Bracewell; the former owner also retained a financial interest in the Blackpool business by virtue of the arrangements arrived at relative to the change of ownership.

From 10th September 1928 London departures increased to thrice-weekly, the terminal moving to United Transport, Southampton Row; Birmingham stage became Bradford Street, where Buckingham Coachworks (from whom Bracewell had recently purchased coach bodies) now acted as Agent. Midland Red was displeased that Bracewell was providing Manchester-Birmingham-London facilities which would compete with proposals by Midland Red and North Western. From 2nd November 1928 the Preston Agent (Scout Motors) abruptly changed: Bracewell's had become aware that Scout was about to commence a rival London service! Withdrawal of Scout's London service after New Year resulted in reinstatement of the Preston firm as Agent, after intervention by Charles Smith Jnr, who had a close friendship with the Watkinson family.

Manchester and Liverpool expresses continued daily through the Winter of 1928/1929, but Liverpool journeys (hitherto run via the Ormskirk road) diverted from 1st January 1929 to call at Wigan and St. Helens in an attempt to attract extra traffic. A fresh application to ply in Manchester, this time from Lena Street Garage, met with another refusal from the City Council.

A short-lived Blackpool-London service by William Salisbury & Sons was incorporated into Bracewell's operation at the beginning of March 1929 (Salisburys becoming Bracewell's Agent), but from 22nd April 1929 Blackpool-London operated daily, with a new feeder from Colne, Nelson, Burnley and Accrington to boost loadings: connection into the main line was at Blackburn. Operation of London journeys via Manchester was discontinued, coaches running from Bolton to Knutsford via Barton Bridge. Midland Red had applied to Blackpool Council to operate seasonal Birmingham-Blackpool expresses itself (as a through service replacing the joint kiss-and-turn facility), but discussions satisfied the larger company that Bracewell was no longer a threat on Manchester-Birmingham section, and Midland Red agreed to resume as Agent for Bracewell's London service – and also to allow him to take over entirely the seasonal route. Accordingly, Bracewell commenced through running to Birmingham on 17th May 1929, heading south on Friday and Saturday, north on Saturday and Sunday.

F. & C. Smith Ltd's Daimler charabanc FR2005 is loaded for an excursion from Blackpool. The 29-seater machine appears to be taking a private party on a trip as the coach is not standing at one of the licensed stands. Charles Smith Jnr. is again in attendance (extreme right), and has arranged for a photographer who specialised for some years in producing souvenir post-card views of excursionists to capture the departure. The small frame on the running board was used to identify the view for the trippers on their return, when he would have available a number of prints for sale. 'Look for number 42 on my board' would be the message. After a morning on the various stands he would move inland to capture tramloads of holiday-makers on the open trams running on the Whitegate Drive circular route and in later years the open runabout buses serving Stanley Park would also receive his attention.

A Colne-bound coach on the London service (one of two operating to Colne on that day) was involved in an accident on the moors between Bolton and Darwen on Friday 12th July 1929: a motor-cyclist emerging at speed from a side lane caused Maudslay FV126 to swerve and mount a bank before falling on its side. No-one was seriously hurt, but the coach was not recovered until the following morning. Reports of the accident reveal that – despite previous notes of withdrawal – Smiths were still carrying London-Manchester traffic at this date: it was stated that some passengers had been dropped in the City, reducing the number involved in the incident.

The seasonal Birmingham route re-commenced on 7th June 1930 as a daily service, leaving Blackpool at 3.30pm (11am on Sundays) and Birmingham at 8.30am (10.30am on Sundays): a new stage was added at Stone. For the first time it continued throughout the winter: from 1st November 1930 timings were adjusted to 9.30am from each terminal. A new seasonal route commenced for 1930: a thrice-weekly Blackpool-Edinburgh via Carlisle and Lockerbie was in operation by 28th July (Wednesday, Friday and Saturday out, Thursday, Saturday and Sunday in) but was not a success, and was withdrawn after operation on 28th September. The London service was enhanced in 1930 by the addition of seasonal feeders from Morecambe and Lancaster to Preston, operated for Bracewell by Atkinson's Dreadnought Motors, and from Clitheroe to Blackburn, operated by a vehicle from the Colne depot.

Application to the Commissioners in 1931 was undertaken separately for Blackpool and East Lancashire-based operations: in Blackpool application was made to continue year-round operation of the Blackpool-Blackburn-Bolton-Birmingham-London, Blackpool-Chorley-Bolton-Manchester, Blackpool-Wigan-St Helens-Liverpool, and Blackpool-Knutsford-Newcastle-Stafford-Wolverhampton-Birmingham expresses, plus excursions and tours. In Colne, application included year-round operation of Colne-Blackburn-Bolton-Birmingham-London express. By the time that the applications were heard both businesses had been incorporated as Jos. Bracewell Ltd, but all applications were granted with only minor adjustment: initial refusal to permit Warrington-Blackpool traffic on the Birmingham-Blackpool service was reversed after a second application, with more thorough evidence in support. Subsequent applications for the Morecambe-Preston and Clitheroe-Blackburn feeders run in 1930 were not allowed (nor was a Morecambe-London application by Atkinsons). After hearing Manchester Corporation's objection, the Commissioner only granted use of Lena Street terminal on notice that a more suitable point must be sought.

News of the sale of Standerwicks to the Combine in November 1932 brought an immediate response from Jos. Bracewell Ltd, and the Blackpool-based portion was offered to the purchasers. This was subsequently amended to include the Colne-London route plus certain limitations to Bracewell's Burnley-based operations (including severe limitation on Burnley-Blackpool and Morecambe traffic, and cessation of all Burnley-Clitheroe excursions). No Blackpool properties were owned by Bracewells: all five premises were still in Charles Smith Jnr's name, and were occupied under leases. A figure of £17,000 was agreed for the purchase, this being substantially lower than the price arrived at for Standerwick's (smaller) business. In part this was due to Bracewell's Accounts revealing less than satisfactory profits: the 1929 net profit of £4,221 had shrunk to £166 in 1930 (after taking into account a loss of £2,008 on disposal of the Lancia fleet), and 1931 profits were little better at £692.

The Blackpool-based fleet of 29 coaches (fifteen Daimler, eight Maudslay, five Leyland and one AJS) to pass to the new owners was revised to include the Colne-based ADC used on the London feeder, one Blackpool-based Maudslay of similar vintage passing to Colne in exchange. Most of the East Lancashire business had to be separated out of the Jos. Bracewell Ltd Accounts, and transferred into a new company – Bracewells (Colne) Ltd – which then formally applied for a transfer of Road Service licences from Jos. Bracewell Ltd: these arrangements were not completed until the year end. These were not the only difficulties: it quickly became apparent that twenty Blackpool-based coaches had never been transferred into the books of Jos. Bracewell Ltd, and were still registered by Joseph Bracewell personally. In addition, they were actually owned (under hire-purchase agreement) by Charles Smith Jnr! In order to correct the book-keeping the sum of £7,000 was deducted from the agreed price of £17,000 and loaned to the Limited Company so that it might formally acquire the machines (and thus enable Bracewell to pay off the outstanding hire purchase balance). Transfer of ownership was concluded on 1st February 1933, with Manager Frank Briggs continuing under a service contract. Immediately following the acquisition, Jos. Bracewell Ltd was placed under management of W. C. Standerwick Ltd: further developments are detailed in Chapter Four.

The main F. & C. Smith stand in Blackpool was on Hornby Road, close to Coronation Street junction, and this 29-seat Daimler, FR2212, is about to depart for the short excursion to Fleetwood, for which the fare was 1s 6d. The arrival of the photographer to record this street-scene for a commercial postcard in the Afond series has prompted the Smith family to pose in front of their charabanc. Charles Snr. stands in the roadway and Charles Jnr. and Frank have placed themselves against the offside wing of the coach. When Charles Jnr. concentrated on his Vance Road stand in 1924, the Hornby Road stand became the departure for Spencer's Motors, but was re-located to the left-hand side of the road adjacent to the Spencer family shop.

Below: Joseph Bracewell decided to revise the C. Smith Motors fleet profile by replacing the chiefly lightweight Lancias by heavier chassis. This Leyland TS2, FR9377, carried a 32 seat Burlingham all-weather body with dual doors and was fitted with sliding windows in the fixed frames. It arrived shortly after the commencement of the London service, and was a regular runner on the new route.

Fleet of Jos. BRACEWELL LTD Fleet Name:C. SMITH MOTORS

Including fleets of predecessor businesses :-
Francis (Frank) SMITH & Charles SMITH Fleet Name: F.& C. SMITH (c1907-1921) Charles SMITH & Charles SMITH Jnr Fleet Name: F.& C.SMITH & CO (1921)
F. & C. SMITH LTD Incorporated 17th November 1921. In Receivership by January 1923. Charles SMITH Jnr Fleet Name: C. SMITH MOTORS (January 1923-July 1928)
Joseph BRACEWELL Fleet Name: C. SMITH MOTORS (July 1928-c June 1931)

NOTE : Joseph Bracewell maintained his original coaching business in Colne (also a branch at Nelson), Lancashire, and the Jos.Bracewell Ltd. company embraced both Blackpool and East Lancashire operations. In general terms, the East Lancashire operations were not part of the sale to Ribble, North Western and Midland Red in 1933, and were transferred to a newly-incorporated company – Bracewells (Colne) Ltd – after grant of licences during 1933. The fleet listed below details only coaches known to have been Blackpool-based.

Registration No.	Manufacturer Type	Aqrd	New	Prev.Owner	Coachwork	Type	Sold	Notes
??	?	1913	1913		?	Ch—	c1920	
??	?	1915	1915		?	Ch—	c1920	
??	?	1915	1915		?	Ch—	c1920	
??	?	c1919?	?		?	Ch—	c1923	
FR1489	Daimler	1919	1919		?	Ch24	c1923	
FR2001-FR2002	Leyland	1920	1920		?	Ch29	c1923	
FR2003-FR2004	?	1920	1920		?	Ch—	c1923	
FR2005	Daimler	1920	1920		?	Ch29	c1923	
FR2006	Leyland	1920	1920		?	Ch29	c1923	
FR2007	Maudslay	1920	1920		?	Ch29	c1923	
FR2079 FR2212	Daimler	1920	1920		?	Ch29	c1923	
FR2486	Leyland	1920	1920		?	Ch24?	c1923	
FR2733	Fiat	1921	1921		?	Ch15	1923	
FR2873	Daimler CK	1921	1921		?	Ch29	1925	
FR2993	Leyland	1921	1921		?	Ch33	1923	
FR4281	Leyland	1921	1921		?	Ch—	1924	
FR4329	Fiat	1921	1921		?	Ch15	1922	
FR4363	FR4378	1921	1921		?	Ch—	c1924	
FR4576 FR4646	Lancia	1922	1922		?	Ch20	1925	
FR4666-FR4667	Lancia	1922	1922		?	Ch20	1925	
FR4705	?	1922	1922		?	Ch—	c1925	
FR4816-FR4874	Lancia	1922	1922		?	Ch—	1926/8	
FR4954	Lancia	1923	1922	a	?	Ch23	1927	a
FR5129-FR5160	Lancia	1923	1923		?	Ch—	1927	
FR5486-FR5545	Lancia	1923	1923	b	?	Ch16/B20	1926/9	b
FR5815-FR5816	Leyland	1924	1924		?	Ch26	1928/9	
FR5862	Lancia	1924	1924		?	Ch23	1925	
FR6199	Lancia	1925	1925		?	Ch—	1927	
FR6516	Daimler	1925	1925		?	Ch—	1928	
FR6517	Lancia	1925	1925		?	Ch—	1927	
FR7137/7170	Lancia	1926	1926		?	C—	1926/8	
FR7200/FR7409	Lancia	1926	1926		?	C—	1927	
FR7442/FR7498	Lancia	1926	1926		?	C—	1927	
FR7800-FR7801	Lancia	1927	1927		?	C20-	1928	
FR7913-FR7914	Lancia	1927	1927		?	C20-	1927	
FR8021-FR8023	Lancia	1927	1927		?	C20-	1928	
FR8095/8097/8209	Lancia	1927	1927		?	C17-/C20-	1927	
FR8268-FR8269	Lancia	1927	1927		?	C25-	1929	
FR8303-FR8304	Lancia	1927	1927		?	C26-	1928/29	
FR8348-FR8349	Lancia	1927	1927		?	C26-	1928/30	
FR8419	Leyland PLSC	1927	1927		?	C35-	1928	
FR8856	Lancia	1928	1928		?	C25-	1930	
FR8955-FR8956	Leyland PLC1	1928	1928		?	C26-	1929/31	
FR9078-FR9080	Lancia	1928	1928		?	C26-	1929-30	
FR9105-9186/9249	Lancia	1928	1928		?	C26-	1930-31	
FR9269/9292-9293	Leyland PLC1	1928	1928		?	C30-/C26-	1929/31	
FR9319	Lancia	1928	1928		?	C26-	1930	
FR9320	A.D.C.	1928	1928		Buckingham ?	C28-	1936	
FR9377	Leyland TS2	1928	1928		Burlingham ?	C32D	1932	
CW7259-CW7260	Maudslay ML2	1929	1927	Bracewell+	?	C26-/C25-	1933	c, d
FR9794/FV 360	Leyland TS2	1929	1929		?	C32-	C31-	e
FV126/FR259	Maudslay ML2	1929	1929		?	C24-	c1934	
FV191/FV260	Daimler CF6	1929	1929		Buckingham?	C28-	c1934	
FV448-FV450	Daimler CF6	1929	1929		Buckingham?	C32-	c1934	f
FV454	Daimler CF6	1929	1929		Buckingham?	C—D	1933	g
FV498-FV500	Daimler CF6	1929	1929		Buckingham?	C26-T	c1934	f
TF1763-TF1764	Maudslay ML6	1930	1930	Bracewell+	?	C20-	1935	h
FV1002-FV1003	Daimler CF6	1930	1930		Buckingham?	C26-T	c1934	
FV1029-FV1030	Daimler CF6	1930	1930		Buckingham?	C26-T	c1934	
FV1067-FV1068	Daimler CF6	1930	1930		Buckingham?	C26-T	c1934	
FV1550	Leyland TS2	1931	1931		?	C24-T		
FV1837-FV1838	Leyland TS2	1931	1931		?	C26-T		
TE2593	Maudslay ML4	1931	1928	Bracewell$	?	C30-	1933	d
FV2358	Maudslay ML6	1931	1931		Burlingham	C26RT		
TF4635	A.J.S.Pilot	1932	1930	Ainsworth	?	C—	c1934	i

NOTES :-
The following 22 vehicles were owned by C.Smith Motors on completion of the sale to Joseph Bracewell on 1st July 1928:
Lancia : FR4874 5545 7137 8268-9 8304 8348 8856 9078-80 9105 9186 9249 9319 (15)
Leyland : FR5815-6 8955-6 9269 9292-3 (7)

The following 29 vehicles were owned by Jos.Bracewell Ltd on purchase by Ribble, North Western & MidlandRed on 1st February 1933:
Daimler : FV191 260 448-450 454 498-500 1002-3 1029-30 1067-8 (15)
A.D.C. : FR9320 (1); Maudslay : CW7259-60 TF1763-4 FV126 259 2358 (7)
Leyland : FR9794 FV360 1550 1837-8 (5); A.J.S. : TF4635 (1)

a	-	Previously lorry of C. Smith Jnr: re-built as Ch23 in 1923, but later Ch20.
b	-	FR5486 was lorry of C. Smith Jnr, but converted to Ch23 in 1924, then variously as goods or hackney while with Smith; FR5545 was later B17-; with subsequent owner was C20-
c	-	Previously in Bracewell's Colne fleet; CW7260 was seated C21 – when used on Bracewell's (Colne-based) extended tour work.
d	-	Returned to Jos.Bracewell Ltd's Colne fleet.
e	-	FV 360 was later converted to C26-T.
f	-	FV 450 was later converted to C26-T.
g	-	Transferred to Jos.Bracewell Ltd's Colne fleet in 1931 (used on Colne-London express): nominally returned to Blackpool fleet in 3.1933, and included in sale (but out-stationed at Colne for Colne-London express).
h	-	Probably up-seated to C26 – when at Blackpool.
i	-	Ainsworth of Accrington was Agent for Bracewell's expresses; at the close of the 1932 season the A.J.S.(Ainsworth's only coach) passed to Bracewell in lieu of nett ticket moneys owed, and Bracewell attempted (unsuccessfully) to take over the Ainsworth excursions licence.
+	-	Transferred from Joseph Bracewell's Colne fleet.
$	-	Transferred from Jos.Bracewell Ltd's Colne fleet.
*	-	Transferred to W. C. Standerwick Ltd 5.1936.

APPENDIX 2 : WOOD BROTHERS (BLACKPOOL) LTD Incorporated 10th August 1920 (as J.W. DEWHURST & CO. LTD: name changed 5th April 1927). Fleet Name:JOHN BULL COACHES

Including predecessor business :- John William DEWHURST (by 1904-August 1920)

John William Dewhurst was operating carriages from Walker Street Livery Stables, Blackpool by 1904 when he took over his father's (William Dewhurst) Livery Stables. He purchased two horse charabancs in 1909, but was refused a transfer of the licences; by 1911 he had at least three horse charabancs running from off-street premises. His first motor charabanc came in November 1913 and he moved to new premises about February 1914, these being the 124 Coronation Street, Blackpool stables recently vacated by F. & C. Smith (Appendix 1) which would become Standerwick Group headquarters from 1933. For 1914 he received two prime stands close by his new premises: at Coronation Street/Reads Avenue junction (horse) and western end of Reads Road (motor). A third stand (south side of Reads Road) was granted in August 1914, but for the reduced pleasure traffic during the Great War the original stands sufficed from May 1915. Dewhurst continued operating throughout the War, and in 1919 he was awarded three motor charabanc licences at Coronation Street.

Planning further expansion, Dewhurst sought outside Capital and a Limited Company, J. W. Dewhurst & Co Ltd was incorporated on 10th August 1920. New money was provided by Ernest Wood, who is believed to have come from Wigan: he was subsequently joined by his brother Walter, and with Dewhurst they formed the Board of Directors. New charabancs resulted in elimination of horse charabancs, the premises now becoming known as Dewhurst's Garage (also later as The Motories) and business included removals and haulage as well as coaching. Dealing was also carried out, including distribution of Beardmore taxi-cabs: some were also operated, and Wedding carriages were available.

In 1921 Blackpool Council granted a fresh stand, at the corner of Reads Road and Central Drive, and perhaps by this time the small garage at this corner was in use by the company; a garage at 7 Palatine Road (where an office had been established) was also in use. In the following year a series of inland excursions was commenced, to Liverpool on Tuesday, Blackburn Market on Wednesday and Manchester on Thursday. By Spring 1925 extended tours for Tradesmens' were operated, and season-end London and Bournemouth tours were run in September. During 1926 Dewhursts joined C. Smith Motors in providing coaches to the fledgling Batty-Holt Motor Tours.

In the early morning of Sunday 16th May 1926 driver Howarth was returning to Blackpool with a Dewhurst Lancia after working from Darwen during Saturday; in a heavy mist he ran into a telegraph pole five miles from home, ending in a field eight feet below the roadway. He was uninjured, leaving the coach to be recovered later, but when the firm arrived to manoeuvre the coach onto the road it was found that all the rugs (and the licence disc) had been stolen.

The Manchester excursion developed into a daily service from Monday 14th June 1926 and was to survive into the ownership of the Combine (1926 saw a short break in operation, with re-commencement from Monday 4th October). On that day a daily express to Liverpool – also to survive into the 'thirties – was commenced, taking the direct road through Ormskirk until October 1929, when it diverted to run via Wigan, Ashton-in-Makerfield and St. Helens to attract additional traffic. Manchester operations expanded to run via Blackburn, Darwen and Bolton from about April 1928, and extended to terminate at Oldham from Whitsuntide 1929, but later route revision saw coaches again running via Chorley instead of Blackburn.

Dewhurst retired from the company in January 1927, leaving Ernest and Walter Wood in control; Dewhurst took dealership activities into his own name, acting in a small capacity as a motor coach dealer. The Woods, meanwhile, changed the company name to Wood Brothers (Blackpool) Ltd (sanctioned on 5th April 1927). Simultaneously the Woods re-introduced the John Bull title that had briefly been in evidence in 1920-1921, quickly extending publicity to refer to the 'Famous John Bull Coaches'.

Operation of the Manchester and Liverpool expresses (competing against several other services) inevitably led to accusations of speeding, and in February March 1928 five John Bull employees appeared at Lytham or Kirkham courts in as many weeks, being fined a total of £15 plus costs. Three employees of rival services also appeared, and were fined £3 each plus costs.

The start of regular weekly London trips by Standerwicks resulted in a hasty decision by Wood Bros to compete, a weekly service commencing on Monday 16th April 1928: like Standerwicks it ran via Preston, Wigan, Knutsford, Newcastle-under-Lyme, Stafford, Lichfield and via Watling Street to Dunstable and St. Albans, even utilising the same London terminal at Russell Square. Wood Bros. ran south on Mondays, returning Fridays, with return fares pitched 2/6d under Standerwick's at 25/-; although described as an express, it was initially a period excursion, without intermediate fares or traffic originating in London. A single fare of (15/-) was available from the following week, when returns reduced to 22/6d.

CENTRAL LANCASHIRE EXPANSION

Meanwhile the Woods had taken a look at occasional operations in Central Lancashire, and in mid-February 1928 appointed Arthur Dinham (a Booking Agent with premises on New Water Street, Salford Bridge) as Blackburn Agent; a series of advertisements in local papers sought hire bookings. An early operation was a Cup Final trip (Blackburn Rovers having won through) and Dinham arranged a personally-conducted excursion at 1.50p. Negotiations to obtain Blackburn premises resulted in early May 1928 the leasing of the yard at the Golden Lion Hotel (Ainsworth Street/Church Street corner), Dinham now acting also as office manager on that site. London and Manchester expresses were immediately diverted to run via Blackburn, Darwen and Bolton; a London feeder from Lancaster (to Preston – probably by taxi) was also offered for a short time. By June 1928 a gentleman's agreement with Standerwicks eliminated fare-cutting, and from 29th June rates were £1 single, £1.5.-d return or £1.10.-d extended return.

Blackburn publicity now featured Wood Bros'. expresses to Manchester and London, with fares also available to from Blackpool at the inconvenient times afforded by the through services, but from 13th May 1928 a daily service from Blackburn (Golden Lion Yard) to Blackpool (The Motories) commenced at 10am (9.30am Saturday), returning at 8pm. Fares of 2/6d single, 4/- return matched local expresses of KCR and East Lancashire Motors but Wood Bros. sought to poach traffic and from 9th July returns fell to 3/6d; Sunday-Friday departure ex-Blackburn being adjusted to 10.15am. Meanwhile, Wakes Week excursions were run by Wood Bros. coaches from Golden Lion Yard.

This activity by Wood Bros. had not gone un-noticed, and the Blackburn-Blackpool express was used in a test case at Blackburn Police Court on 27th July 1928. On 17th June a constable observed from the highway a Wood Bros. coach standing in Golden Lion Yard: booking a ticket at the yard office he boarded the coach. The prosecution contended it made no difference whether the coach was on (or merely visible from) the highway: the chalked board was solicitation to ply for hire and rendered the service illegal; as no licence had been granted summonses had been issued. The Bench ruled against Wood Bros. on 3rd August; as the prosecution was a test case the company was fined a nominal £1, and costs awarded against the driver and booking agent.

Wood Bros. withdrew its advertisements, but from 11th August revised publicity appeared for Dinham's Blackpool service, with bookings taken at Dinham's 9 New Water Street office (some 50 yards from Wood Bros'. yard); by this means coaches were not visible to the public until after a ticket had been purchased, and the Blackburn authorities (still unhappy about the intruder) were powerless to act further. Wood Bros. meanwhile applied for six licences: at

FV9685 was purchased in September 1928, and had a Burlingham all-weather dual- entrance body seating 24 on a Leyland TS2 chassis as seen right. By this date most all-weather coaches had fixed window-pillars and a coach-built back, enabling them to operate almost as a full-coach when closed up. Prior to Christmas 1928, Wood Bros. returned FV9685 to be up-graded for use on the Blackpool-London express, principally by fitment in the rear of a toilet unit. Entrance was gained through a central door in a mahogany partition into a passageway that led to the emergency exit. Doors led off left and right, one to a folding washbasin, and the other to a chemical closet. The main portion (as seen above left) was fitted with parcel nets above the windows, each pillar carrying a mirror and ornamental electric lamp, while four circular electric lamps and four bell-pushes were fitted along a board running down the centre of the roof. The rear door was now blocked off and side seats fitted at the rear to permit circulating space by the toilet door. Eelsewhere the seating was arranged two-and-one, to reduce overall capacity to 20. This was the first toilet-equipped coach to run Blackpool-London, and for a couple of years Wood Bros. was elevated to the position of premier operator on the route. The device on the coach side is now a Tiger!

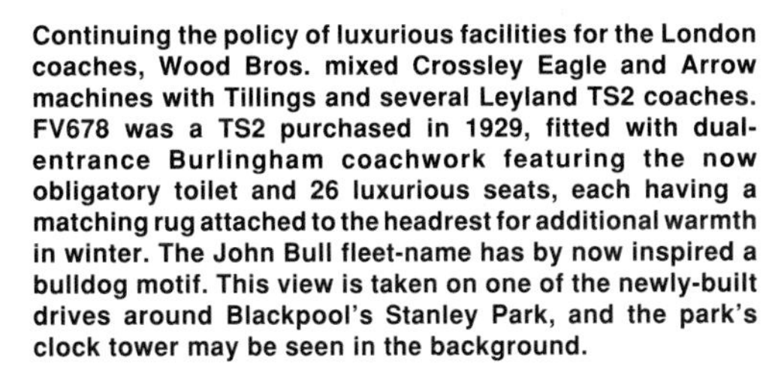

Continuing the policy of luxurious facilities for the London coaches, Wood Bros. mixed Crossley Eagle and Arrow machines with Tillings and several Leyland TS2 coaches. FV678 was a TS2 purchased in 1929, fitted with dual-entrance Burlingham coachwork featuring the now obligatory toilet and 26 luxurious seats, each having a matching rug attached to the headrest for additional warmth in winter. The John Bull fleet-name has by now inspired a bulldog motif. This view is taken on one of the newly-built drives around Blackpool's Stanley Park, and the park's clock tower may be seen in the background.

The London service coaches halted for afternoon tea north-bound in Knutsford at 4.35pm, and the photographer has captured the scene as two coach-loads disembark and hurry across the square to the Canute Cafe, where kettles will be boiling to ensure the travellers can be refreshed in the thirty minutes allowed before they resume their journey. FV1689 is a 1931-built Leyland TS2 with Burlingham 25-seat dual-entrance body fitted with toilet, and the coach in front is probably one of FV1859 or FV1860, similar machines (but with a single rear entrance) built later in that year. Note the well-wrapped luggage deposited in the roof boxes.

Blackburn Watch Committee meeting on 27th August this was summarily refused, and subsequent applications for Blackburn excursion licences in 1929 and 1930 were similarly unsuccessful.

Meanwhile, Wood Bros. had been expanding in Central Lancashire, using Harry Harwood, Station Garage, Darwen, a coach operator and hirer of Crossley touring cars. Harwood was licensed in Darwen and also (through Dinham) in Blackburn at holiday times. Now Harwood acted as Darwen Agent for Wood Bros: their coaches ran for Harwood to expand his programme at holiday times, and in particular commence a series of Holiday Expresses to Scarborough and North Wales on Darwen, Accrington and Blackburn Wakes Week Saturdays. These ran in 1928 on 14th, 21th and 28th July (returning one week later), and again in subsequent years, so incensing the brothers Holden (Barrie at Oswaldtwistle and Edric at Accrington) that they banded together in 1929 to launch services competing against Wood Bros./Harwood operations. It is of interest to note that Harwood adopted the fleet name John Bull also, and was subsequently to own at least one of the Wood Bros. coaches. Broadly similar arrangements were probably made in other towns, although details are lacking: certainly Wood Bros. had built up a network of excursion bases in East Lancashire by February 1931, when licensing passed to the Commissioners.

FURTHER EXPRESS DEVELOPMENTS

In Blackpool, 1928 saw changed arrangements for touring operations, as the Batty-Holt contract was terminated when that firm decided to operate its own coaches, but as previously Wood Bros. ran its own extended tours at Tradesmans, the 1928 operation covering Edinburgh, Scarborough and Shakespeare Country & Wye Valley. Daily excursions ran to Southport, Morecambe, Windermere and Keswick, plus a wide variety of less frequent destinations.

Wood Bros. continued to improve the London express: from 10th September 1928 the weekly service improved to run south on Monday and Friday returning on Tuesday, Friday and Saturday: southbound journeys diverted between Lichfield and Daventry to call at Birmingham (and shortly afterwards Coventry); as arrangements had not been fully completed in Birmingham, only single fares (12/6d) were at first available. From Tuesday 23rd September London departures ran from Central London Coaching Station, Crescent Place: this was to bring problems to the *entente* with Standerwick as Lyne, Frank & Wagstaffe now represented both operators in London. Birmingham was now fully served, a stage at Hen & Chickens Hotel, New Street, enabling return fares to be offered.

Declining excursion traffic towards the close of the touring season gave rise to thoughts of finding further work for the coaches and from Monday 24th September 1928 a new daily service running Blackpool-Leeds commenced, calling at Burnley, Todmorden, Hebden Bridge, Halifax, Elland, Huddersfield, Brighouse and Bradford, and competing with existing services by W.Armitage & Sons and Walker Taylor & Sons. Departure was at 9am ex-Blackpool, 5pm ex-Leeds, but curiously it was to be some months before arrangements were made for a stage in Blackburn. See Appendix V for further details.

Three luxuriously-appointed Leyland TS2 coaches (centrally heated, with armchair seats, lavatory and wash basin, reading lamps, press button bells, table and rugs etc) were purchased between September and December 1928 to upgrade London services and these were to bring Wood Bros. the accolade of becoming the premier route from the Fylde to the Capital for a period, until others found it necessary to follow suit. Meanwhile the difficulties between Wood Bros. and Standerwick were again resolved by agreement: from 6th November 1928 Standerwicks moved into the Central London Station (Wood Bros. remained in situ until 26th November, when new arrangements were concluded for Road Travel Bookings Ltd, Bush House, Aldwych to act as Agent and terminal station); in exchange Standerwick withdrew from Birmingham and Coventry, leaving that traffic to Wood Bros. – at least for that winter.

Daily Blackpool-London operation was introduced first by Wood Bros, from 17th December 1928: initially advertised as a Christmas New Year facility, daily loadings were sufficiently encouraging to ensure that reversion to three journeys per week did not take place, although from 15th January until 19th March 1929 no service ran on Sundays. By the latter date, the route into Birmingham was revised: initially diverting from the original routing at Lichfield to reach Birmingham via Sutton Coldfield, the new diversion commenced at Stafford, serving Cannock and Walsall.

The 1929 season saw Wood Bros. coaches spreading their wings even further, with a May approach to the Oldham Council for licences to ply from the Palace Garage, Union Street as an extension to the Blackpool-Manchester expresses: Oldham was one of the more co-operative authorities and granted five licences (Lancia FR7904 requiring alterations to its seating). The tenant at Palace Garage was John Eastwood, who ran an Oldham-Blackpool express and in 1929 arrangements for interavailability of tickets were agreed, although it is not believed that Eastwood journeys, which left Oldham at 9am, returning at 7pm ex-Blackpool, ran via Manchester or Bolton. Wood Bros. ran on these timings to supplement Eastwood's fleet at Wakes Week but were the subject of police complaint when a constable found the crews sleeping in their vehicles on the street at Mumps after they had been positioned on the Friday night starting the holiday (Palace Garage having closed for the night by the time they arrived in town). For 1930 no less than thirteen Wood Bros. coaches were licensed to support Wood Bros and Eastwood express journeys from Oldham.

In about September 1929 a Colne-Burnley-Accrington feeder for the London service was commenced (joining the main route at Blackburn), competing with Bracewell's feeder . Wood Bros. feeder coach may have been provided by John Mitton, from whose garage the route commenced; in any case it was withdrawn early in 1930, by which time Wood Bros. was reportedly diverting their main-line London coaches beyond Bolton to run via Manchester City Centre: when, in March 1930, the City Council finally refused to licence the diversion it had probably ceased!

In November 1930 Wood Bros. was contemplating a Blackpool-Newcastle on Tyne express: Lancaster Council granted short-term approval, but the service did not commence. From 22nd December 1930, however, a daily Blackpool-Birmingham service was started, leaving Blackpool at 11am, Birmingham (Smithfield Garage) at 8.15am; this was almost certainly commenced to tap traffic from David Roberts'Empire Motors route which had ceased a couple of days earlier on bankruptcy of the proprietor (in this it was doomed to failure as traffic looking to join Empire coaches was more likely to find Lansdowne's existing Blackpool-Birmingham service, which left from a stand adjacent to Roberts' Empire Hotel site). Wood Bros'. new Birmingham route ran via Wigan and Warrington, but ceased shortly after the New Year and did not re-commence until 1st April 1931, when Blackpool departure was retimed to 1.30pm and it was diverted to run via Preston, Blackburn and Bolton.

The brief operation of the Birmingham service had introduced Wood Bros to the former Empire agents in Wigan and Warrington and it seems that on suspension of Blackpool-Birmingham journeys early in January 1931 some duplicate London-bound coaches were diverted via Wigan and Warrington to carry the remaining Empire passengers, and also offer journeys through to the Capital. No precise date for commencement of this diversion has been established (first mention in Blackpool is on 21st March 1931, but it must have been operating prior to 19th February to satisfy the Commissioner).

ROAD TRAFFIC ACT APPLICATIONS

Application for licences was made for the two London expresses, Blackpool-Leeds; Blackpool-Manchester-Oldham; Blackpool-St Helens-Liverpool; Blackburn-Blackpool; plus the re-routed Blackpool-Blackburn-Birmingham (now described as seasonal). All were granted apart from the Birmingham route, which objectors claimed had not previously been operated as now requested: in December 1931 the application was withdrawn. The Manchester/Oldham route differed from the 1930 service operated: Wood Bros. had ended coordination with Eastwood and found new Oldham premises at Victory Garage. Journeys at 9.30am and 6pm ex-Blackpool, 9am and 5pm ex-Oldham were sought, but after substantial opposition had been heard only the 9.30am ex-Blackpool and 5pm ex-Oldham were granted. The Manchester halt (outside Lewis's store) was opposed by Manchester Council, and under pressure from the Commissioner Wood Bros. sought in July 1932 to move into the Corporation's Parker Street Bus Station (and also use Fingland's Coach Station). Manchester objected *post facto* when Wood Bros coaches began to use Parker Street; the Commissioner arranged for the stop to be moved to Aytoun Street (outside the former Goodfellow terminus at Maiden's Garage). In Liverpool the terminus was not suitable, and a move from Exchange Station to MacLachlans Garage at Pier Head was agreed in December 1932, although a request for additional journeys at 0930 ex-Liverpool and 1900 ex-Blackpool was denied.

A feeder service from Fleetwood to Blackpool had also been sought: this had been run in connection with London and Leeds routes, but it was now requested that it should also link with the Liverpool and Manchester/Oldham routes. Vociferous objection was upheld but Wood Bros. subsequently carried Manchester traffic on the feeder and it was refused on renewal in 1932, leading to applications in February 1933 for the four routes involved to be individually extended to Fleetwood. The Leeds and London extensions were approved, but Manchester and Liverpool disallowed, by which time Wood Bros. was in new hands.

Application for excursions was also complicated, the basic licence at Blackpool covering three stands (Coronation Street, 1 Reads Avenue and Palatine Road) and also linking to five East Lancashire stands as the twelve excursion coaches might commence from any of the eight stands. The main East Lancashire site was at Golden Lion Yard Blackburn, with satellite stands at Darwen, Great Harwood, Accrington and Clitheroe, reflecting the wide area of activity by the company in the inland area.

The acquisition by the Combine of W. C. Standerwick Ltd on 11th November 1932 was not well received by the Directors of Wood Bros and they quickly arranged, through the intermediary of Mr W. Blackhurst, to alert Ribble that they were willing to discuss a sale of their company also. Major Hickmott was quickly on the scene, and after consultation with North Western and Midland Red it was agreed that the purchase would proceed jointly; day-to-day operations would be transferred to the Standerwick company, who would manage the Wood Bros. (Blackpool) Ltd business. In these circumstances only three Directors were appointed: Major Hickmott (Ribble), J. W. Womar (North Western), and O. C. Power (Midland Red). The Agreement for sale of the company was effected on 1st February 1933, consideration being £25,750.

Detailed changes after this date are included under Standerwick (Chapter Four), but here it should be noted that in February 1935 the joint ownership of this company ceased, and the shares of North Western and Midland Red were purchased by Ribble. After formal transfer of excursion licences and vehicles to Standerwick in December 1935, ending trading, the company was entered into liquidation in 1937.

Fleet of J. W. DEWHURST & CO. LTD Name changed to WOOD BROS (BLACKPOOL) LTD from 5th April 1927. Fleet Name: JOHN BULL COACHES

Including fleet of predecessor business:-John William DEWHURST (by1904-1920)

Registration No.	Manufacturer Type	Aqrd	New	Prev. Owner	Coachwork	Type	Sold	Notes
FR1029(1)	?	1913	1913		?	Ch—	1914?	a
FR1029(2?)	Leyland	1919	1919		?	Ch24	?	b, c
FR1718	Leyland	1919	1919		?	Ch24	?	c
FR2638/FR2756	Leyland	1920	1920		?	Ch—	1925/7	c
FR4327	Leyland G5	1921	1921		?	Ch29	1922	
FR4754	Leyland G7	1922	1922		?	Ch33	1927	
FR4785	Lancia	1922	1922		?	Ch20	c1930	
FR5193	Thornycroft	1923	1923		?	Ch—	1926	
FR5823/FR6169	Lancia	1924	1924		?	Ch23	1927/30	
FR6529/6673/6731	Lancia	1925	1925		?	Ch—	1927-30	
FR7156-FR7157	Lancia	1926	1926		?	Ch—	1929	
FR7727	Leyland PLC1	1926	1926		Burlingham	C26D	1930	
FR7904-FR7905	Lancia	1927	1927			C23-	1929	
FR8143 FR8263	Lancia	1927	1927		?	C22-/C25-	1929	
FR8791 FR8850	Leyland PLSC3	1928	1928		Burlingham	C26FT C31-	1930/32	
FR9092 9094 9283	Lancia	1928	1928		?	C26-	1930	
FR9093	Albion PNA26	1928	1928		?	C26-	1930	
FR9393	Tilling B10B2	1928	1928		?	C26-	1931	
FR9685 9725 9727	Leyland TS2	1928	1928		Burlingham	C24D	1931	d
FR9960	Crossley Eagle	1929	1929		Burlingham	C25-T	1930	
FV40 48	Leyland TS2	1929	1929		?	C32-	?	
FV49	Leyland TS2	1929	1929		?	C26RT	?	
FV173	Albion PNC26	1929	1929		?	C26-	?	
FV 25/ FV 418	Tilling B10B2	1929	1929		?	C20-/C26-T	?	
FV 677	Crossley Arrow	1929	1929		Burlingham	C26FT	1932	
FV678	Leyland TS2	1929	1929		Burlingham	C26DT	*	
FV 925	Leyland TS2	1930	1930		Burlingham	C26-T	*	
FV 926	Crossley Arrow	1930	1930		Burlingham	C26-T	1932	
FV 972-FV 973	Tilling B10A2	1930	1930		Burlingham	C32- by	1936	
FV1061-FV1062	Tilling B10A2	1930	1930		?	C32-	by 1936	
FV1124	Leyland TS2	1930	1930		?	C24-T	by 1936	
FV1125	Leyland TS2	1930	1930		?	C26-T	*	
FV1500-FV1501	AEC Regal	1930	1930		Burlingham	C25-T	*	
FR2873	Daimler CK	1930	1920	Sutcliffe	?	Ch19	1931	e
FV1689	Leyland TS2	1931	1931		Burlingham	C25DT	*	
FV1690-FV1691	AEC Regal	1931	1931		?	C32-	*	
FV1859-FV1860	Leyland TS2	1931	1931		?	C25RT	*	
FV2385-FV2386	Leyland TS2	1931	1931		?	C26RT	*	
FV1840	AEC Regal	1932	1931	Batty-Holt	Burlingham	C26-	*	f
FV3093	AEC Regal	1932	1932		Duple	C28RT	*	
FV3167	AEC Regal	1932	1932		Burlingham	C28RT	*	
FV3394-FV339	Leyland TS4	1933	1933		Burlingham	C28FT	*	
FV3396	AEC Regal	1933	1933		Burlingham	C28FT	*	

NOTES :-The following 18 vehicles were owned by Wood Bros. (Blackpool) Ltd on purchase by Ribble, North Western & Midland Red on 1st February 1933:
Leyland: FV678/925/1125/1689/1859/1860/2385/2386/3394/3395 (10); AEC: FV1500/1501/1690/1691/1840/3093/3167/3396 (8)

a - Probably commandeered by War Dept in 1914; the charabanc body may have been retained to be placed on the 1919 chassis that bore the same number.
b - Appears to have Ch— body & Registration Number from the 1913 vehicle.
c - The charabancs numbered FR1029/FR1718 may have been re-registered in 1921 with the numbers FR2638/FR2756, but this is not confirmed.
d - In 12/1928 FR9685 (at least) was re-built to C20FT, with 2-and-1 seating and four inward-facing seats over the rear wheel arch.
e - May have been acquired in a dealer capacity, and not operated.
f - Re-seated to C27- at unknown date.
* - Transferred to W. C. Standerwick Ltd 10.1936.

Right: FV3167 was a 1932-built AEC Regal with rear-entrance 28-seat coachwork for the London service. The Burlingham style has become more flamboyant, with decorated window-pillars and a more exotic waist-band. The destination box is split into three, the two small top boxes carrying the words John and Bull, while illuminated side screens carry the legend John Bull Luxury Coach Travel. The Bulldog motif remains, but the animal is only distantly related to the one depicted in 1929!

Facing page: Two further Leylands followed Dewhurst's earlier purchases in 1921/2 and FR4327 (the 1921 acquisition) is seen working an excursion out of Accrington for Dewhursts, who forged links with operators in Central Lancashire, including Blackburn, Darwen, Accrington and their satellite townships. Generally, operations were in the form of hiring to local coachmen, but if sufficient business was not found a Wakes Week raid on a town would bring additional revenue. The charabanc is seen leaving the Great Eastern Hotel in Arnold Street, Accrington.

APPENDIX 3 William SALISBURY & SONS LTD Incorporated 23rd May 1927 Fleet Name: PRIDE OF THE NORTH MOTORS

Including predecessor and acquired businesses: William SALISBURY c1909-June 1927 John Esau JENKING 1895-July 1936

William Salisbury was born in Preston and became apprenticed as stable-man and carriage driver with Hardings, the premier Preston horse proprietors. Hardings was, until the coming of the electric trams, the largest provider of horse omnibuses that plied along the main highways, and was a very reputable firm. Salisbury moved to Blackpool about 1909, becoming a carriage proprietor and operating landaus in the town. In 1915, however, he felt the time had come to transfer to motor transport and sold his landau to Dennis Ryan, the proceeds providing him with cash to obtain, in July 1915, his first motor charabanc, which he ran from Empress Garage in Cross St (near Pleasant Street junction), Blackpool; he also ran motor taxis from premises on Topping Street, Blackpool.

After the Great War ended Salisbury built up his fleet, operating Maudslay, Leyland and Lancia charabancs by 1921 and adding Daimler and Reo machines to 1925. In the 1921 motor coach stand arrangements his business had been allotted a stand on Pleasant Street (Warbreck Road junction: Warbreck was later renamed Dickson Road), and land adjacent to this stand was taken to provide off-street loading. Salisbury's sons (William Jnr and Alfie) were also active in the business (now formally known as William Salisbury & Sons Pride of the North Motors) and by 1922 the brothers were conducting extended tours, a speciality being a week-long London tour. In May 1924 the business was able to boast that the entire fleet was equipped with pneumatic tyres, and in 1925 the first saloon coach, an Albion, was acquired.

In common with many Blackpool operators, Salisburys found much work in the inland towns and the coaches could be found at Wakes week in Preston and Accrington for several seasons. In 1926 the Accrington operation was sufficiently well-established for advertisements to appear in local papers, publicising both a period excursion to Blackpool (three separate departures at 8.30am 1pm and 5.30pm) and excursions during the week to the Lake District and Grange from four agents. About this time the Salisbury business became associated with Thomas Hoyle of Crawshawbooth, who acted as agent: Salisburys still worked occasionally out of Rossendale as late as 1934! This latter association appears to have come about through Charles Smith Jnr (himself associated with Hoyle); between 1925 and 1927 Smith cascaded five of his Lancia coaches to Salisburys.

The Salisbury business was converted into a Limited Company on 23rd May 1927 with William and his two sons as Directors. The association with Hoyle was productive: in that year Salisburys were working Wakes traffic out of Burnley, Oldham and Manchester additionally, and the foray into the latter city resulted in the launch of a daily express Blackpool-Manchester (via Chorley and Bolton) from Saturday 1st October 1927. Unlike many of his Blackpool competitors, however, Salisburys were actively working traffic originating in the city at peak times. His Blackpool-based passengers were, from 16th January 1928, able to alight near Piccadilly when Salisburys commenced using Rochdale Canal Co's yard on Dale Street. The ex-Smith Lancias were regular – and speedy – runners on the express, as a series of prosecutions confirm: in one case William Salisbury Jnr was timed at over 35mph! The expresses allowed about six hours in Manchester, and in one speeding case it was disclosed that Salisbury was returning a party of Blackpool express drivers (including some from rival services) to the resort to avoid them hanging about in the city during the long layover. On this occasion his speed was said to be 40mph!

From Good Friday (6th April) 1928 daily Liverpool expresses were commenced, but an announcement on 17th November 1928 informed the public that the route was cancelled until further notice. Meanwhile, from Monday 22nd October 1928 a weekly express to London was opened (return from the Capital was on Saturdays): the route continued through the winter but it seems that it was not a success, and after a period in which passengers were carried on Bracewell's C. Smith Motors service Salisburys withdrew and acted as agent for Bracewell's service.

The Manchester service continued satisfactorily, and from January 1929 new Leyland Tiger coaches (centrally heated, and with reading lamps) took over the operation. Salisburys were still attempting to carry Manchester-based traffic additionally, but application for licences in January 1929 was curtly refused by Manchester's Watch Committee. In Blackpool fleet expansion had outgrown Empress Garage and an additional depot (on Cocker St) was leased in March 1929. Tradesman's Holiday in May 1929 produced particularly good trade, and Salisburys ran out of coaches: in a rare announcement the company regretted that the Manchester express was 'postponed' for the two days of the holiday! In October 1929 the express provided winter-time connection with Underwood's Sheffield-Manchester service (not giving particularly convenient connections, however, with the wait in Manchester over six hours). In January 1930 renewed application to Manchester for licences to legalise the existing traffic originating in the city was made without success. Not to be discouraged, Salisburys immediately applied for excursion licences, but without their own premises in the city this attempt was doomed to failure also. From 13th April 1930 an attempt to improve usage of the Manchester coaches was to have been made by a doubling of the service, with weekday departures ex-Blackpool at 9.30am and 3.30pm, and ex-Manchester at 1pm and 6pm, but intensive advertising in the fortnight prior to commencement brought no bookings and the scheme was deferred until July, when it proved sufficiently successful to be repeated in 1931. At the end of 1930 yet another unsuccessful licence application was made in Manchester, but the 1931 application for Road Traffic licences brought an end to journeys commencing in the City, for the Commissioner only sanctioned departures at 9.30am ex-Blackpool and 6pm ex-Manchester, the service also calling (from July 1931) at Fingland's new Manchester station on Gt.Bridgewater Streeet. In evidence, Salisburys stated that they had carried 24,000 passengers in 1930 and their business employed 23 drivers.

On 12th September 1931 the company suffered a serious blow with the death (at age 31) of William Salisbury Jnr who was, at the time of his death, the youngest member of Blackpool Town Council: his place on the Council was taken by brother Alfie following the by-election held later in the year.

In addition to the Manchester express service, Traffic Act licences were granted for excursions from Pleasant Street with 15 vehicles; the licence included a substantial number of extended tours. The loss of much of the East Lancashire work under the Act was partly compensated by a new group of excursions from Gornall's Garage, Hambleton, with pick-up points in Out Rawcliffe, Pilling, Stalmine and Preesall: this was granted in January 1933. However, some business from out-of-town sources continued, as evidenced by reports of a collision between a Salisbury coach and a motor-cycle combination in June 1932, the coach being engaged in a private hire from the Prospect Mill, Prospect Street, Bolton.

Meanwhile, in August 1932 Salisburys applied for an extra halt in Manchester (Parker Street Bus Station) on the express: this was refused, but the following year intermediate stages were allowed in Blackpool and, in conjunction with the resolution of problems between Salisburys, Stephensons, Lansdownes and M. & H. Motors (plus services of Wood Bros. and Bracewells, now under management of Standerwicks), extra en route stops through Pendlebury and Salford were allowed. Salisburys made the most of their independence at this time by emphasising their non-Combine status in publicity. The Blackpool-Manchester service was finally withdrawn at New Year 1935, as part of the arrangements for sale of the company described below.

William Snr and Alfie became disenchanted with the new order during 1934, not least because of a competitive situation in Dickson Road area, where combine-owned Armitage, and predatory moves by John Jenking and Lansdowne Motors Ltd were making operations more difficult. Initially planning to extend competition with Jenking by purchasing the small Cleveleys business of William Whiteside, they finally decided to dispose of their coaching business at the end of 1934, and Ribble was interested in taking over. The Salisburys wished to retain their car hire and car sales operation, which also worked from the Pleasant Street site and this presented something of a difficulty. Salisburys suggested that Ribble might be able to make available the Progress Garage at 98 Dickson Road, which was little used at that time apart from Armitage's Yorkshire express, but Ribble was under pressure to find a new location for the Armitage excursions, which left from a street-side stand on Lansdowne Crescent and were under threat from Blackpool Corporation: it seemed that it might be necessary to apply to re-locate Armitages' excursions to run from the garage.

The problem was resolved by William Salisbury approaching Mrs Clara Wood (owner of Lansdowne Hotel) who let the back yard of her hotel to her son James as a stand (fronting Lansdowne Place) for his Lansdowne Motors Ltd coaches. Salisbury knew that following a dispute between Wood and his mother she had terminated the rental agreement with Lansdownes: now he persuaded her to allow Armitages to relocate their stand onto her land. This cleared the way for sale of Salisburys to Ribble Group for £15,000 (plus transfer of the Progress Garage lease to W. & A. Salisbury) in February 1935, and the Salisbury coach business became a Standerwick subsidiary to preserve the Goodwill. From this time publicity was handled by Standerwicks and appeared on a joint basis.

There were echoes of the deal between Salisbury, Armitage and Mrs Wood in February 1936, when the Commissioner enquired into the reason for Lansdownes running from a Lansdowne Place street stand, having been replaced by Armitage coaches on the hotel yard: he was apparently satisfied at the circumstances and permitted Lansdownes to remain temporarily on-street; attempts to relocate Lansdowne on Derby Hotel Car Park, or to return to the Lansdowne Hotel site, proved unsuccessful and it was 1938 before a permanent site (on Ormond Avenue, Gynn Square) was found.

In July 1936 the business of John Esau Jenking was acquired by Ribble and as this was located close to Salisburys' headquarters it was absorbed into Salisburys, eleven coaches being transferred. However, only three Albions were considered worthy of long-term retention, the remainder being sold when new coaches arrived in 1937. Jenking had bases in Cleveleys and Fleetwood, bringing Salisburys into new areas, but in summer 1937 it was decided to close down Salisburys into the Standerwick company, and the licence grants were made on 5th June 1937. However, as the season was well under way closure was deferred, and joint advertising finally ceased on 21st October 1937.

John Esau JENKING QUEEN OF THE NORTH MOTORS

John Esau Jenking was the archetypal sand-grown transport operator, spending most of his working life in the industry: 'Johnny Jenks', as he was familiarly called by friends and colleagues, was a well-known character throughout the town – and beyond. He commenced his career well before the coming of the motor charabanc, driving a four-in-hand waggonnette from Blackpool to Fleetwood Market by 1895, and later operated carriages (probably two waggonnettes) which he sold to Walker Taylor in March 1915. In January 1914 he had purchased his first motor charabanc and operated from a stand in Queen Square. This charabanc was commandeered for military use but in June 1915 he typically requested the Watch Committee to issue a licence (and allocate a stand) for a replacement vehicle that he had not then purchased! Jenking then set about rectifying his omission: first he purchased a licensed horse-charabanc from Yates & Sykes and then he took delivery in July 1915 of a new Star charabanc. Returning to the Watch Committee he requested transfer of the horse charabanc licence to himself, and then traded his new licence for a motor charabanc licence! The bemused Committee duly allocated him a stand in Banks St (adjacent to the Promenade). In August 1916 a second stand was refused but a new Maudslay charabanc was authorised in June 1919 to ply from Banks Street/Lord Street corner (where he had a mews garage).

Establishing an office at 5 Springfield Road, Jenking continued to ply from his stand and garage on Banks St; he was a family friend of the Salisburys (as well as a competitor) and adopted the name Queen of the North Motors in 1923 in response to Salisbury's Pride of the North Motors title, even running his London extended tour when Salisburys advertised their own. When it became necessary for his Maudslay charabanc to be returned to the manufacturer for a major overhaul Jenking ran a single-fare only excursion to Coventry - and points en route! The arrival in 1925 of the first of several Albion vehicles saw the addition of an extra stand, at Warley Road, the Springfield Road premises becoming a garage, and a further small depot (on Lord St) was leased the following year, when another Albion arrived.

Commencement of a Manchester express by Salisburys in October 1927 was watched with interest by Jenking, and by 3rd March 1928 Jenking had commenced his own route, running from Banks St and Springfield Road stands via Chorley and Bolton, terminating in Manchester on Market St (outside the doors of Lewis's store). By 21 April he had extended back to commence at his new stand on Bispham Road (cnr.Coronation Road), Cleveleys; in October 1928 he appointed a Fleetwood agent and further extended the Manchester route to start from Lord St (cnr.Poulton Road). In 1928 the Motor Coach Owners Association sought to eliminate fare cutting, but Jenking (although a member) did not comply, and his Manchester service was cut from Association publicity until he returned to the agreed fares. The Manchester express was still running at Christmas 1928 but is thought to have ceased shortly after New Year.

A stand at Carshalton Road (off Dickson Road) was in use by Spring of 1930, and in this year Jenking attempted to obtain licences for nine Albion coaches to run a proposed express from Oldham: the Watch Committee sought further information on his proposals, but he was too busy to reply! His application to the Commissioners was for excursion licences: the sites at Cleveleys and Fleetwood, plus in Blackpool from Banks St, Cocker St (cnr.Lord St), Carshalton Road and Warley Road. All except Cocker St were granted (for ten coaches) but in February 1933 he proposed a return to the Springfield Road stand, renewed his attempt for Cocker St and requested a new site at Cheltenham Road (cnr.Egerton Road)! The latter two were granted after much complaint by others (not least Salisburys) but Springfield Road was firmly declined.

His 1933 application was partly in consequence of a disciplinary hearing called by the Commissioner in December 1932, who had receiveda large number of reports of irregular operation by Jenking. The chief accusations were: regular operation from Springfield Road (which was not a stand); unlicensed destinations from Cleveleys stand; unlicensed excursions from Darwen and from Farnworth (Bolton); operation of the Blackpool-Fleetwood excursion at one shilling (the authorised fare was 1/6d). All were admitted, but Jenking was allowed a further opportunity to conform to the new Act. Some confusion was later evident in October 1935 when Jenking was summoned for operating out of Fleetwood with cut-price excursions: he had run to Knaresborough and to Windermere at a price alleged to be approximately half the authorised fare. His explanation that the trips were in the nature of a private hire rather than excursions could not be substantiated by any documentary evidence but the Magistrates were inclined to be lenient and dismissed the cases on payment of costs.

At the start of the 1936 season he decided to retire from coaching and arrangements were made to sell his business to Ribble; his Blackpool stands formed a circle around Salisburys' Pleasant St site and it was decided that Salisburys should absorb the Jenking business; this was approved by the Commissioner (perhaps with a sigh of relief) in July 1936. Johnny Jenks did not entirely sever his connection with the industry, for he continued as a coach dealer in Blackpool for a few more years.

Two 29-seat Maudslay charabancs, FR1440/3 were placed in service during 1919. In this view FR1443 is standing at the junction of Pleasant Street with Warbreck Road – the latter was later re-named Dickson Road. The Salisbury stand was located here until pressure from the Watch Committee persuaded him to secure a plot of land slightly away from the corner to enable loading to take place off-street.

John Esau Jenking's first post-war charabanc was a small Maudslay machine seating 19. This appears to have a second-hand body adapted for dropping onto the new chassis – perhaps this body had been stored since his 1914 machine was commandeered. One of Jenking's licensed stands at this time was at Banks Street, and Jenking poses in front of this charabanc on nearby Princess Parade. In later years he was to assume a greater girth, prompting the Traffic Commissioner to remark in reply to a complaint by Jenking 'that other operators were forming a ring round him and trying to crush him' in May 1933 "that they would have to be rather weighty to achieve any such aim!"

Fleet of W. SALISBURY & SONS LTD Fleet Name: PRIDE OF THE NORTH MOTORS

Including Fleet of predecessor business:

William SALISBURY Trading as: Wm.SALISBURY & SONS ;PRIDE OF THE NORTH MOTORS .

Fleet No. 1936	Registration No.	Manufacturer Type	Aqrd	New	Prev. Owner	Coachwork	Type	Sold	Notes
-	?	?	1915	1915		?	Ch—	?	
-	FR1440	Maudslay	1919	1919		?	Ch29	1921	
-	FR1443	Maudslay	1919	1919		?	Ch29	?	
-	FR2701	?	1920	1920		?	Ch—	1927	
-	FR4296	Leyland	1921	1921		?	Ch29	1926	
-	FR4740	Lancia	1921	1921		?	Ch23	?	
-	FR5794	Leyland	1924	1924		?	Ch23	1927	
-	FR5814	Daimler CK	1924	1924		?	Ch23	1929	
-	FR6586	Reo	1925	1925		?	Ch19	1929	
-	FR6587-FR6588	Lancia	1925	1925		?	Ch—	1929	
-	FR5862	Lancia	1925	1924	C.Smith	?	Ch23	1928	
-	FR6737	Albion PF24	1925	1925		?	C16-	?	
-	FR7108	Lancia	1926	1926		?	C—	1929	
-	FR5486	Lancia	1926	1923	C.Smith	?	Ch16	1928	
-	FR7442/FR7498	Lancia	1927	1926	C.Smith	?	C20-	1931	
-	FR7913-FR7914	Lancia	1927	1927	C.Smith	?	C20-	1931	
-	FR8097/FR8209	Lancia	1927	1927	C.Smith	?	C20-	1931	
-	FR9711-FR9712	Leyland TS2	1928	1928		?	C31-	1932-3	
-	FR9941	Tilling B10B2	1929	1929		Burlingham	C26-	1934	
-	FR9279/FR9339	Tilling B10B2	1929	1928	S&J Wood Ld	Burlingham	C25-C26-	1932-3	
-	FR9151	Tilling B10B2	1930	1928	S&J Wood Ld	Burlingham	C26D	1935	
-	FV301	Tilling B10B2	1930	1929	S&J Wood Ld	Burlingham	C—D	1935?	
-	FR8856/FR9319	Lancia	1930	1928	J.Bracewell	?	C25-C26-	1932	
-	FV905-FV906	Reo	1930	1930		Burlingham	C20F	c1934	
29-34	FV1662-FV1667	AEC Regal	1931	1931		Burlingham	C26R		
35	FV2681	Leyland TS4	1932	1932		Burlingham	C28R		
-	FV2896	AEC Regal	1932	1932		Burlingham	C32R	1934	
36	FV2920	AEC Regal	1932	1932		Burlingham	C32R	*	
37	FV3455	Leyland TS4	1933	1933		Burlingham	C28R	*	
38- 40	FV4483/4548-4549	AEC Regal	1934	1934		Beadle	C32R	*	
85- 86	FV5741-FV5742	Leyland TS7	1936	1936		Eng.Electric	C31F	*	a
1- 2	FR9120/FR9264	Albion PFB26	1936	1928	J.Jenking	?	C24- C22-	1937	
3	FV 268	Albion PNC26	1936	1929	J.Jenking	?	C26-	1937	
4	FV 329	Albion PNC26	1936	1929	J.Jenking	?	C28-	1937	
5	LG4593	Leyland TS2	1936	1931	J.Jenking	?	C—	1937	
6	FV1688	AEC Regal	1936	1931	J.Jenking	Burlingham	C28F	1937	
7- 8	FV1855 FV1877	Albion PMB28	1936	1931	J.Jenking	?	C28-	1937	
92	FV3655	Albion Valiant	1936	1933	J.Jenking	Burlingham	C32R	*	
93- 94	FV4910-FV4911	Albion PK115	1934	1934	J.Jenking	Burlingham	C24R	*	
3	RN7777	Leyland TS7	1937	1936	Ribble	Duple	C31F	*	b
5	RN7779	Leyland TS7	1937	1936	Ribble	Duple	C31F	*	b
9	RN7784	Leyland TS7	1937	1936	Ribble	Duple	C31F	*	b
14- 15	RN7997-RN7998	Leyland TS7	1937	1937	Ribble	Duple	C31F	*	b
17	RN8000	Leyland TS7	1937	1937	Ribble	Duple	C31F	*	b

NOTES :

a - Allocated (but did not carry) Ribble numbers 1465-1466.

b - 17 Leyland TS7 chassis (FV8027-FV8041 FV8558-FV8559) were ordered for Standerwick & Salisbury but delivered to Ribble: Ribble 1525-1529 1531-1537 (new 1936) and 1652-1656 (new 1937) were transferred to Standerwick Salisbury, but the 1936 chassis had new (1937) bodies fitted (the twelve-month old bodies were placed on the 1937 FV-registered chassis).

* - Transferred to W.C.Standerwick Ltd in 07.1937

After a massive modernisation programme in 1931, when most of the former C. Smith Motors Lancias were replaced by a fleet of six 26-seater Burlingham-bodied AEC Regals, Salisburys purchased two further Regals in the following year to complete the task. These later deliveries were FV2896 and FV2920 but the Burlingham coachwork fitted carried 32 seats in the newer vehicles, for use primarily on the Blackpool-Manchester express service. Illuminated indicator boxes display the destination and the company name – very necessary in 1932 with other Blackpool operators competing with Salisbury on the Blackpool-Manchester run each day. The Stephenson-Lansdowne joint service picked up at Gynn Square nearby and Bracewell, Wood Bros and M. & H. Motors also ran from the town. All used the Manchester-Pendleton-Pendlebury-Bolton road for at least some journeys and competition was fierce.

John Esau JENKING Fleet Name:QUEEN OF THE NORTH MOTORS

Registration No	Manufacturer Type	Aqrd	New	Prev. Owner	Coachwork	Type	Sold	Notes
?	?	1914	1914		?	Ch--	1914:	
CW1252	Star	1915	1915		?	Ch24	?	
FR1747	Maudslay	1919	1919		?	Ch19	?	
FR5971	Lancia	1924	1924		?	Ch--		
FR6668 FR6737	Albion PF24	1925	1925		?	Ch19	c1927	
FR7277	Albion PFA26	1926	1926		?	C--		
FR7504	Albion PV26	1926	1926		?	C23-	1927	
FR8187 FR8289	Albion PFB26	1927	1927		?	C22-/ C25	1929/33	
FR8255	Lancia	1927	1927		?	C20	1928	
FR8316 FR8413	Albion PFB26	1927	1927		?	C24	1931 33,	
FR9120/FR9264	Albion PFB26	1928	1928		?	C24/C22-	*	
FR9387	Albion PFB26	1928	1928		?	C24	1934,	
FV 268	Albion PNC26	1929	1929	S.& J.Wood	?	C26	*	
FV 272	Albion PNC26	1929	1929		?	C26R	c1934,	
FV 329	Albion PNC26	1929	1929		?	C28 -	*	
CA7972	Albion	?1929	?,	?	?	C--	?	
FV1855/FV1877	Albion PMB28	1931	1931		?	C28	*	
FV1922	Albion PH49	1931	1931		?	C20	1934,	
FV3655	Albion Valiant	1933	1933		Burlingham	C32R	*	
LG4593	Leyland TS2	?1933	1931	Goodfellow	?	C--	*	
FV4910/ FV4911	Albion PK115	1934	1934		Burlingham	C24R	*	
FR7376	Halley QX	1934	1926	Riding		C26	1935	
FV1688	AEC Regal	1935	1931	Armitage	Burlingham	C28F	*	

NOTES: Absorbed in fleet of Wm.Salisbury & Sons Ltd in 7 36

APPENDIX 4 : WRIGHT BROTHERS (BURNLEY) LTD Incorporated 21st January 1921

The company was set up to carry out the business of Funeral Directors: day-to-day operation was in the hands of W. W. Wright, assisted by his brother H.Wright who was also licencee of Boot Inn, Parker Lane, Burnley. A third brother (a local vicar) had an interest in the business but was not a Director. By 1927 Wrights was interested in a second Funeral business: James E. Whalley Ltd. The company's garage was located on Turf Street, Burnley. From 1922 a 19-seat Lancia charabanc was operated, and four years later the coaching section was expanded: two 26-seat Burlingham-bodied Leyland Lionesses were purchased and commenced a daily service Nelson-Burnley-Padiham-Lytham-St Annes-Blackpool, where they used Horsfall & Salthouse's Coliseum Garage. The service loaded outside Burnley office at Boot Inn Yard (Parker Lane/St James St corner), authorised on Burnley Corporation's excursion licence, but in May 1928 the Corporation issued a separate express licence for the daily journey. The service closed seasonally in October 1926 but re-opened from 14th December for the Christmas period, and to assist the often meagre trade Wrights added traffic from the resort to East Lancashire, with a Blackburn halt for expatriate resort passengers.

The fleet expanded in 1927 allowing extended tours to Torquay to leave weekly from Burnley, Nelson, Colne, Rossendale, Accrington and Blackburn: tours became an important activity in the years that followed. Establishment of Rossendale agents prompted Wrights to commence a daily Bacup-Rawtenstall-Haslingden-Lytham-St Annes-Blackpool route from 3rd September 1927, and the end of the Blackpool season prompted applications to run a Burnley-Rawtenstall-Manchester express. It is believed that a service ran briefly about Christmas 1927 but difficulty in securing licences caused withdrawal by February 1928, after attempts had been made to commence at Colne.

Wrights soon became known for its high-quality operation: a former Rossendale resident recalled that their tour and express customers were usually folk who regarded themselves as a cut above the rest (he included his aunt in this category). The masses travelled on the competing Holts Yelloway service, described as cheap and cheerful in comparison to Wrights, who used the slogan 'Travel the 'Wright' Way' for many years.

1928 saw a resumption of the Torquay tour, leaving weekly from 1st July to 19th August, and the Nelson-Blackpool express was extended back at Whitsuntide to commence at Colne: coaches now left at 8.30am and 1.30pm, returning at 1pm and 7.30pm. Special late trips ran during the Blackpool Illuminations, returning at 9pm or 10pm. The Bacup-Blackpool express was extended too: coaches en route from Burnley depot now picked up at Weir, and from July a stop was made at Accrington. The failure of the Manchester route had not deterred Wrights, and by late September 1927 plans for a Colne-Liverpool express were laid, but licences were not forthcoming.

Further new services were planned from both Colne and Bacup to Morecambe and to Southport, all of which followed the same valley routes as Blackpool expresses, and commenced with one daily journey on 1 April 1929. From 11 May 1929 Colne-Blackpool increased from two journeys to four, ex-Colne at 8.15am, 11.30am, 2.30pm and 5.30pm and ex-Blackpool at 8am, 11.30am, 2.30pm and 7.30pm or 8pm. By this time a double-deck vehicle was in stock, and this was almost certainly reserved for use on the Colne-Blackpool 8am and 2.30pm journeys from Colne, which carried the heaviest loadings. In July 1929 proposals were made to increase Bacup-Blackpool to four journeys, but the authorities would only sanction two, and services left Bacup at 8am (returning at 8pm) and on Saturday, Sunday and Tuesday at 1.30pm (returning at 10pm). In this year also period return expresses left from both Padiham and Accrington, running to Colne or Bacup via reverse routes to the other expresses, then on to Scarborough.

The usual Torquay extended tour was joined in 1929 by a new Ilfracombe tour, and as the season drew to a close renewed attempts to start a daily Colne-Nelson-Burnley-Padiham-Liverpool express were made: this time the local authorities were persuaded to issue licences (Burnley insisted that it should leave from the Cattle Market rather than Parker Lane stand), and operation began about January 1930. Wrights also sought a daily Padiham-Burnley-Nelson-Colne-Keighley-Bradford-Leeds service, but in the face of almost universal opposition this proposal was dropped.

At the 1930 licensing meeting Burnley sought to move all expresses from operators' stands to Cattle Market, but Wright Bros (and the competing Eastwood company) were successful in defending their current stages. Wrights Blackpool and Morecambe expresses now called en route at Whalley; Morecambe & Heysham Council required Wright Bros to quit its Harbour Garage terminal (on Grove Street adjacent to the Promenade) in favour of the new municipal Omnibus Station situated inland at Euston Road. Wrights objected but the Council made the use of their station a condition of the licence. In Rossendale new efforts to expand the Blackpool route were successful when a 5pm journey ex-Bacup was approved to run seasonally from 2nd June until 31st October. At Blackpool coaches still called (and parked up) at Coliseum Garage, but extended to serve Talbot Mews for passengers requiring a more central point.

The expresses from Colne and Bacup to Southport did not re-commence in 1930, having suffered from poor traffic in 1929, but a period excursion was continued at Wakes Weeks. The Scarborough period returns resumed weekly in high season: the Accrington leg now ran as a feeder, joining the Padiham-Scarborough main line at Skipton. Colne-Liverpool continued daily (by now terminating at Mount Pleasant), but application for an additional stop at Accrington was refused in October 1930. In that month application for routes Colne-Nelson-Burnley-Padiham and Bacup-Rawtenstall-Haslingden-Accrington to Preston met with little support, the District Advisory Committees suggesting that Preston be made a halt on the existing Blackpool route. By the time that Wrights received the refusals their applications to accede to the DAC suggestions were too late as licensing had already passed to the Commissioners. In a similar manner application for a new Todmorden-Blackpool route was deferred by Todmorden Council until the watershed had passed – and then refused!

THE ROAD TRAFFIC ACT – AND PROBLEMS

Other operations and activities had also been undertaken in 1930: Wright Bros acted as Burnley agent for the abortive Wood Bros (Blackpool) Ltd Colne-Blackburn feeder to its London expresses (Appendix 2). Operation of Wakes Week feeders by Wright Bros. coaches were also a feature: these ran to Manchester to join the Welsh Express of The Creams (Lancashire) Ltd (a subsidiary of Brierleys' Creams, Llandudno) serving Rhyl, Colwyn Bay and Llandudno; and an express to Torquay (probably that of Stephen Wade's Wade-Ways service). In Summer 1931 holiday-week feeders from Burnley and Rossendale to Manchester connected with Hodgetts'Ani-Way express to Torquay (Wade having ceased some time previously), but Wakes-week expresses from East Lancashire to North Wales were run directly by both The

Creams and Wrights, the latter having discovered that demand for an independent North Wales service warranted through coaches. The new licensing system did not lend itself to these inter-company feeders and a battle for licences ensued as both Wright Bros. and The Creams sought to secure grants from the Commissioner.

Wrights was successful in retaining a Colne-Llandudno operation (although The Creams initially secured period excursion facilities in Burnley these were lost in 1933 in an attempt to revise these into an express, with a feeder from Accrington and Rossendale linking in at Bacup; 1934 proposals to reinstate linking period excursions were similarly rejected). In Rossendale, Wrights was refused permission to continue after the 1931 season. The feeder to Manchester for Torquay became superfluous when Hodgett was refused licences to continue operations late in 1931.

These difficulties apart, Wrights was generally successful in its applications to continue, all expresses being confirmed (including Padiham-Scarborough, although the Accrington feeder was refused). Colne-Liverpool (which was applied for as a seasonal operation, with a subsequent application for all-year operation to resume) became a target for Ribble opposition in the Traffic Court, and the all-year proposal was withdrawn at the hearing. The grant for seasonal operation (on 12th March 1932) was qualified by loss of all intermediate stops (Nelson, Burnley, Padiham and Whalley), leaving Wrights little option other than withdrawal (about 7th May 1932) of the remaining part of the service.

Application for the proposed Todmorden excursion licence was refused by the Yorkshire Commissioner but Burnley excursions and extended tours (including Padiham and Whalley) were granted, as was an April 1932 application to take over the excursions operated by Horsfall, Salthouse & Co from Coliseum Garage, Blackpool. This firm operated a four-vehicle tours programme, and managed the coach and car park on the Coliseum site: a substantial part of their work had been operation of coaches for the tours programme arranged by Lytham-based E.F.Parkinson, who had recently transferred his business to Standerwicks. Horsfall, Salthouse & Co had taken the Coliseum site on lease in 1921 and operated from there until the decision to sell, in January 1932. Wrights had, of course, been a substantial customer of Coliseum Garage, using it as the Blackpool depot almost from commencement.

The shares of the Halifax-based coaching company Robert Edwards & Co.Ltd were acquired by the Wright brothers about 1932, and the company operated as a subsidiary of Wright Brothers (Burnley) Ltd. Certain vehicles were transferred to the new acquisition, which continued in Wrights' ownership after the Burnley business was sold by the family in January 1934. The Edwards company was, however, sold to Hebble in October 1934.

A decision by Ribble in early 1933 to re-route the express acquired from Croisdale's Brunshaw Motors (Todmorden-Holme Chapel-Water-Rawtenstall-Haslingden-Blackpool) to run Todmorden-Rawtenstall via Bacup signalled the start of a further period of aggression by the larger company: objection by Wrights and Yelloway prevented the re-routed Ribble service from picking up at Bacup for Blackpool, but Ribble next sought new Wakes Week expresses from both Water and Loveclough to Blackpool and to Morecambe (via Rawtenstall) plus a series of similar routes to both resorts from townships in the Burnley area: Worsthorne, Fence, Barrowford, Higham and Sabden. These were clearly predatory, seeking to erode traffic presently using Wrights expresses to Blackpool and Morecambe, and the smaller company countered by lodging a similar series of applications. After an acrimonious hearing both sets were dismissed in June 1933 by the Commissioner, but Wrights were much dispirited by the situation and at the close of the season took action to place their business on the market. The reputation of the company was such that Ribble was to purchase for £22,500 the entire shareholding (from 10th January 1934), and to retain goodwill the company was continued as a Ribble subsidiary. One Bedford coach was on order at the time of purchase and the contract was completed under Ribble ownership; Ribble also introduced two new Leyland coaches to Wrights fleet in 1934. These three vehicles were allocated (but did not carry) Ribble fleet numbers 1491-1493.

In March 1934, application was made by the new owners to restore the Accrington-Llandudno expresses as a Wakes Week service, running via Haslingden, Rawtenstall and Bacup; a similar application covered Accrington-Scarborough via the same routing, but the Commissioner reiterated his disapproval once again. After continuing through the 1934/1935 seasons, it was decided to merge Wright business with Standerwicks as part of the new arrangements for that company, and application was lodged for the expresses and Burnley excursions to be taken over: the grants were made on 12th October 1935, and Wrights fleet was transferred to Standerwicks two months later. An exception to these transfers was the extended tour operation, which was taken over by Ribble (along with those of East Lancashire Motors) in order to create a touring base that might subsequently be welded together to enable Ribble to compete more effectively with the independent touring companies. Wrights excursion base at Coliseum Garage, Blackpool was not transferred to Standerwick, although from the 1936 season Standerwick coaches were used on hire to Wrights: the reason for this arrangement appears to have been the reluctance of Ribble to risk losing parts of the licence if exposed to the objections of the Blackpool coaching fraternity. Wrights remained in being, receiving revenue from coaching carried out on its behalf by Standerwick, and also retaining ownership of the Burnley garage; the Blackpool Coliseum freehold was purchased by Blackpool Omnibus Stations Ltd (jointly-owned by various Associated Companies) and developed into the Coliseum Coach Station. Wrights excursion licence at the Coliseum was finally transferred to Standerwicks from 11th August 1948, and the ownership of the Turf Street, Burnley garage was disposed of, enabling the company to be finally wound up during 1949.

Wright Bros original Lancia char-a-banc was joined in 1926 by two Leyland Lioness coaches which were chiefly used to inaugurate a daily express service from Nelson and Burnley to Blackpool. The first of these was CW6956 which was fitted with coachwork seating 25 but this was later altered to 26. This pre-delivery view taken by Leyland's photographer clearly shows the folding door fitted over the front entrance and the sliding windows that provided ventilation on warm summer days. Note the electric lights fitted on the window uprights: these were quite a novelty in 1926. The intention of Wright Bros to use the coach as a service vehicle (rather than a touring coach) is demonstrated by the fitting of a destination box, although the Blackpool sign appears to be a permanent display. Lettering for Wrights'Pullman Service appears along the waist, and for some years the company referred to its coaches as Pullman Two etc (this being the number associated with this particular coach).

Pullman number 9 was a Leyland Lion, a design that did not often survive in coaching fleets for long, as operators preferred the faster Tigers that followed from the Leyland stable. This particular example, new in 1928 and registered CW8266, was the sole example to enter the Wright Bros fleet, receiving a body by Strachan and Brown with the unusual opening roof panel system associated with that firm's products. The interior view, below, shows the almost all-weather coach effect when the panels were removed in fine weather. Patterned shades now cover the electric lights and a bell-push is fitted, again emphasising the service nature of much of Wright Bros operations. The wide-looking emergency door at the rear is fitted with a seat, which presumably swung out if the door was opened. The seats are comfortably upholstered with arm-rests, a nice feature on a coach intended to run an express route taking less than two hours to complete. The entrance is again fitted with a door of the folding variety. Outside, a rudimentary luggage rack is fitted and it is of interest to note that period passengers to Blackpool and Morecambe were offered a van delivery service to transport their baggage to their chosen accommodation.

Fleet of WRIGHT BROTHERS (BURNLEY) LTD Incorporated : 21st January 1921

Fleet No.	Registration No.	Manufacturer			Prev.Owner	Coachwork	Type	Sold	Notes
		Type	Aqrd	New					
1	CW4381	Lancia	1922	1922		?	Ch19	1927	
2	CW6956	Leyland LC1	1926	1926		Burlingham	C25F	1934	a
3	CW7102	Leyland LC1	1926	1926		Burlingham	C26R	*	
4/6	CW7206/CW7496	Leyland LC1	1927	1927		Burlingham	C28R/C26-	*	
5	SN5972	Albion PM28	1927	1927	?	?	C—	?	
7	CW7706	Albion PK26	1927	1927		?	B29-	1933	
8	TD8897	Leyland LC1	1928	1927	?	?	C—R	*	
9	CW8266	Leyland PLSC	1928	1928		Stchn & Brwn	C32-	?	
10	CW8442	Leyland PLC1	1928	1928		Burlingham	C29-	*	
11	CK3841	Leyland PLC1	1928	1927		Burlingham	C—R	*	
12	CW9144	Leyland PLC1	1928	1928		Burlingham	C26-	*	
13	CW9243	Leyland TD1	1928	1928		Leyland	H51R	1932	
14	TE5711	Leyland TS2	1929	1928	Leyland	Leyland	B26-	?	b
19/16-17	HG 608-HG 610	AEC Regal	1931	1931		Burlingham	C32R	*	
18	HG 611	AEC Regal	1931	1931		Burlingham	C32R	1932	c
15	HG 754	Bedford WHG	1931	1931		Duple (?)	C14-	1932	
21	HG 995	AEC Regal	1932	1932		Burlingham	C32R		
13?	HG1281	Bedford WLB	1932	1932		Duple (?)	C20-	1932	d
20?	FR8232	Dennis F	1932	1927	Hsfl,Salthse	?	C26-	1933	e
23/22	FR9157-FR9158	ADC	1932	1928	Hsfl,Salthse	?	C26-	1934	
24?	FR9945	Daimler CF6	1932	1929	Hsfl,Salthse	?	C—	c1934	
-	HG1332 AEC	Regal	1932	1932		Burlingham	C32F	1932	f
25?	HG1760	Bedford WLB	1933	1933		Duple	C20F	*	
26?	HG2063	Dennis	1933	1933		Duple	C32-	1933	d
20	HG2368	Bedford WLB	1934	1934		Duple (?)	C20F	*	g
27-28	HG2758-HG2759	Leyland TS6	1934	1934		Eng Electric	C31R	*	h

NOTES:

- a - Later re-seated to C26F.
- b - Formerly Leyland demonstrator.
- c - Burnt out & scrapped.
- d - Transferred to subsidiary Edwards fleet in Halifax.
- e - Converted to lorry of subsidiary Edwards fleet in Dinnington.
- f - Hired for a period in 1932 from Tillotson (dealer) to cover vehicle shortage following fire destroying HG 611. Later operated by Thompson 'Victory Services', Shiremoor.
- g - Purchase completed after acquisition by Ribble: allocated (but did not carry) Ribble number 1491.
- h - Purchased by Ribble: allocated (but did not carry) Ribble numbers 1492-1493.
- * - Transferred to W.C.Standerwick Ltd in 12/1935 and allocated fleet numbers 9-12 14/16/15/17-22 in late 1936.

A fleet of four new AEC Regal coaches joined the Wright Bros fleet in 1931: these were HG608-HG611, numbered 19 16-18 respectively. The first three arrived in March 1931 but the last was not taken into stock until September. The allocation of number 19 to the coach that was registered first is curious and it may be that this machine was used as a demonstrator by Burlinghams, who constructed the 32-seat rear-entrance bodies for all four vehicles. Double display boxes are fitted to these vehicles: the boxes above the drivers' cabs carried the Wright Bros names, and those over the bonnets were fitted with blinds. In this view Nos. 16 and 17 (nearest the camera) show Morecambe and Liverpool respectively and are both lettered on the roof panels for the daily expresses to Blackpool, Morecambe and Liverpool. Numbers 18 and 19 appear not to be so lettered, and may have been the regular runners for the extended tour operation. Number 18 was only to survive for about one year as it was burnt out, and scrapped in August 1932. The remaining three passed to Standerwicks in December 1935, operating for their new owner for another two seasons. The switch to AEC coaches from Leyland by Wright Bros (and many other North West and Yorkshire operators) is explained by the Burnley Dealers (Tillotsons) giving up their Leyland Agency in favour of new arrangements with the London chassis builder.

APPENDIX V : SOME OTHER RIBBLE GROUP ACQUISITIONS

This Appendix gives some account of two Blackpool businesses in which Ribble had an interest but from which only part of the operations were transferred to Standerwicks.

(a) W. ARMITAGE & SONS LTD Incorporated 6th February 1929
Fleet Name: PROGRESS MOTOR SERVICES

Including predecessor businesses:

William ARMITAGE)
William ARMITAGE & Josiah Olivant MANN)
C. B. ARMITAGE, J. R. ARMITAGE & J. O. MANN)

1913-March 1929 Fleet Names: COUNTY MOTOR COMPANYWilliam ARMITAGE & SONS PROGRESS MOTORS

William Armitage was a Yorkshireman, born in Huddersfield, who moved to Blackpool about 1913 and as William Armitage & Sons, opened a motor garage at 98 Dickson Road, Blackpool, under the title County Motor Company. A Commer charabanc the Progress was purchased and run from a stand on Hornby Road (cnr.Central Drive); by 1915 the fleet had grown to three, with a second stand outside the Savoy Hotel at Queens Promenade. After the Great War two charabancs were running, from Hornby Road and outside County Garage; here County Motor Company was selling Ruston Hornsby motor cars. As early as September 1920 Armitage was advertising extended tours to Scarborough or Devon. The 1921 revisions to stands resulted in Progress coaches running from the Cocker Street Dickson Road junction.

In 1924 the motor garage and dealership were re located to Raikes Parade and the Dickson Road premises became solely a motor coach depot: probably at that time the business was formally split, with William Armitage taking County Motor Company, and his sons C. B. and J. Armitage becoming proprietors of the William Armitage & Sons coaching business (still using the fleet name Progress Motors). At some stage between this 1924 re arrangement and 1927 a capital investment in the Progress coaching business was made by Mann's Motor Service (Bradford based hauliers) and Josiah Olivant Mann became an additional partner (and General Manager). By July 1924 Armitages attempted to establish a booking office and depot at Progress Garage, 138 Lytham Road but the location was too close to the well established premises of S. & J. Wood Ltd (Seagull) and the venture was short-lived.

A weekly service to Hebden Bridge, Halifax, Huddersfield, Bradford and Leeds commenced on Saturday 1st November 1924, the return journeys running on Tuesdays; a parcels service to these towns was in operation by the end of November. The service developed into express routes competing with broadly similar services by Walker Taylor & Sons and Wood Bros. John Bull: these routes will be examined in more detail later in this Appendix.

Josiah Mann was driver of Albion coach FR8085 on the Blackpool Leeds express on Monday 8th August 1927 when, in a torrential downpour at Brearley (between Mytholmroyd and Halifax), the Progress vehicle skidded into a Halifax Corporation tramcar; the coach was badly damaged and several seats were torn from the coach. Most of the passengers were injured, one Leeds man being killed. After recovery, the vehicle was repaired and continued in service until 1931.

The business was transferred into a Limited Company (W. Armitage & Sons Ltd) incorporated on 6th February 1929, initial directors being the Armitage sons and J. O. Mann (who was also Managing Director). The fleet in 1929 comprised nine Albion coaches (including three former demonstrators) and the Yorkshire expresses had become the major work of the business: the number of passengers carried annually on the two routes now approximated to 70,000 (peaking in 1931 at 79,000).

From Saturday 7th October 1929 Armitages introduced a daily service from Blackpool to Blackburn, Accrington, Haslingden, Rawtenstall, Bury, Heywood and Rochdale, reducing after a week to Wednesdays and Saturdays. The service survived until Christmas but had gone by Saturday 4th January 1930.

Applications lodged under the Road Traffic Act showed that Armitage excursions were still leaving from Cocker Street stand (also from Dickson Road garage): after objections were presented a licence allowing five coaches to run from Lansdowne Crescent was confirmed. A limited one coach programme from a site at the seaward end of Victoria Road, Cleveleys was also approved and a new application for a similar licence from the Promenade at Fleetwood was granted in January 1933.

However, the new Act was to bring problems in the operation of the expresses, and it became necessary for major changes to be implemented in order to maintain this important section of the company.

(b) WALKER TAYLOR & SONS LTD Incorporated 2nd March 1933
Fleet Name: PRIDE OF THE ROAD MOTORS

Including predecessor businesses:

Walker TAYLOR c1904-November 1924)
Mrs.Hilda TAYLOR November 1924-May 1928)
E. H. & T. H. TAYLOR & Mrs Hilda Taylor May 1928-March 1933)

Fleet Names: WALKER TAYLOR & SONS and PRIDE OF THE ROAD MOTORS

Walker Taylor was a Yorkshireman who came to Blackpool for health reasons about the turn of the century: he was a Livery Stable owner and carrier, working from George Street, Blackpool in 1904 and from premises in Cookson Street by May 1907. At that time he purchased a two horse charabanc The Pride of the Road and was allotted two routes: a circular to Singleton returning via Weeton, and a morning excursion to Wrea Green. After conveying visitors to Blackpool Aviation meeting in August 1910: his licence was suspended (for unspecified misdemeanours) for one week!

By 1911 his horse charabanc was running from the Royal Hotel (by the Tower at Adelaide Place): the Singleton excursion was now run in the afternoon, having been replaced by a morning trip to Cleveleys and Poulton. He commenced running a motor charabanc in May 1913 from a stand at Winifred Street Adelaide Street junction; a second motor charabanc was added in February 1914, running from Chapel Street (junction with Coop Street) close to the railway bridge. The motors were initially kept at the Taylor residence (68 Albert Road), but in April 1915 he rented Claremont Garage on General Street. The previous month Taylor had purchased two horse waggonnettes from John Jenking, trading their licences with the Watch Committee against a licence for a third motor charabanc, which ran from Jenking's former Queen Square stand. He attempted in August 1915 to transfer his Chapel Street stand to Banks Street (where Jenking had been granted a new stand) but this was refused, as was a June 1916 application for a fourth motor charabanc stand.

Fuel shortages in 1917 resulted in withdrawal of two motor charabancs in favour of a resumption of horse transport: the Pride of the Road and the two ex Jenking carriages (one now named The Clarence after new stables rented at the Clarence Hotel on Albert Road) ran from Queen Square and Winifred Street stands. The third waggonnette operated from the Clarence stables (replacing Chapel Street). A return to peace time conditions enabled the three motors to be returned to service, using the three stands granted in 1917. By this date the Claremont Garage had been given up as the Clarence stables were in use as the motor garage!, Taylor (now living at 136 Albert Road) obtained no less than ten Buckingham bodied Daimler charabancs in May 1920: three were used to to replace earlier machines and the remaining seven were sold off to other operators. Using the Pride of the Road name for his fleet a series of day and extended tours was run, including an 11 day trip to London, Brighton and South Coast. The 1921 licence re arrangement placed Taylor's stand at the Albert Road Central Drive corner.

Excursions to Yorkshire were commenced on 4th March 1922 and these developed into an express service that competed with Armitages and Wood Bros. also John Bull: details of these operations will be found below.

The business was to receive a severe blow, however, on Wednesday 30th July 1924 when Walker Taylor was seriously injured in an accident at Clarence Garage: whilst marshalling his coaches a brewers motor lorry arrived, and in attempting to manoeuvre the vehicle clear of his fleet he was pinned to the garage wall by the starting handle of the lorry, receiving injuries from which he died two days later. For the succeeding three months the business ran under control of the Executors, passing to his widow (Mrs. Hilda Taylor) in November 1924.

A curious case brought at Clitheroe in September 1927 brought Mrs Taylor before the Magistrates charged with having a motor coach exceeding a width of 7ft 6in: she reported that the vehicle (probably one of the 1924 short Daimler chars a banc) had been re bodied and passed by the Blackpool authorities, but the Clitheroe police had determined in a spot check that the vehicle was 7ft 6½ in wide! The case was dismissed on payment of costs. In May 1928 Mrs Taylor introduced her sons into the business, the proprietors becoming E. & T. H. Taylor and Mrs. Hilda Taylor.

Applications under the Road Traffic Act confirmed the excursions from Clarence Garage but problems were encountered with licensing of the expresses, leading to major changes to this part of the business.

(c) ARMITAGE AND TAYLOR'S YORKSHIRE EXPRESS OPERATIONS

Walker Taylor & Sons was the first of the Blackpool operators to commence a service to Yorkshire, running a period excursion to Huddersfield from Saturday 4th March 1922 as a weekend trip returning on Monday; this was repeated at approximately four weekly intervals and by 14th April 1923 charabancs were calling en route at Halifax. These excursions probably ceased for the summer but from 25th October 1924 they were extended to Leeds via Bradford and increased to run weekly; return journeys now ran on Tuesdays. From 15th November 1924 the service ran on alternate weeks to Halifax via Bolton, Manchester, Oldham and Huddersfield (Bradford and Leeds were only served on alternate weeks via the original route). Operation again ceased for the summer in mid May 1925, but resumed from 26th September 1925, running weekly through to Leeds by the original route only, and some traffic originating in Yorkshire was being conveyed by special journeys operated at Christmas.

Meanwhile, Armitages had commenced a weekly service to Hebden Bridge, Halifax, Huddersfield, Bradford and Leeds on Saturday 1st November 1924, return journeys running (as Taylors) on Tuesdays; a parcels service to all these towns was offered by Armitages before the end of November. The Armitage service appears to have ceased at the end of May 1925 but re commenced on 3rd October 1925, from which date it was split, each branch running weekly: Blackpool-Hebden Bridge-Halifax-Bradford-Leeds, and Blackpool-Bolton-Manchester-Oldham-Huddersfield. From 15th May 1926 the 1924 routing was resumed and operation increased to Wednesday and Saturday (coaches now completed a round trip on each operating day).

From Saturday 3rd July 1926 Armitage increased to daily; additional stops were added at Burnley and Todmorden, but within a week journeys on Tuesday, Thursday and Sunday were deleted. A four days a week operation continued until 23rd October 1926, the Wednesday and Saturday winter service then resuming to 28th May 1927. Taylors had improved their express to run a return trip each Monday, Friday and Saturday from Friday 2nd July 1926, and the two ran rival services throughout that Summer; Taylors reverted to Tuesday and Saturday operation from November 1926.

From Saturday 21st May 1927 Armitage re commenced on Monday, Wednesday, Friday and Saturday, while Taylors ran on Monday, Wednesday, Thursday and Saturday, but within a few days the two reached agreement to co ordinate and Taylors ran on Tuesday, Thursday and Saturday, removing competition except on Saturdays. A Friday evening Taylor positioning journey at 5pm returned to Blackpool from Leeds the following morning; after a few weeks this journey was retimed to leave at 9am and ran through the summer period, and again over Christmas.

From 1st September 1927 Armitage increased to daily, connecting at Leeds with Leeds & Newcastle Omnibus Co's Harrogate, Darlington and Newcastle on Tyne route. The Winter service (now Monday, Wednesday and Saturday) commenced on 28th November 1927, an additional Friday service resuming from 20th April 1928, but from Maundy Thursday (5th April), over the Easter holiday, a return journey commencing from Leeds was operated by Armitage for the first time. This was repeated at Whitsuntide, continuing daily through the summer; however the return trip starting from Blackpool still ran on four days only until Saturday 8th September, when twice daily operation commenced (9am and 6.30pm ex Blackpool). Taylor's Easter 1928 service saw resumption of daily return journeys from each end; the Summer period produced several experimental variations before a daily return journey from each end was re established on Saturday 8th September 1928 (9am and 6pm ex-Blackpool; 9am & 2.15pm ex-Leeds); by this date Burnley and Todmorden were also served.

The revised timings had only been in operation for a few days when Wood Bros. launched their own Blackpool Leeds route on Monday 24th September 1928, leaving the resort at 9am and returning at 5pm daily: both Armitages and Taylors (both run by ex-patriate Yorkshiremen) regarded Wood Bros with hostility and it was some time before any question of cooperation with the newcomer was considered. Wood Bros. express was seasonally expanded in May 1929 to twice daily (ex Blackpool 9.30am and 4.30pm retarded to 6pm from July 1929 and ex Leeds 9am and 3.15pm); the company did not reintroduce the extra journeys in 1930.

Meanwhile, from 25th October 1928 Armitage's Blackpool departures were revised to 9am and 4.30pm for winter (the 6pm timing was resumed for subsequent Summer periods). Armitage had opened a small garage – the Progress Garage – in Huddersfield and a new service (at the 9am timing ex Blackpool only) diverted (or connected, depending upon traffic) at Huddersfield to serve Heckmondwyke, Batley, Dewsbury, Wakefield and Barnsley. Taylor's winter service commenced on 27th October 1928, leaving Blackpool at 2pm on Monday and Wednesday, 9am on Tuesday, Thursday and Friday, and 9am and 2pm on Saturday; returns from Leeds were at 2.15pm. Sunday journeys were added in May 1929 at 9am and 4.30pm, but from 8th June 1929 the service ran daily at 9am, with 2pm departures on Friday and Saturday to position coaches for a 9am service out of Leeds on Saturday and Sunday.

Several Yorkshire operators were of course now in competition, the main opposition coming by 1929 from Holdsworth Motors (Hebble) from Halifax and Hanson from Huddersfield (each leaving Blackpool at 2pm and 6pm); Hanson had earlier responded to Armitages morning timing from Yorkshire towns by adding a morning journey (with evening return) from Blackpool, but failed to attract custom and it had gone by July 1929. J. Bullock & Sons (1928) Ltd ran daily from Wakefield, while Lancashire and Yorkshire Motors Coast to Coast express offered a daily service from Barnsley, with connections from Doncaster and from East Coast resorts. Robert Barr Ltd was running Leeds Blackpool, while West Yorkshire had commenced from Bradford in 1928 (extended back to Leeds in 1929) and Ribble would commence Blackpool Leeds expresses in 1930.

From Saturday 17th May 1930 Armitage commenced a third daily journey: 2pm Blackpool-Leeds (connecting with Leeds and Newcastle Omnibus Co to Newcastle), but the connection caused problems and by October departure had been advanced by an hour to 1pm. All departures now also served the Wakefield Barnsley route: the 1pm only reached Dewsbury but the 6pm terminated at Wakefield. Increasing loadings on the 9am ex Blackpool enabled Barnsley passengers to be offered a direct run from Huddersfield at peak times, but on quieter days Barnsley traffic continued to be routed via Wakefield. Leeds departures were also increasingly sophisticated: the morning journey now left at 8.30am (with an associated 8.45am ex Wakefield), while the afternoon journey left Leeds at 2pm (Saturday), 3pm (Monday Friday) or 5pm (Sunday), with associated journeys from both Barnsley and Wakefield.

Taylors 1930 service left Blackpool daily at 9am and 2pm, with an extra seasonal journey at 6pm; journeys left Leeds at 9am and 1.45pm, with a seasonal 5.30pm timing. As a response to changes in the Armitage service, Taylors' route was split at Halifax in mid October 1930, coaches running direct to Bradford and Leeds, or via Elland and Huddersfield to terminate at Brighouse.

THE ROAD TRAFFIC ACT AND OTHER PROBLEMS

Applications were lodged in early 1931 to continue the five Yorkshire expresses operated by Armitages, Taylors and Wood Bros: while these were granted by the North Western Commissioner the backing applications ran into serious problems before the Yorkshire Commissioner. He was concerned at the indirect nature of the Blackpool operators' services, which diverted to serve the many towns in industrial Yorkshire; he also took the view (not taken into account in the Act) that traffic originating in Yorkshire should be handled by Yorkshire operators. In due course he sanctioned the five routes (all had grandfather rights under the Act) but imposed severe duplication limitations that made a nonsense of the more realistic figures set by the North Western Commissioner. Additionally Armitage and Bullocks were ordered to co ordinate between Wakefield and Blackpool. Armitage and Taylor were forced to bring Wood Bros into discussions regarding the problems, and all three continued to run as before pending hearing of their Appeal. Incredibly the Minister upheld the Yorkshire Area grant in a September 1932 decision and the three were obliged to consider alternative plans to continue.

Meanwhile, in 1931 extra Illuminations journeys (1pm from both Bradford and Dewsbury, returning at 10pm) had been operated by Armitages between 17th September and 20th October: these special journeys attracted an average of 27 passengers per coach, with a total of 1,332 passengers carried on the five Saturday operating days. Armitages applied to continue in 1932 and the Commissioners approved the journeys, which had apparently operated in 1931 without sanction. As an adjunct to the loss of the express services Appeal, Armitages sought a new excursion licence from their Venn Street, Huddersfield garage, in October 1932, hoping to regain some of the lost express traffic through excursions to Blackpool and other destinations (including Chester and Manchester) and also to establish a base as a Yorkshire operator, but the numbers objecting to this move caused a withdrawal prior to the Hearing.

A revised operating plan for Blackpool Leeds operation was put before the North Western Commissioner in November 1932 and heard at Blackpool on 1st March 1933: it provided for a Blackpool Leeds pool, with Wood Bros running the 9am departure ex Blackpool and 3.15pm ex Leeds, Taylors at 2pm ex Blackpool, 9am ex Leeds (plus in summer 6pm ex Blackpool), and Armitages at 4.30 (winter) or 6pm (summer) ex Blackpool and 8am ex Leeds. Only Wood Bros journeys called at Blackburn and Accrington, while Armitage and Taylor timings also served Brighouse (variation to Taylors' Blackpool Brighouse route, proposed to continue in summer only, had been withdrawn prior to the hearing). In reality a co ordinated service was proposed: each journey was applied for by a single operator, although tickets were inter-available and receipts shared in agreed proportion to compensate those running less popular timings. Armitages' Barnsley service would continue to leave Blackpool at 9am, returning at 2pm (duplicating Wood Bros' Leeds times as far as Huddersfield); the other timings had been withdrawn in favour of Bullocks Wakefield-Blackpool journeys and all Armitage and Bullock Wakefield journeys now co-ordinated with inter-availability of tickets. The Leeds pool would be managed for the three partners by Josiah Mann of Armitages and would reduce overall mileage by one third; the Yorkshire Commissioner had accepted the scheme. After hearing the proposal the North Western Commissioner approved the applications, which came into effect on Saturday 15th April 1933.

Even before the applications reached the Commissioner the position had changed radically with news of Standerwicks' sale to the Associated companies, and the decision of Wood Bros. and Bracewells to offer their businesses for sale also. Thoughts of a partner in the new pool becoming controlled by the Associated companies was not palatable to Armitage or Taylor, and both also opened negotiations with Ribble. This company (now operating jointly to Leeds with West Yorkshire) negotiated with a view to purchasing for other interested companies and it was decided that West Yorkshire, Yorkshire (Woollen District) and Yorkshire Traction would also participate. The position of Taylors (a partnership) differed from the other purchases in hand, and to avoid the necessity of a formal application to the Commissioners it was agreed the partners would incorporate a limited company and transfer their licences as a preliminary to the sale. Walker Taylor & Sons Ltd was incorporated on 2 March 1933 and the subsequent licence transfers were authorised on 3rd June 1933, enabling formal sale to be completed on 1st July (technically back dated to 15th April, the date of sale of Armitages). The Armitage business was sold for £10,700 and Taylors for £13,500; Josiah Mann was retained as Manager and Taylors operated under Armitages' management, that company also controlling Wood Bros. Leeds journeys. Operation of the Armitage and Taylor excursions were little changed, although the stands at Lansdowne Place and Albert Road were interlinked, enabling coaches to run from either. Josiah Mann left his position as Armitage Manager after twelve months, in April 1934, and from this time publicity for the Armitage group was undertaken by Standerwicks and joint advertisements regularly appeared for the five companies in the two Blackpool groupings.

Pool expresses continued in their joint form while plans were formulated by the new owners for greater rationalisation of Yorkshire Blackpool services to effect further economies and achieve better vehicle utilisation. Accordingly a proposal for a much enlarged pool was placed before the Commissioner on 21st December 1933: this involved a merging of the existing services of the Blackpool pool operators, plus their owners Ribble, West Yorkshire, Yorkshire (Woollen District) and Yorkshire Traction and Hebble (now associated following purchase by the railway), and plans for joint operation by the eight companies of ten new expresses were presented: these would replace existing operations, the scheme involving a saving of some 100,000 miles annually. The North Western and Yorkshire Commissioners adjourned the hearings to confer, and subsequently rejected the proposals, largely on the strength of railway opposition; a subsequent Appeal by the eight companies was rejected by the Minister in November 1934. Despite this the companies completed a formal Pool agreement and in January 1935 prepared a second submission this time for nine routes but still retaining operation by the ten pool partners. On 1st February 1935 Ribble published a pool timetable, although it contained only the existing individual, joint or Blackpool pool services, without universal interavailability of vehicles or ticketing.

In the meantime, in a parallel move to changes that were taking place within the Standerwick group, application was made in April 1935 for the excursion licences of Armitage and Taylor to be transferred to Standerwicks, and this was approved in August 1935, leaving Armitages and Taylors licensed solely to operate the Blackpool pool expresses. Just prior to this in a move related to the sale of Wm. Salisbury & Sons Ltd to Standerwick Armitages had evacuated the Dickson Road garage, transferring the starting point of their Leeds and Barnsley expresses to Talbot Mews.

The enlarged pool hearing took place in April 1935, following which the North Western and Yorkshire Commissioners adjourned once more to confer, eventually presenting a modified scheme involving the enforced inclusion of certain non Associated companies in the winter timetable (including Armitages' partner Bullocks on the Wakefield route), and exclusion from the Pool of the three Blackpool companies Armitage. Taylor and Wood Bros), reducing the number of full partners to five. After argument the Associated companies were obliged to agree, enabling the new Yorkshire Blackpool pool services to commence on 1st November 1935. The licences issued to Armitages, Taylors and Wood Bros. were withdrawn, and the companies subsequently entered into liquidation during 1936.

W. ARMITAGE & SONS LTD Fleet Name: PROGRESS MOTORS .

Including fleets of predecessor businesses :-
William ARMITAGE (1913-1924))
C. B. & J. R. ARMITAGE & Josiah Olivant MANN (1924-1929))
Fleet Names: W. ARMITAGE & SONS; PROGRESS MOTORS

Registration No.	Manufacturer			Prev.Owner	Coachwork	Type	Sold	Notes
	Type	Aqrd	New					
??	Commer	1913	1913		?	Ch29	c1916	
??	?	1915	1915		?	Ch—	c1918	
??	?	1915	1915		?	Ch14	c1924	
FR1785	Maudslay	1919	1919		?	Ch28	1927	
FR2514	AEC	1920	1920		?	Ch—	?	a
FR4640	Vulcan VSC	1922	1922		?	Ch19	1927	
??	Lancia	1923	1923		?	Ch20	?	
FR5318	Albion PF24	1924	1924		?	C19-	1928	
FR5813	Star	1924	1924		?	C23-	1927	
HS3571	Albion PF24	1925	1925	Albion	?	C—	c1930	
FR7464	Albion PFA26	1926	1926		?	C20-	1930	
FR8085	Albion PFB26	1927	1927		?	C20-	1931	
FR8849-FR8931	Albion PFB26	1928	1928		?	C24-	1932/31	
GD5306	Albion PFB26	1928	1927	Albion	?	C20-	c1933	
GD8694	Albion PM28	1928	1928	Albion	Pickering	C32R	1930	
FR9951	Albion PR28	1929	1929		?	C29-	1935	b
FR9952	Albion PNC26	1929	1929		?	C26-	1935	b
FV 79	Albion PR28	1929	1929		?	C32-	c1932	
FV 971	Albion PMB28	1930	1930		Burlingham	C32R	1935	b
FV1069	Willys Overland	1930	1930		?	C14-	1931	
FV1685-FV1688	AEC Regal	1931	1931		Burlingham	C28F	1935	b
FV1908	Albion PH49	1931	1931		?	C20-	1935	b
FV2547	AEC Regal	1932	1932		?	C32-	1935	c
FV3169	Albion PV70	1932	1932		Burlingham	C32F	1935	c

NOTES :

a - Originally a lorry; converted to Ch— at unknown date (probably after 1923).
b - Passed to YorkshirePool operators in 2/1935, but not taken into stock: sold elsewhere.
c - Passed to Yorkshire Traction Co.Ltd in 2/1935.

Walker TAYLOR & SONS LTD Fleet Name: PRIDE OF THE ROAD MOTORS .

Including fleets of predecessor businesses :-

Walker TAYLOR Fleet Names: WALKER TAYLOR & SONS; PRIDE OF THE ROAD (1913-1924)
Mrs. Hilda TAYLOR Fleet Names: WALKER TAYLOR & SONS PRIDE OF THE ROAD (1924-1928)
Edward H.TAYLOR, T. Harold TAYLOR & Mrs. Hilda TAYLOR Fleet Names: WALKER TAYLOR & SONS; PRIDE OF THE ROAD (1928-1933)

Registration No.	Manufacturer Type	Aqrd	New	Prev. Owner	Coachwork	Type	Sold	Notes
??	?	1913	1913		?	Ch—	?	
??	?	1914	1914		?	Ch—	?	
CW1251	Star	1915	1915		?	Ch25	1920	
??	?	1916	1916		?	?	Ch—	?
FR2629	Daimler ?	1920	1920		Buckingham	Ch—	?	
??	Daimler	1920	1920		Buckingham	Ch—	?	
??	Daimler	1920	1920		Buckingham	Ch—	?	
FR4270	Leyland S6	1921	1921		?	Ch33	1928	
FR5953-FR5954	Daimler	1924	1924		?	Ch20	192/ 31	a
FR7854	Lancia	1927	1927		?	C20-	1931	
FR9088	Tilling B10B	1928	1928		?	C28-	1935	b
FR9089	Tilling B10B	1928	1928		?	C26-	1932	
FR9953-FV 134	Tilling B10A2	1929	1929		?	C32-	1935	b
FV1000	Leyland TS2	1930	1930		?	C30-	1935	c
FV1057	Leyland TS2	1930	1930		?	C30-	1935	d
FV1692	Leyland TS2	1931	1931		BurlinghaM	c30F	1935	e
FV1749-FV1750	Leyland TS2	1931	1931		?	C30-	1935	c
FV1999	Leyland TS2	1931	1931		Burlingham	C30R	1935	f
FV2651	Leyland KP3	1932	1932		Burlingham	C20F	1935	b
FV2658	Leyland TS4	1932	1932		Burlingham	C30F	1935	e

NOTES:

a - Some (at least) may have been rebodied C-- about 1927
b - Passed to West Yorkshire Road Car Co.Ltd in 02 1935.
c - Passed to YorkshirePool operators in 02 1935, but not taken into stock: sold elsewhere.
d - Passed to Hebble Motor Services Ltd in 03 1935.
e - Passed to Yorkshire Traction Co.Ltd in 02 1935.
f - Passed to Yorkshire (Woollen Dist) Transport Co Ltd in 02 1935.

Armitages operated excursion stands in Fleetwood and Cleveleys, the latter positioned at the seaward end of Victoria Road by the Clock Tower and pierrot show. In this 'thirties view three coaches are by the site – a Walker Taylor & Sons Ltd coach (probably Leyland Tiger FV1999) stands nose in, with a normal control Albion of Armitages just visible behind the Clock Tower. To the right is one of Armitages four 1931 AEC Regals with Burlingham coachwork (FV1685-1688). From 1933, when the Associated companies took control, Armitages managed the Taylor fleet and presumably inter-hiring took place as required. What is interesting is that the RTA licence only permitted one coach to work from the Cleveleys stand each day!

A small fleet of four 28-seater Burlingham-bodied AEC Regals purchased by Armitages in 1931 was followed by a single 32-seat example in the following year. This view shows one of the 1931 examples, seen here in a view taken for Burlinghams and issued by Armitage as a post card advertising the daily Leeds expresses. This example was posted in Bradford in 1935, and was probably handed out by the agent with tickets or leaflets. The seating was arranged with two inward facing seats for three passengers over the rear wheel arch and these may not have been the most comfortable for passengers taking the four hour long through journey! The front entrance is equipped with a folding door.

INDEX

- J.Abbott & Son (Blackpool) Ltd 47
- C.B.& J.Armitage 'Progress', Blackpool 111 112 **114**
  - Express Carriage Services:
    - Blackpool-Leeds 111 112
- William Armitage 'Progress', Blackpool 111
- W.Armitage & Son Ltd, Blackpool 26 29 102 104 111 112-113
  - Express Carriage Services:
    - Blackpool-Leeds 111 112-113
    - Blackpool-Barnsley 112
    - Blackpool-Rochdale 111
- Associated Motorways 58 61
- Atkinson 'Dreadnought Motors' Morecambe 98
- Robert Barr Ltd, Leeds 112
- Batty-Holt Touring Svces, Blackpool 97 100 102
- Birch's Motor Services Ltd, Knott End 44
- Blackpool Motor Coach Owners 12 16 19
- Richard Blackhurst, Blackpool 97
- Blair & Palmer Ltd, Carlisle 54
- Joseph Bracewell 'C.Smith Motors' 21 70 71 97-98 **98**
  - Express Carriage Services:
    - Blackpool-Birmingham 97 98
    - Blackpool-Edinburgh 98
    - Blackpool-Liverpool 97 98
    - Blackpool-London 97 98
    - Blackpool-Manchester 97 98
    - Colne-London 97-98
- Jos.Bracewell Ltd, Colne & Blackpool 22 24-28 31 98
  - Express Carriage Services:
    - Blackpool-Birmingham 26-28 31 98
    - Blackpool-Liverpool 26-27 98
    - Blackpool-London 26-28 31 98
    - Blackpool-Manchester 26-27 98
    - Colne-London 26-28 31 98
- Bracewells (Colne) Ltd, Colne 38-39 98
- Frank Briggs 26 36 **36** 49 64 97 98
- Bristol VRLL coaches **45** **59** 61 **62** **63** 63-64 **69**
- British Transport Commission **41**
- Buck's Motors, Swinton & Manchester 97
- J.Bullock & Sons (1928) Ltd, Wakefield 112 113
- Edward Butterworth, Blackpool **10** 14 92
- A.Christy (Bolton) Ltd, Bolton **37**
- Coliseum Garage/Station, Blackpool 22 107 108
- Commercial Motor Users Association 16
- County Motors (Lancaster) Ltd, Lancaster 71
- Creams (Lancashire) Ltd, Rochdale 107-108
- Hugh Croisdale 'Brunshaw Mtrs' Burnley 108
- Crosville Mtr Svces Ltd 24 38-39 65
- Cumberland Mtr Svces,Ltd 54
- James Davis Ltd, Preston 72 73
- John William Dewhurst, Blackpool 100
- J.W.Dewhurst & Co.Ltd see Wood Bros (Blackpool) Ltd
- William Dewhurst, Blackpool 100
- Arthur Dinham, Blackburn 100 102
- East Lancashire Mtrs Ltd, Blackburn 29-30 **31** 100
- John Eastwood, Oldham 102
- P.Eastwood Ltd, Burnley 107
- Easy Way Holidays **13**
- Robert Edwards & Co.Ltd, Halifax 108
- Empire Motors (Roberts), Blackpool 20 21 102
- Empress Motors, Preston 71
- Fylde Coaches Ltd, Cleveleys 30
- 'Gay Hostess' coaches **43** **47** **52** **53** **54** 55-56 57 **59** 61
- Gore's Tours, Southport **11**
- Joseph Hanson & Son, Huddersfield 112
- Harry Harwood 'John Bull', Darwen 47 102
- Hebble Motor Services Ltd, Halifax 108 113
- Hilton, Sharpe & Co.Ltd, Blackpool 96
- Barry Holden, Oswaldtwistle 102
- Edric Holden, Accrington 102
- Holdsworths 'Hebble', Halifax 112
- Holt Bros (Rochdale) Ltd, Rochdale; later Yelloway Mtr Svces Ltd 10 19 21 25 27 **40** 42 44 64 77 107
- Horsfall, Salthouse & Co, Blackpool 22 30 107-108
- Thomas Hoyle, Crawshawbooth 96 97 104
- Imperial Motor Services, Liverpool 27
- J. E.Jenking 'Queen of the North'Blackpool 31-32 104-105 **105** 111
  - Express Carriage Services:
    - (Fleetwood)-Blackpool-Manchester 105
- Kenyons, Coleman & Robinson Ltd B'burn 22 29 30 **30** 32 100
- Adam King, Stretford 97
- Lancashire & Yorkshire Motors, Barnsley 112
- Lancashire United Tramways Ltd; later Lancashire United Tpt & Power Co.Ltd, then Lancashire United Transport Ltd 10 19 29 **32** 42 44 55 64
- Lansdowne Motors Ltd, Blackpool 20 21 26 102 104
- Leeds & Newcastle Omn.Co Northallerton 112
- Llandudno Motor & Garage Co. Ltd **6**
- London Coastal Coaches Ltd 22 48 49
- M.& H. Motors Ltd, Blackpool 19 22 29 33 **32** 104
- Robert MacKay 64
- MacShanes Motors Ltd, Liverpool/London 20 22
- Josiah Olivant Mann 111 113
- Wm.Marshall & Son Ltd, Blackpool 29 32
- Midland Red (B.M.M.O.Ltd) 21 24-28 31 39 49 55 56 96-97 102
- John Mitton, Colne 102
- Geo Moore & Sons (St Annes) Ltd 46
- Motors (Blackpool) Ltd, Blackpool 11
- N.B.C. Computer Services Ltd 92
- National Travel 64
- National Travel (North West) Ltd see North Western Road Car Co.Ltd
- Nell Gwynne Coaches, Bodenham 22
- North Manchester Motor Coaches Ltd 64
- North Western Road Car Co.Ltd; later National Travel (North West) Ltd 19 24-28 29 **32** 42 44 55 56 61 64-65 102
- S.Owen & Sons, Blackpool **16**
- T.H.Parker Blue Bird Coaches, Oldham 26 42
- Edwin F. Parkinson, Lytham 21-22 108
- Pilot Motors Ltd, Preston 71
- Potteries Motor Traction Co.Ltd 56
- Preston Embee Motors Ltd, Preston 85
- Ribble Motor Services Ltd 19 24-29 31-33 **32** 36 **37** 38-39 42 44 47 54 56 58 64-65 71 73 74 78 79 80 102 104 105 108 112 113
- Ribblesdale Coachways Ltd, Blackburn 38-39
- Rishton & Antley Motor Co.Ltd, Accrington 72
- Robin Hood Coaches, Nottingham 22
- Robinson 'Royal Blue', Scarborough **17**
- W Salisbury 'Pride of the North', Blackpool 104 105
- W.Salisbury & Sons Ltd, Blackpool 30 31-32 97 104 105 **105** **106**
  - Express Carriage Services:
    - Blackpool-Liverpool 104
    - Blackpool-London 97 104
    - Blackpool-Manchester 104
- Scout Computer Services Ltd 92
- Scout Motor Services Ltd, Preston 27 36 39 48-49 **50-51** **53** 54 **54** 55-57 77-78 **77-78** 79-80 **80-82** 82 **83-84** 85 **86-91** 92 97
  - Express Carriage Services:
    - Blackpool-Birmingham 48-49 55-58
    - Blackpool/(Darwen)-London 36 48-49 55-58 77-78 79 97
    - Blackpool-Oxford-(London) 54-55 56-58
    - Colne-London 48-49 54 55-58
    - 'Gaytours' expresses 55
    - Keswick-London 54 55-58
    - (Preston)-Southport-London 58
  - Stage Carriage Services:
    - Blackpool-Peel 82 92
    - Blackpool-Preston-Burnley 85
    - Blackpool-Preston-Rochdale 85
    - Blackpool-Warton 85
    - (Gt.Eccleston)-Wharles-Kirkham 85
    - Lea-Preston-Frenchwood 82 92
    - Preston-Blackpool 78 79 80 82 85 92
    - Preston-Lytham 85 92

Preston/Blackpool-Salwick 82 85 92
Lytham-Preston-Burnley 85
John Sharp, Manchester 27 97
'C.Smith Motors', Blackpool see Joseph Bracewell
Charles Smith (Snr), Blackpool 96
Charles Smith Jnr, Blackpool 70 71 72 73 96-97 98 100 104
Express Carriage Services:
Blackpool-Liverpool 97
Blackpool-Manchester 96 97
Francis (Frank) Smith, Blackpool 96
F.& C.Smith, Blackpool 70 **95** 96 **98** 100
F.& C.Smith & Co, Blackpool 96
F.& C.Smith Ltd, Blackpool 96 **96 97**
James Smith, Wigan 21
James Smith & Co.(Wigan) Ltd 21 77
Southdown Motor Services Ltd 39
Spencer's Motors, Blackpool 97
Edward Victor Standerwick 14-18 **14** 20 22 24-26 29 36
Frank Standerwick 45-46
Walter Clinton Standerwick 14-20 **14-17**
W. C. Standerwick Ltd **8 9** 12 18-22 **18-23** 24-32 **24 26 27 29 33-35** 36 **37** 38-39 **39-42** 42 **43** 44 **44-47** 46-49 **48-53** 54-57 **54-56** 58 **58-60** 61 **61-63** 63-65**65 69** 92 96 98 100 102 108 113
Express Carriage services:
Bacup-Blackpool 30 36 38 **38**
Bacup-Morecambe 30 36 38
Banbury-Morecambe 39
Barrow-London 61
Blackpool-Birmingham 21 25-28 31 48-49 55-58 77
Blackpool-Eastbourne 39
Blackpool-Liverpool 18 19
Blackpool-London 18-21 24-28 31 36 48-49 55-58 77 100 102
Blackpool-Manchester 18 19
Blackpool-Oxford-(London) 54-55 56-58 61
Colne-Blackpool 30 36
(Skipton)-Colne-Eastbourne 38 39 61
Colne-Llandudno 30 38
Colne-London 31 36 38 48-49 55-58 61
Colne-Morecambe 30 36 38
Colne-Oxford 61
Colne-Pwllheli 39
Fylde Coast pool **40** 42 44 64
'Gaytours' expresses 55
Keswick-London 54 55-58 61
Padiham-Scarborough 30 38
(Preston)-Southport-London 58
Stage Carriage services:
Blackpool-Salwick 92
Stephenson Bros, Blackpool 26 104
Josiah Street Ltd, Blackpool 96
R. Strickland, Blackpool 14 17
Swift Fleet Motors Ltd, Salford 10 96 97

E.,T.H.,& H.Taylor 'W.Taylor & Sons', Blackpool 102 112-113
Express Carriage Services:
Blackpool-Huddersfield-(Leeds) 112-113
Blackpool-Brighouse 112-113
Hilda Taylor 'W.Taylor & Sons' Blackpool 112
Express Carriage Services:
Blackpool-Huddersfield-(Leeds) 112

Walker Taylor 'Pride of the Road', Blackpool 104 111
Express Carriage Services:
Blackpool-Huddersfield 111 112
Walker Taylor & Sons Ltd, Blackpool 26 29 32 113
Express Carriage Services:
Blackpool-Leeds 113
T. Towler (Lytham) Ltd 46
Travel Corner, Blackpool 45 64
Trent Motor Traction Co.Ltd 55

Underwood Express Ltd, Sheffield 104

Matthew Wade 'Majestic Motors', Preston 71 72
Waddington & Son Ltd, Blackpool 32 **33**
J.G.Warburton Ltd, Blackpool 92
Warwick Computer Systems Ltd 92
James Watkinson 'Scout' Motors 21 25 70-74 **70-77** 77
Express Carriage services:
Blackpool-London 70-77
Keswick-London 73
Stage Carriage services:
Preston-Blackpool 71-74
J.Wearden & Sons Ltd, Blackburn 38-39
Webster Bros, Wigan 21
West Yorkshire Road Car Co.Ltd 29 112 113
Western S.M.T.Co.Ltd 54
Alfred Whiteside Ltd, Blackpool 46
William Whiteside, Cleveleys 30 104
Whittaker Bros (Blackpool) Ltd 85
Wood Bros (Blackpool) Ltd 'John Bull'; prev.J.W.Dewhurst & Co.Ltd 12 19 20 21 24-28 31 92 100 **101-102** 102**103**107 112-113
Express Carriage Services:
Blackpool-Birmingham 102
Blackburn-Blackpool 28 100
Blackpool-Liverpool 26-27 100
Blackpool-Leeds 26 102 112-113
Blackpool-London 26-28 31 100 102
Blackpool-Newcastle on Tyne 102
Blackpool-Manchester-Oldham 26-27 100 102
Colne-London 102
S.& J.Wood Ltd 'Seagull', Blackpool **7** 17 29 32 111
Wright Bros (Burnley) Ltd 22 30 32 44 107-108 **108-110**
Express Carriage Services:
Accrington-Scarborough 107 108
Accrington-Llandudno 107-108
Bacup-Morecambe 30 107-108
Bacup-Preston 107
Bacup-Southport 107
Burnley-Manchester 107
(Colne)-Burnley-Blackpool 30 107-108
Colne-Liverpool 107-108
Colne-Llandudno 30 107-108
Colne-Morecambe 30 107-108
Colne-Preston 107
Colne-Southport 107
Padiham-Leeds 107
Padiham-Scarborough 30 107-108
Todmorden-Blackpool 107
(Weir)-Bacup-Blackpool 30 107-108

Yates & Sykes, Blackpool 105
Yelloway Motor Services Ltd see Holt Bros (Rochdale) Ltd
Yorkshire Traction Co.Ltd 29 113
Yorks (Woollen Dist) Tpt Co.Ltd 29 113

PHOTOGRAPHIC CREDITS

Peter Deegan	50(lower) 83(upper) 90
Peter Deegan Collection	6 7 8 9(upper) 10 11 14-17 33(lower) 37 38(lower) 42 45 46 49 51(centre & lower) 53(lower) 55 56 58 79(lower) 89(lower) 91(lower) 92(lower) 96 97 98(upper) 101(lower) 102 105 114
R.Downham	43(lower) 59 60 61(upper) 62(lower) 63 65 69
J.B.Horne/English Electric	29
The late R.F.Mack	9(lower) 40 41(lower) 51(upper) 79(upper) 82
T.B.Maund	83(lower) 88(centre)
National Motor Museum	19 95(upper) 101(top left & top right)
R.E.C.Collection	21 24 26 27 30 31 33(upper) 38(upper) 53(upper & centre) 54 73(upper) 75 87(upper) 89(centre) 91(upper) 95(lower)
Senior Transport Archive	18 20 22 23 32 34 35 39 41(upper & centre) 43(upper) 44(upper) 47 48 50(upper) 52(lower) 62(upper) 70-72 73(lower) 74 76-78 80(upper) 81 84 86 87(lower) 88(lower) 89(upper) 98(lower) 101(upper & lower centre) 103 106 108 109 110
R.L.Wilson	44(lower) 52(upper) 61(lower) 80(lower) 87(centre) 88(upper) 91(centre) 92(upper)

Timetables, hand-bills, leaflets, 'on hire' window sticker and "Gay Hostess" Food Waybill are all from Peter Deegan Collection